Stay Soft, Get Eaten

MITSKI

Stay Soft, Get Eaten
The Complete Biography of Mitski Using Her Own Words
by Jared Woods
proofreading by Milz Dechnik
cover photo by David Lee (CC Attribution 2.0 Generic license)
Published by The Goat's Nest Publishing
ISBN 9798282538090
ASIN B0F7G2CJ96
JaredWoodsSavedMyLife.com

THIS BOOK IS PROUDLY WRITTEN BY A HUMAN WITHOUT THE USE OF AI

DEDICATED TO MY PATREON SUBSCRIBERS

Aaron, Adam, Ahmed, Ama & Ross, Ammr, Bert, David, Diana, Gina, Jo, Kez, Lenka, Lonnie, Marcus, Michael, Milz, Ryan, Saily, Tony, Wilmie, and Xen

THANK YOU FOR SUPPORTING A STARVING AUTHOR

Join the team! *patreon.com/legotrip*

CONTENTS

"I sound like an asshole. If someone heard what I was saying, didn't know who the fuck I was, and didn't care, they would truly be like, 'Who the fuck does she think she is? Why's she talking like she's fucking special?'" [2]

- MITSKI

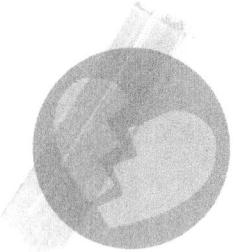

INTRODUCTION

Imagine the tip of a paintbrush, saturated with blue, kissing down to the canvas. With sweeping motions, it curves and flows, patiently adding layers of soft elegance to itself.

Now watch as the lid of a spray can pops off, rattling from a shake and then vomiting a brutal red across the scene, hissing aggressively as it distorts everything it touches.

These two colours connect. They merge. The paint consistencies are too different to coexist yet they are forced together, dripping into a puddle of confusion below. Do you see that? The place where they meet? That is Mitski.

Mitski is a mixed medium of contradicting components at war within herself. This observation has plenty of nuances, but without a doubt, her cultural roots are the most focused upon by her and the media. She is one part Japanese, one part American, and no two countries could be so distinctly dissimilar. The reserved, polite nation of Japan. The loud, arrogant nation of the USA. Japan's indirect subtlety of communication. America's confrontational candour. The East's reverence in conformity. The West's push for individualism. The respectful bow. The authoritative handshake. These weighty influences set an early stage for Mitski where she could never fully identify as one thing or the other, automatically the outsider wherever she may find herself.

This amalgamation has manifested in numerous ways throughout Mitski's personality, art, and perception of the world. Constantly uprooted, never belonging anywhere, Mitski's childhood was crushed by immense isolation, and yet she is now revered around the globe by millions of strangers. She is willing to crack herself open and expose her most profound thoughts through lyrics and candid interviews, and yet she is so immensely private that much of her personal life remains shrouded in mystery. These two worlds are forever colliding within Mitski, a tumble of paradoxes that have snowballed into her signature musical expression. Songs like hers are not only a result of a special mind but also of unique circumstances.

What sets Mitski apart from other artists is that she is, above everything else, about her craft. She never actively tried to become a superstar, but thankfully, due to some cosmic justice at work, she became one. Much to her dismay, the TikTok generation swallowed her up, and the belly of the internet tore her to pieces, only to stitch her back together as the emotional spokesperson for the sad. Like so many things in Mitski's story, her greatest gifts sharpened the cursed side of the sword, too.

Stay Soft, Get Eaten is the complete biography of Mitski. From her accolades that amplify louder per her every album to her passion for the creative study of music itself. From her unabashed exclamations of her opinions to her almost-paranoid protection of individual details. From her yearning for worldly acceptance to an overwhelming cult-like fanbase suffocating her close to death. Together, we take each step along Mitski's growth by allowing her to tell her own tale through quotes from hundreds of interviews, articles, and social media posts, while scrubbing the deepest crevices within her powerful discography. In this book, the words are taken straight from Mitski's brain and into the hands of her fans, finally helping us all to unpick the rich enigma that is Mitski.

"I don't show even the people I love most, but I'll show you this darkness in me." [1]

- MITSKI

Part One
THE EARLY LIFE
OF MITSUKI LAYCOCK

1.1.
MEET THE MIYAWAKI FAMILY

"My name is Mitski. That's spelled M-I-T-S-K-I, like the MIT ski team." [3]

- MITSKI

Mitsuki Laycock. That was Mitski's name at birth. Say "Mitsuki" out loud and you're probably pronouncing it wrong. It is identical to "Mitski". The mispronunciations were most likely what encouraged her to drop the "U". Here's that scoop from Scot Moriarty, who worked with Mitski during her first record.

"At some point, she'd told me, like, 'Yeah, just spell it that way', [...] I think she specifically said people would always call her Mit-su-ki. And she was, like, 'that's not how it's pronounced.'" [4]

- SCOT MORIARTY

According to The Fader, she sometimes refers to herself as "Bitchski", which might be worth mentioning. As for "Laycock", she no longer uses that either, opting to replace it with her mother's surname "Miyawaki." No matter, as we all know her by the mononymous "Mitski", a decision she regrets.

"Seeing my name just reminds me of the world. It's just not mine anymore. I am a foreigner to myself now." [2]

- MITSKI

Mitski was born on September 27th, 1990. That makes her a Libra, a zodiac categorisation she chats about regularly.

"I'm a Libra. I don't want to make this about astrology, but I'm very focused on balance." [5]

- MITSKI

"[My] ascendant sign is Scorpio. Scorpios are very intense and dark with something mysterious about them. That's how people see me at first. [My moon sign is] Capricorn [...] the goat that steadily climbs mountains. I persevere. I'm very stubborn. I work hard. Am I making sense?" [6]

- MITSKI

While astrology may have dictated Mitski's personality from the stars, her life on Earth appears far more influenced by where she was born: Japan.

"I was born in Mie [Prefecture] which is just, like, nowhere countryside." [7]

- MITSKI

We gradually start to unwind the greater Mitski picture when we learn that the family actually resided in the Democratic Republic of the Congo during this time.

"[My mother] flew her pregnant belly to Japan, gave birth, and then took her newborn child and flew back to Africa." [8]

- MITSKI

"I was born in Japan but only because my mother wanted me to have Japanese citizenship secured. The moment I was born, she took me back to the Democratic Republic of Congo, where my parents were living." [9]

- MITSKI

"It was crazy of her to do that, to carry an unborn child in her stomach while she's travelling from Africa to Japan, give birth, fly back to Africa. I was almost born in the plane, according to my mother. Although I don't know how accurate that was! And then, once she'd recovered, we just went back." [10]

- MITSKI

"This is so private, but I was a C-section. I came out at 10 a.m. sharp. That's why I'm so orderly. I'm just, like, 'Let's go!'" [11]

- MITSKI

The first Mitski detail we learn is that, when it comes to Mitski geography, nothing is simple. However, it's worth noting that she did spend some of her younger years in Japan, mentioning Kobe City once or twice. Her first language is Japanese.

"I lived with my grandma who lives in the way countryside. So I feel like I experienced Japan a lot." [9]

- MITSKI

"I think I spent a total of 5-6 years in Japan. Even though I was living abroad, I attended a local Japanese school until the 6th grade of elementary school." [12]

- MITSKI

Digging up information about Mitski's family is a complex treasure hunt. What we do know is that her mother is Japanese and her father is American. They are retired and might live in suburban Pennsylvania where some of Mitski's possessions are still stored. She also has a little sister who is a Gemini and lives (or may have once lived) in the UK. According to Mitski, that sister is...

"...a really good person." [1]

- MITSKI

Other than that, Mitski has kept this side of her life surprisingly well private.

"The stuff I'm not candid about is when it affects other people. I have people in my life who aren't in the public, and I don't feel like I have a right to talk about them when they never consented to this dynamic." [1]

- MITSKI

However, she has offered glimpses of insight into her parents' professions.

"My mother's a glass blower so that's where I got my artistic temperament." [13]

- MITSKI

As for her dad, well, that is a source of greater intrigue...

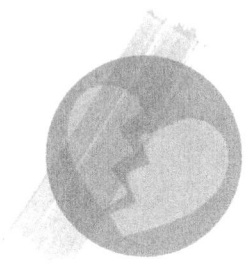

1.2.
MOVING AROUND

"My dad worked for the State Department. I lived in a dozen countries. I could list them, but it would make me sound like an asshole." [14]

- MITSKI

Mitski's father's job is the reason why the family relocated so often.

"[My father is] a Foreign Service Officer so we moved to a different country every year, or every other year. I have a Japanese passport and a US passport but that's the extent of my knowledge of where I'm from." [15]

- MITSKI

"I just tagged along with my father [...] It's not because of anything I've accomplished. Growing up, I moved along with him." [16]

- MITSKI

Due to this line of work and Mitski's vagueness around details, there are rumours that her parents may have ties with the CIA.

"I wouldn't say yay or nay, but they might be! At least one of them..." [7]

- MITSKI

As for the locations themselves, you'll find most publications agreeing that she lived in over 13 countries around the world. But after further investigation, this figure may be an exaggeration.

"That was a number I threw out randomly and then it's stuck in the press but I actually don't know. I never really counted." [7]

- MITSKI

"I went to 13 schools. But some of those schools were in the same country, so I don't know. But I've also lived in countries without going to school there. I have never really counted. I should tally them up." [15]

- MITSKI

Alright, but here are the ones we do know for certain: China, Czech Republic, Democratic Republic of the Congo, Malaysia, Turkey, and the USA (Alabama and Virginia states specifically). She has also hinted at India and Taiwan. Interestingly, of these, Malaysia stuck out to her the most.

"I was in a Japanese school in Malaysia when I was in... I don't remember what years [...] sixth grade, fifth grade, something." [9]

- MITSKI

"I miss Malaysia a lot because that was three consecutive years I lived in one place, which was a big deal for me. It's summer all year round and I was a kid, so I identify a lot with that place. I identify with the mix of cultures, and how it's Malay and Chinese and Indian. But the thing is, if I go back there, I'll be a foreigner. I won't belong there. So in my heart, I can think of it as home, but it never will be home. I feel like my whole identity—every place I feel like I belong to, I don't actually belong to, you know? I don't belong anywhere. I think that's the consistent theme for me. I think that really affects how I write songs, how I perceive the world" [16]

- MITSKI

1.3.
EARLY BRAIN SHAPINGS

"I'd run into the parent in the kitchen and small-talked, and put breakfast together for myself while everyone else was sleeping. I was that kid." [1]

- MITSKI

As the above quote would indicate, Mitski always had some fire of confidence within her, which would serve her well as a stage star. Nevertheless, her constant moving naturally unsettled her roots, which played a monumental role in moulding her personality through different levels of isolation. In many ways, this is the core of Mitski's story.

"I didn't even make friends because I knew it would be goodbye in a year. Everyone else just thought I was different and weird. When people looked at me they couldn't recognise any of the history of me, like, 'Where is she from? What's her ethnicity? Who is she?' I just didn't make sense to anybody." [6]

- MITSKI

"I never learned how to make friends. I never learned how to make those compromises you have to make if you wanna stay friends. You gotta learn how to forgive, to say sorry. I just did exactly what I wanted. It's scary to me to not do everything I want to do. It's like I'm somebody else." [17]

- MITSKI

"You can't earnestly say goodbye every year. I would move every year. You can't survive becoming attached every year, and having to say goodbye every year. So yeah, I learned to kind of float above that, and accept that I don't have any roots." [18]

- MITSKI

"When you're a kid, especially, it just gets to be too much to become attached to people or places and then be torn away from it. You just stop attaching yourself. And I think that's the source of a lot of my loneliness. Sure, it's that I didn't grow up in one place. I didn't have consistency. But, also, I had created a wall so that nothing came in or out. And that creates loneliness." [19]

- MITSKI

On that note, Mitski does recognise how this unique upbringing fed into her unique musical gifts.

"I grew up moving around so much [so] I was always an outsider. And being an outsider makes you very objective about everything. You almost see yourself how other people see you and your beauty. I learned to be objective about even subjective things, like about my emotions. And I have learned how to observe myself from the outside. I think that's what's made me so clinical about these emotional

personal things because I'm able to kind of separate myself from my own emotions and describe them accurately."[20]

- MITSKI

"I've always been an outsider and what you learn when you're an outsider is that you're always watching. It teaches you to be very observant and it also teaches you to look at yourself objectively, or look at yourself how other people are looking at you. Because when you have to pitch yourself, you have to really quickly judge how other people are seeing you in order to form a positive impression of yourself. And that not only made me feel like I have to cram all my ideas into one second but also made me very aware of myself, and very observant, and also very objective. That's been very helpful in my songwriting because when you write songs, you have to, in a way, be objective about your own really subjective things in order to describe them. You have to walk that tightrope of being very subjective while also being very objective."[11]

- MITSKI

"I moved to a different country on an average of every year to every other year, and each new place had a completely different set of customs and languages. Different people would handle this differently, and because I lived nomadically while I was growing and learning about the world and myself, I think I learned to connect and communicate by not relying on culture-specific customs to guide me. That is, because each culture has their own ideas about good and bad, right and wrong, polite and improper, I just gave up on looking for answers in my environment and instead turned inward to my instincts, to the core of me. I'm going on and on because I think *this is consequently how I've come to write and perform music as well. I've learned to write instinctually, to truly listen to what my gut is saying instead of what is correct according to music theory or popular opinion. I try to produce every note and every word because it somehow feels 'right' deep within me."* [21*]

- MITSKI

"It's not good to dissociate. I'm not trying to recommend it. But I think it's a coping mechanism I adapted and adopted into my life from a young age because I moved around a lot, and nothing felt like it was in my control. I was often in places I didn't know and I didn't understand. So in those moments, I would just go into my head and I would make up stories. I would make up songs and that would be a way for me to comfort myself. That's kind of been a skill I've developed." [22]

- MITSKI

"It's shaped my identity at my core and that informs my music. A lot of it is to do with leaving—saying goodbye—and going to a new place and not belonging. I think those are big themes in my music, objectively!" [10]

- MITSKI

Speaking of her musical future, Mitski considers herself a late bloomer as an artist. However, we can map out several clues that she was on the right path from quite a young age.

1.4.
MIGHT CONTAIN
TRACES OF MUSIC

"I'm Japanese and I'm not Japanese. I'm American, I'm not American. I moved around a lot so I'm not from anywhere. I found that being good at music gave me some kind of purpose. Or gave me something to say, 'Well, I'm here.' And then I could present my music and be, like, 'That's why I'm here.' Often I would feel like I'm not allowed to be somewhere or I don't belong somewhere, [but now] I could stand my ground and go, 'Oh no, but this is what I can contribute.' And that's what music became to me." [13]

- MITSKI

On the timeline of many musicians, there is a parental musician influence on top. But in Mitski's story, it was less obvious than that.

"I don't really have any musicians in my family [...], but my father was kind of an amateur ethnomusicologist, where he genuinely enjoyed really pretentious field recordings of [different] culture's music. He really loved Appalachian folk and all Irish and Scottish folk. He loved all the different music from Latin America [...] he loved throat singing music, Mongolian and Tibetan music... a lot of stuff that you would pretend to like just to be cool, he genuinely loved that stuff. So it would just be playing in my household and that's what I'm familiar with and that's now genuinely what I like as well." [13]

- MITSKI

While her parents may not have had any direct musical abilities, they still nurtured an eclectic mix of artistic appreciation within their growing daughter. She has recalled a numerous spectrum of genres wafting through her household.

"I think my influence comes from whatever entered my brain when I was younger and I was still forming. I had no choice of what came into my brain. A lot of my mother's 70s, 80s Japanese pop music. And my father, who's a big ethnomusicology guy, he listened to a lot of Smithsonian Folkways recordings. So it was a mix of those with whatever pop music was around me or whatever pop music was on MTV abroad. So whatever pop music is, like, five years late." [23]

- MITSKI

"I always go back to Japanese nursery rhymes that I grew up with. It's weird, those are the things that you can't shake. So if you have children, I suggest you make them listen to really good music at infancy, because that's what is stuck with them for the rest of their lives." [11]

- MITSKI

"My mom used to sing me a lullaby. I'm not gonna sing it for you because that's just for me." [25]

- MITSKI

More importantly, when Mitski showed an interest in music, no matter how slight, her parents were open to this exploration.

"They were always hands-off but supportive, in that they never pushed me towards anything [...] my parents learned early on that I will just do as I do and there's not much they can do about it. So they kind of just let me go and let me do my thing. I took a few piano lessons as a kid but it didn't last; I just learned piano from doing it over and over on my own, because I didn't have many friends and there was always a keyboard in the house." [26]

- MITSKI

"A lot of musicians talk about how they were into music from the start. They always wanted to be musicians. It wasn't like that for me. I didn't think of it as a job or a career. It was just something that was constant. I moved around so much, and music was the one thing that couldn't be taken away from me. I could just do it on my own terms, and I could learn so much about it. You can never learn enough about music. So it was always a part of my childhood, but it wasn't a conscious part of it in any way." [26]

- MITSKI

"I just really enjoyed singing. I spent a lot of my life in transit [...] a lot of times in cars or just in new houses [where] there's nothing. I would just sing to myself. I wouldn't have any friends [but]

music would keep me company. So that's kind of how I
naturally became good at it." [13]

- MITSKI

"Music is something that you don't need things for. It can be inside
you without anything. And that's how I started singing. Not to sound
too cheesy, but things come and go. Any kind of material thing
can be taken away from you. But music can't be taken away
from inside your head. So it really became kind of like a family
member, and a great love, and a friend, and a place to live,
and everything for me." [27]

- MITSKI

"We always had a keyboard in the house and I messed around with
that. I always loved music. Early on, I caught on to the fact that I
was pretty good at it so I had a music education in that I always took
music classes. Like, advanced music classes." [9]

- MITSKI

Despite the transient nature of her life, Mitski did take part in musical activities
offered by her schools.

"I always loved music, but the first moment I remember crying to
music was in first grade. We were singing the theme song to that
movie Castle in the Sky, and I just started crying. Not because of
anything that's sad in the song, but just being overwhelmed by how
beautiful I thought it was. And all the kids in class were, like, 'Why
are you crying?' And I didn't really understand why." [28]

- MITSKI

"I don't remember the first official show I ever played. But I do remember the first public performance I did. It was in first grade, the school musical. It was a Japanese school and it was a Japanese play called Juu-San Biki No Neko which means 'Thirteen Cats'. And we were all cats. They did a good job. Everybody got a solo. I got a solo." [29]

- MITSKI

Mitski also sang in the choir through most of her school life.

"I remember I auditioned in seventh grade for a short solo part. The teacher and everyone looked at me. I was like, 'Oh, this is something I can do.'" [1]

- MITSKI

"I had always been in Japanese school. But in seventh grade, my parents put me in English-speaking school and I didn't speak much English. I was having a hard time. But I joined a choir and that's where people started to say, 'Hey, Mitski, you have a good voice!' And that was my entry point... or not really my entry point because I didn't... I still didn't have many friends. But it gave me a reason to be there. Me being able to sing gave me permission to exist or be like, 'Well, this is why I'm allowed to be here', or why I'm allowed to be in choir, because I'm contributing. I think that was how it started. And then ever since, I felt like I didn't have anything else. I wasn't good at anything else. So I fixated on music from then on and then I just kind of went with it." [11]

- MITSKI

"I grew up in choirs and I was always an alto and I was always singing the weird harmonic parts that don't make much melodic sense.

It's funny, all the songs I remember singing in choir, I can't really sing them on my own because they're weird alto parts that don't make sense without a soprano." [30]

- MITSKI

As we shall later learn, there were still many years to go before Mitski wrote her first official song. But when pressed for answers, one may find there are many baby Mitski songs that are so rare, that nobody has ever heard them.

"I've said in interviews that the first time I wrote a song officially was when I was either 17 or 18. But now I'm remembering that the first time I wrote a song without knowing I was writing a song was first grade, second grade. [I was] a small child at the school bus stop waiting for my bus. I just made up a song to myself about how excited I was to go to school. I'm not going to sing it for you because that's between me and my child self." [29]

- MITSKI

"I was always making up songs in my head, so it's hard to tell when I wrote my first song exactly." [31]

- MITSKI

1.5.
FINDING IDENTITY IN ALL THE WRONG PLACES

"If I ever found a place where I belonged, that in itself would be an identity crisis to me." [32]

- MITSKI

One advantage of forever changing schools was that Mitski could test out being whoever she wanted.

"This was a tiny bit before social media was really a thing so I could really show up anywhere and be nobody and start from scratch. So I, like, truly experimented. For one school I was the popular girl. For another school I was the party girl. For another school I was strictly academic, like completely nerdy. Another school, I was kind of punky." [7]

- MITSKI

One of the funniest stories of Mitski's chameleon years was when she sang Whitney Houston's rendition of Dolly Parton's "I Will Always Love You" on stage.

"There was one school in Virginia. I went there and I decided I'm not going to talk to anybody. And so the whole year, I didn't talk to anybody. I was that weird girl who just literally wouldn't talk to anyone. And at the end of the year, I entered the talent show and I sang 'I Will Always Love You.' I killed it. I thought that was funny. [...] I just loved watching the audience reaction, just their faces changing as I sang. From, like, that quiet new kid who's never talked to anyone to 'oh shit, wait, she's actually...!' And then I left the school." [7]

- MITSKI

"When I was planning it, I'd envisioned it as much more cinematic and funny and grand. But the actual execution of it was much smaller in cinematic scope. I was just singing this melodramatic song to confused and alarmed faces." [33]

- MITSKI

"I was pretty quiet, and no one knew me. So I would go on stage at a talent show and people would be like, 'What is going on? Who is this girl?' And then I'd leave. It would always be a fun little joke I played with myself." [34]

- MITSKI

Reportedly, this was not the only time Mitski performed this shock show, having once delivered a rendition of Stevie Wonder's "Lately". However, she forgot the piano chords, but continued anyway, singing a cappella.

"People thought I was being extra and just really belting." [34]

- MITSKI

As fun as this all sounds, it wouldn't take a therapist to predict these games coming with a serious price.

"I was like, whatever, fuck it—I'm never going to meet any of these people ever again, and they don't know who I am. I'll try on this person and see if I am this person, and then if I'm not, that's fine, there are no consequences, because I can just start over at the next place. In the long run that really fucked up my brain in terms of my identity. But that's how I led most of my adolescence." [16]

- MITSKI

"Doing that every year of my life kind of fucked me up in the long run because it was like... 'who am I?'" [7]

- MITSKI

"[It] was great for me as a teenager when I didn't know who I was. So I could just be every kind of extreme, knowing that, if it's not who I am, I would leave anyway. And even though that fucked me up in the long run, I also discovered that I am all of those people. I'm not one person. I'm many people in one body [...] There's a dichotomy and there's all these different emotions at the same time. I'm comfortable with that because I learned early on that I am all of those people. I'm everything and that's fine." [11]

- MITSKI

"I think that actually helps my songwriting because I get to write from different perspectives probably a lot more easily than people who lived in one place." [9]

- MITSKI

1.6.
CLASSIC TEENAGE DEPRESSION

"When you're a teenager, everything is dramatic. It's the end of the world every day. My music is the result of not being that teenager anymore but still being sad. The world goes on, and you're not important. There's a lesser sense of, I'm the protagonist, this is a great tragedy. It's more, my sadness is living here, I have to deal with it, I wish this weren't happening, but I'm used to it." [14]

- MITSKI

High school is a difficult ordeal for anyone, but within the tumble dryer of Mitski's displaced existence, her physical insecurities and yearnings for love happened with additional intensity.

"I just burnt myself all up hating myself for not being beautiful and perfect. I felt like if I could just be pretty, then someone would find me and take me to my life." [2]

- MITSKI

"I spent all my teenage years being obsessed with beauty, and I'm very resentful about it and I'm very angry. I had so much intelligence and energy and drive, and instead of using that to study more, or instead of pursuing something or going out and learning about or changing the world, I directed all that fire inward, and burnt myself up." [33]

- MITSKI

"In tenth grade—this says a lot about how developmentally delayed I was—I had in my mind that it was the proper thing for me to have a love interest. And you'd see in movies where two characters instantly see each other and are, like, 'I'm in love!', and then it just cuts to them on a date or interacting. So, in my brain, I interpreted that as, if I just keep looking at this boy, that's how it will start. A lot of my adolescence was like that. Me thinking I was doing the right thing by re-creating a movie scene that I'd seen but then realising that's not how it happens in real life." [33]

- MITSKI

"As a teenager, I didn't want to be alive. Everything was so hard. I just wanted to be dead. I didn't have anything I was good at, because I didn't know I could make music yet. And I didn't fit anywhere. And I took a lot of risks, and I just did a lot of things where I didn't take care of myself." [33]

- MITSKI

"I never thought I'd grow old. I thought I'd die young." [9]

- MITSKI

Eventually, in the tenth grade, she decided to grab her independence with both hands and move to Alabama... by herself.

"There was a performing arts school in [Birmingham] Alabama that I wanted to go to. So I went alone." [7]

- MITSKI

"Ninth grade I was living and going to school in Japan [and] I wanted to study music more. The school I was going to just didn't have that big of a music thing. And it was also just wanting to get away, you know? Like, I was, what, 15? 16? I just wanted to be on my own and I wanted to [...] be, quote-unquote, 'independent'. So I applied to a bunch of performing arts high schools in the US without really thinking of geography [...] and then [The Alabama School of Fine Arts] took me. They had a housing thing. They had a pretty good support system for kids who were from far away. So I could just go and not have a car and, just, you know, go to school there." [9]

- MITSKI

The Alabama School of Fine Arts (ASFA) is known for music as well as visual arts, theatre arts, creative writing, math, science, and dance. According to Newsweek, it was the fourth Top High School of 2003. And while I don't doubt Mitski has become their primary boasting point, there were other famous students under their name, such as actor Ajiona Alexus, author Suzanne Collins (*Hunger Games*), actor Laverne Cox (*Orange Is the New Black*), and musician William Brent Hinds (former lead guitarist for Mastodon).

"I had a lot less freedom in Birmingham, Alabama, just because I didn't have a car. I realised you really do need a car to get anywhere. And also, because I was a minor in America, I was very closely supervised. Abroad minors... well in the countries I lived in anyway...

could just run around. So I was oblivious to the fact that you can't do whatever you want." [9]

- MITSKI

"I found that Birmingham was... I don't want to say it's sad because I'm sure it's a beautiful city. I don't know it that much. But what I found was a lot of desolation, or just not enough money. And, again, Alabama itself [...] the countryside, or the landscape is beautiful. But Birmingham was a hard place to be in as a young person. So I felt like it was actually a little stifling. And also the room I lived in had Pepto-Bismol pink walls with no window." [9]

- MITSKI

Well, you know what they say: when the going gets tough, just quit. Which is exactly what Mitski did.

"My parents are maybe a little too trusting but very hands-off. And I just said, 'I'm not going to school' and they're like, 'okay'." [9]

- MITSKI

"I went to four different high schools. Freshman year, I was in Japan. 10th grade, Alabama. 11th grade... I actually ditched school and didn't go to school for a year because I was, like, 'I'm not learning anything, I'm just not gonna go.'" [9]

- MITSKI

"I hated it. I felt like I wasn't learning anything. I felt like I could teach myself more than I was learning in school, so I was, like, 'fuck it.'" [7]

- MITSKI

Moving back to Japan, she entered the working world.

"I worked as a waitress at a Korean barbecue place. And on weekends, I'd go to museums. I'd go on little day trips to other parts of Japan. I learned to party a little bit in Japan. It's safer." [7]

- MITSKI

Thankfully, her smarts kicked in soon enough.

"After a while, I realised that, being in the Working World, people treated me like shit because I didn't even have a degree. I was just a high schooler not in school. And I was, like, oh, it's not about learning anything in school. It's just getting that degree. So I was, like, I need to go back to school to get a degree." [7]

- MITSKI

"You need to go to school so that people don't treat you like you're an idiot. So I went back to school and that was in Virginia." [7]

- MITSKI

"For 11th grade, I went to a school in Virginia, Falls Church. That was a blur." [9]

- MITSKI

"I was really good in school because I learned early on that if your grades are really good then teachers can't say shit to you. Even if you're kind of a bad kid, they can't scold you because you're, like, 'Well, look at my grades. I'm doing everything you want me to do, so fuck off.' So, kids out there, just keep your grades up and then you can do whatever you want!" [7]

- MITSKI

After Virginia was military school in Ankara, Turkey, where Mitski graduated.

"I graduated early. I went to a military-based school. And I had enough credits to graduate. [It] took a few months, and I was, like, 'Wait! I can graduate! I don't need to be here!' I went up to the principal. I was, like, 'Can I just get out of here? You don't want me here. I don't want to be here.'" [7]

- MITSKI

"I just went to the principal's office and I was, like, 'Can I just have a degree?' And she was, like, 'You know, no one's ever done that, but I guess if you have all the credits.' So I graduated early." [9]

- MITSKI

1.7.
MITSKI THE J-POP STAR?

One of the weirder periods in Mitski's early life was when she nearly tumbled into the music industry from the completely wrong direction. As the story goes, a talent manager snapped her up with the full intention of packaging her as the next big pop singer in Japan.

"[He wanted me to be a] cute young girl artist. Or, not artist, pop idol. At a certain point, I just turned to him and said, 'All the songs you're giving me are really bad. I don't want to sing any of this.'" [35]

- MITSKI

The "talent manager" hit back, asking Mitski to write something better.

"I couldn't. Because I wasn't writing at that point and I didn't even consider the fact that I could write anything." [35]

- MITSKI

Who knows how deeply this exchange affected her, but it wasn't long after this that Mitski took the reins of her own musical destiny.

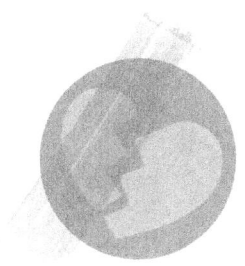

1.8.
THE FIRST SONG

"As I continued to sing, I felt uncomfortable singing other people's songs. I wanted to express my own emotions, but I felt uncomfortable using other people's words. So I decided to try writing songs to express my own thoughts and feelings. I was about 17 years old at the time. I didn't even have the desire to write my own songs or form a band until I was about to go to college." [12]

- MITSKI

"When I first started to write songs, it was because I really wanted to sing, and I couldn't find any songs that I could freely sing the way I wanted to. But now it's just become something I do. I don't feel like myself if I'm not doing it. As for who I make music for, it's primarily for myself, but I am very conscious not to write self-indulgent music. I am, after all, trying to say something in my songs, and there's no use in saying anything if it's not actually communicated." [36]

- MITSKI

From the very beginning, the piano was Mitski's weapon of choice. Hence, it's only fitting that's where her songwriting journey truly began.

"I took a few piano lessons, but that was very short-lived. And then I just fucked around with the keyboard in the house once in a while. I became familiar with it. So not many things have been conscious decisions for me. That was just what was available." [9]

- MITSKI

"I had the musical education, I just wasn't writing songs. Or I didn't think that it was something I could do, you know? I wasn't really brought up to believe that one could just be an artist." [9]

- MITSKI

"I didn't start writing music until much later [...] a lot of musicians start really young. But, for me, I started writing really 17, 18. I really enjoyed singing but I found that none of the songs that I encountered actually said what I wanted to say. I was singing in order to express myself." [13]

- MITSKI

And now the moment you've all been waiting for: when Mitski wrote her first song, drunk, while living in Ankara, Turkey.

"When I started writing music, I was a teenager getting drunk a lot. And I would just sit at the keyboard for hours while I was drunk." [9]

- MITSKI

"I had a keyboard in my room, and I just sat down and started writing this song for the first time. And I thought, 'This is something I can

do? That's amazing.' Suddenly, there was something that was coming out of me that I could sing. And it was just such a rush." [33]

- MITSKI

That song—*her very first song*—was later recorded for her debut. It became known as "Bag of Bones".

"By the time it was done, my heart was pounding like I just saw the rest of my life. I was fucking doomed." [8]

- MITSKI

The "fucking doomed" comment picked up some press and Mitski later clarified what she meant.

"Doomed to pursue it. Now I had a taste of... I don't know. I'd touched God, I felt like. And once you feel that, you can't keep living your life like it didn't happen. I felt like I finally found some mysterious inner-spring, and I had to keep pursuing it." [26]

- MITSKI

"I'm sure a lot of teenagers experience this. I didn't see a purpose in myself, and then I was able to write this song. It was just a relief." [1]

- MITSKI

From this point on, it was music or death.

"I've always felt a lack in everything else in my life. So I kind of... clung to music? Clinged to music? Clung to music?" [28]

- MITSKI

"I'm fundamentally just someone who needs to give myself to something. And so I decided on music." [33]

- MITSKI

"I think it was less of, like, 'I can make my own music' realisation, and more, like, 'I can't do anything else' realisation. I always loved music and I always sang, but I didn't realise it could be a job until I realised I didn't want to do anything else. And so I had to make it my job. I had to make it work" [27]

- MITSKI

"I kind of realised I have to do music. It's not even a choice. I have to figure out a way to do it." [37]

- MITSKI

"It was my little secret garden that I tended to. No one else was allowed in. Things get lost, or break, or disappear. People come and go. But my songs, my writing, it was mine." [2]

- MITSKI

On a side note, ever wonder what Mitski might've been if she hadn't chosen the music path?

"I would also love to be a writer because I feel like you can work truly independently. With music you have to work with other people in order to make it happen. But with writing you can create worlds just with yourself." [11]

- MITSKI

"I really loved geology. I might [have been] a geologist. What I really love is categories. This is why I love biology. I was good at it in school. This is why I love tarot cards. This is why I love astrology. Because there you can put all these things in categories and name them. And I really like rocks. Not so much a crystal person, I'm not really keen on the magical qualities of rocks. I just like how they came about." [11]

- MITSKI

1.9.
MUSICAL INFLUENCES

"[My least favourite question is] 'What's your influence?'
But I realised that's probably just me. I still haven't really figured
out my influences." [38]

- MITSKI

Roundabout here feels like a decent place to dump the strew of names that have been associated with Mitski's art.

"I basically only listened to pop music. Mariah Carey, Britney Spears,
Backstreet Boys, NSYNC, Christina Aguilera, you name it. A lot of
Disney club people. And a lot of Disney songs, too. Just traditional
pop songs. But then, when I tried to sing them, or when I tried to
do something like what the popstars were doing, it just didn't seem to
work. It didn't seem to match up with what I was doing." [39]

- MITSKI

Mitski's taste was quite typical to your average millennial listener, but if you had to pick out one name she adored the most, nobody can challenge Mariah Carey.

"My first album I ever bought was Mariah Carey. I think it was the Singles album and I love her." [27]

- MITSKI

"Sometimes I think we forget how amazing she is. She's my hero." [40]

- MITSKI

"Her melodies are so good. Her music is pleasing even to a child's ears [...] but more than anything I just couldn't believe what she was doing with her voice. I'd never heard anything like it." [39]

- MITSKI

"I would like to just be on the viewing side of that one-way mirror when Mariah Carey is writing and making a song. I don't want to intrude on it, I don't need to be part of it, I would just like to see how the magic happens, because she's just amazing. She's an amazing singer, but a lot of people don't give her credit for how great of a writer she is. I just want to be in the room when she's making a song." [41]

- MITSKI

"I don't like my voice. I got into singing because other people said they like my voice. But then I would listen to my own voice and I'd be like... really? Like this? I think what it is, is that [...] when I was younger, I was listening to Mariah Carey and Christina Aguilera and my voice sounded nothing like that. So I thought my voice was bad because my standards was Mariah Carey, which is impossible. I think that

sets a precedent for the rest of my life. My standards are way too high. I always feel like I could sing better. And it's yeah. It's just a matter of like, 'Okay, we don't have much more studio time. You have to cut it off.'" [11]

- MITSKI

"I loved Mariah Carey, but I never thought, 'I'm going to be the next Mariah Carey.'" [42]

- MITSKI

If you enjoy Mitski slobbering all over Mariah Carey, search for the *This Is The Greatest Song I've Ever Heard In My Entire Life* podcast, the episode "Mitski Learned How To Sing From 'Always Be My Baby'".

Mitski also loved Britney, but we all did.

"My favourite Britney song is 'Oops, I Did It Again.' Because of the video. The red latex suit. I don't know if it's latex, but that was shocking. And the skit in the middle? The best thing about early 2000's music videos was the skit. 'Well, baby, I went down and got it for ya...'" [43]

- MITSKI

Besides Britney and Mariah, another poppier name you may hear from Mitski is The Spice Girls, but there's more to that story...

"Truth be told, I just liked The Spice Girls at the time because this neighbour girl I was hanging out with was really into Spice Girls. I thought it was the thing that I had to keep up with." [39]

- MITSKI

Nevertheless, pop was life for little Mitski.

"I'm passionate about pop because that's what I grew up on. I didn't have any idea about the DIY scene. I didn't know anything about independent music at all until I got to college and I saw other people my age performing rock music. I was like, 'Oh, there's this whole other aspect to music that's not pop.' I was very much a pop child. It has to do with being abroad, and, you know, I grew up without the internet, for a while anyway. What I had access to was what was on MTV, or what was on the one English-speaking channel, and that was usually the Top 40 stuff. The reality is, all that most people in the world have access to is the major label stuff. We can discount it all we want, but the reality is that it affects many people's lives. It's important to look at it, and talk about it, and listen to it." [44]

- MITSKI

"I grew up on purely top 40 music. I would always be abroad, in a lot of countries where everything came late. So I'd get the top hits from like a year before or two years before. And so I tend to relate to people who are a little older than me, because I grew up on their media." [7]

- MITSKI

"I'm not that different from the masses. In terms of musical taste, I tend to agree with the majority on what's good and what's not. I love Ariana Grande's 'God is a Woman'. I assume that if something clicks for me, there will be other people for whom it would click, too, because I'm not that extraordinary. It's the same with songwriting. If you write what works for you and what's true to you, you

can count on you not being so special that no one else would have felt that way." [45]

- MITSKI

"I love The Cardigans." [27]

- MITSKI

"Pop music is what everyone can access. It's frustrating that a lot of it is the lowest common denominator of 'What will everybody like? What is the safest thing to do?'" [17]

- MITSKI

As she evolved into a bigger human, so did her palate, and we come across those artists that appear more inline with Mitski's signature indie alternative style. Without a doubt, the name that comes up more than any other is M.I.A.

"My favourite artist in the world is M.I.A. But I feel like if I collaborated with her, I would ruin it. I would just taint her. I don't want to lower her." [46]

- MITSKI

"I randomly found her first album when I think I was 13 or 14. Her music was so different and I connected with it so strongly and immediately. I think she just continues to inspire me because she always seems to be doing exactly what she wants to do regardless of opposition. That's not to say she's trying to offend anyone. I don't think she's ever trying to do anything to be inflammatory, she's just doing exactly what she feels is right or she thinks that she should do. It doesn't really seem to matter to her whether people want her to do that or not, and I just find that so inspiring." [47]

- MITSKI

"I was a junior high school student living in Kobe when I first heard M.I.A. When I was killing time at a small local record shop, I happened to see the cover of M.I.A.'s debut album there, and I was attracted to it, so I bought it without even checking the sound. When I listened to that album, my life changed. I became a fan of her. She makes music that no one else makes, and I've been following her ever since. Every time she releases an album, I realise how great she is. Her music itself is far removed from others. Her fashion and statements are all unique, and it took five years for the world to catch up with her. I think her charm is that she is ahead of her time." [12]

- MITSKI

"M.I.A is my big hero. She's been my hero since her first record came out [...] she does whatever the fuck she wants. She's a major artist, she's a woman of colour, she comes from a very different background than what you'd expect from a pop artist, and she's very vocal about that. She's so openly political and says what she wants, but she gets away with it because, number one, her music is amazing, and number two, what she's saying is always very important and, oftentimes, correct. It resonates with people. I love how she does something and, at the, moment people are, like, what the fuck is she doing? Then, two, three years later, other pop artists are doing the same thing or just copying what she was doing." [46]

- MITSKI

"She was just doing something totally different from everybody else. She was so free. And listening to her music, I was, like, 'Oh, maybe I can just do what I want.' I was inspired by her—not trying to make music like her, but just in the ethos of it all. Like, 'Oh, actually, none of what anyone did before me matters, I just need to find what I'm good at.'" [39]

- MITSKI

"[I love] M.I.A and Björk, and just a bunch of artists I don't sound like. But I think I'm drawn to [them] because they do their own thing. They're very independent in their philosophy." [27]

- MITSKI

Björk comes up a lot too. Why?

"Because she's been doing her damn thing for 30 damn years!" [48]

- MITSKI

"At first [Björk] terrified me because it's just too much tiny little sounds. Too much 'ting ting ting ting' instead of full chords. But I came back around to her, around late high school, early college." [39]

- MITSKI

"Björk opened up a world of music to me. Her music taught me how there are a million different ways to put sounds and thoughts together, and that music doesn't actually have to sound like anything that's been traditionally accepted as music." [81]

- MITSKI

"I love Björk. I think a lot of people can relate. When she sings, you see a landscape. I think that's what I love about her voice. You feel, *like, if there was no electronics or digital anything, she can be a messenger singing out messages to the next town over. And a lot of her... I forget the term for it, but when she, like, stretches her voice, oftentimes she doesn't have vibrato. It's just a pure tone. It's a little raspy. I love that."* [11]

- MITSKI

To emphasise the point: when asked the classic question of which three celebrities she'd love to have over for a meal, Björk was one Mitski's choices.

"I would love Iggy Pop at the table because his deep groveling voice would be really soothing in the morning. I think Björk would be great at brunch. And the third guest I'll have is Lassie. I would really enjoy watching Lassie eat human food and be, like, 'I can really have this?'" [52]

- MITSKI

Along with M.I.A. and Björk, she has mentioned Micachu and J-pop singer Shiina Ringo, because...

"They all do what the fuck they want, and do it well." [53]

- MITSKI

"There's this one artist called Micachu. I would love to collaborate with her, sincerely. Because everything she does is so left field. She comes from a classical background and she recently did the soundtrack for Under the Skin which was beautiful." [46]

- MITSKI

"There is a Japanese artist, Shiina Ringo, her [album is] Kalk Samen Kuri no Hana. Maybe someone out there will be inspired to write that down and look it up, but it's my favourite album in that there's so much attention to detail, so many instruments. It was a great feat for her as a solo artist to make, so I think I was turned to that album." [44]

- MITSKI

Pop remains important to Mitski, finding joy in the more modern sounds of Charli XCX, Empress Of, and some K-Pop for good measure.

"[Is Charli XCX] some kind of genius?" [45]

- MITSKI

"[Empress Of's] melodic contours are so cool!" [3]

- MITSKI

"There's a K-pop song called 'Call Me Baby' by this group called EXO, and the chord progressions in that is just fascinating." [28]

- MITSKI

But she also gravitates to some more classic rock sounds, such as Jeff Buckley, Bruce Springsteen, Prince, Johnny Cash, and, of course, Iggy Pop.

"[I] like people like Johnny Cash and Iggy Pop. People who have very, very simple—almost stupidly simple—lyrics. It's actually very hard to express everything you want to express in five words or ten words. I look up to them for that because it's actually very difficult to be simple and effective. I don't know who said it, but someone said that truly intelligent people, people who truly understand their subject, can

describe and explain it to a five-year-old, or a six-year-old. That's important for me to keep in mind. I want to take really complex ideas and describe them in simple enough terms for everyone listening to understand." [44]

- MITSKI

"I actually really like Iggy Pop and Johnny Cash and people who write lyrics that are so simple. Because often I think the hardest thing is to take the muck inside you, the complicated thing and simplify it into, like, three words. I think Iggy Pop and Johnny Cash do that very well. Maybe they do it instinctively. Maybe it's not so thought-out. I don't know, I've never talked to them about their process. But those are writers I'm attracted to." [11]

- MITSKI

"I don't really listen to pop-country, but I like really, really old country that's closer to folk. Like Johnny Cash, who is considered country. There's also this one song by Brandi Carlile called 'The Eye' that I was just listening to today. But I wouldn't say I'm, like, a fan. Saying you're a country fan has implications." [55]

- MITSKI

"I love Bruce Springsteen and Prince, just like all these artists that are very unique that I don't sound like." [23]

- MITSKI

"Honestly? Yoko Ono. I think she has had it hard. It was not her fault at all! Everyone just needed a scapegoat slash target, and there was this Asian girl who John was in love with. And they're, like,

'Fuck her!' when she's actually a great artist in her own right. Her poetry is amazing." [11]

- MITSKI

"I was always disappointed that the stuff that was coming out of me sounded so different from what I liked to listen to. I always thought that meant that my music was bad. But I came to realise it's just different." [9]

- MITSKI

One would correctly assume that Mitski has many other influences that are not quite so predictable, but her love for jazz may come as a surprise.

"This makes me sound like an asshole but I've just been listening to jazz. I don't think I can listen to anything remotely similar to myself and my music anymore because I start analysing it or I start listening to it as an artist. With jazz I can just fully appreciate it and absorb it as music, as a whole. And I think jazz is deep and beautiful, so that's what I've been listening to lately." [47]

- MITSKI

"I'm actually listening to a lot of [Charles] Mingus, which makes me sound like an asshole. The jazz artist. Because it's so different from what I make and especially when I'm on tour, I'm playing my music all the time, I wanna listen to something that's nothing like what I'm making. And also, a lot of it just doesn't have words so I just want to have something that's like going without having to focus on a lyric or anything. A lot of jazz at the moment." [56]

- MITSKI

Classical, too.

"Of course, a big formative piece for my high school years was 'The Rite of Spring' by Stravinsky. That was another thing that was, like, 'Ohhh, you can do anything!'" [39]

- MITSKI

An even bigger stunner is her in-depth passion for hip-hop.

"I could go on and on about how great Chance the Rapper is, but I would prefer it if everyone just went in and listened for themselves. Everything in the album Coloring Book is artful. It's really good music." [3]

- MITSKI

"Young Thug is underrated. He does shit that no one else is doing. The way he raps and sings and makes sounds like he doesn't seem concerned with sounding good. He just wants to express something. He just wants to push the envelope." [40]

- MITSKI

"I love how Young Thug doesn't seem like he's thinking about what sounds pretty. It's more, 'How can I use my voice as an instrument and make this interesting?'" [14]

- MITSKI

"If Drake sampled me, that would be great. Just saying." [46]

- MITSKI

"Drake thinks he's underrated and no amount of love we show him will ever convince him otherwise. It's just something that he has to figure out for himself." [40]

- MITSKI

She has expressed further love for Vince Staples and even more so for Run the Jewels.

"I'm not in any position to talk about rap music or hip-hop because I'm not in that world, [but Run the Jewels is] such a return to what hip-hop or rap is supposed to be about. Because, like, Killer Mike talks about real stuff. And it goes back to the Public Enemy age, when they were still about rebelling. And that's actually punk rock." [23]

- MITSKI

Expanding on that, she said the best album of 2014 was...

"Run the Jewels 2." [48]

- MITSKI

And the best concert?

"Billy Elliot, the Musical." [48]

- MITSKI

Of course, Mitski still has love for her loud guitar music. She was once spotted wearing a hoodie from drone metal band Sunn O))). She also takes many interview opportunities to praise other rock bands, big and small.

"[I love punk rock band] Ceremony. The first [album] I listened to is Rohnert Park, like most people. They sound like 'ahhhhh!'" [57]

- MITSKI

"Spirit of the Beehive is a band. Actually, I think they're my favourite band. They're a Philly band. We played a DIY house show together and I've been following them since. They would make weird soundscapes but then suddenly open up to a super pop melody that you can sing along to and then go back to weird. I think it's very beautiful." [57]

- MITSKI

Want to dig deeper? The pit of Mitski's influences truly is bottomless, with some of the more obscure names including Arthur Russell, Beverly Glenn-Copeland, Vangelis, Ikue Asazaki, and Bartók to name a few.

"I feel like Bartók actually writes great melodies that we can learn from today. It's just like folk melodies. Bartók's very pop. And classical is one of those things, I think, where it actually does sound good on vinyl. That's kind of the impression I get. There's less bass. Heavy bass is what kind of fucks up vinyl sounds and this doesn't really have it." [57]

- MITSKI

"On one hand, I relate really strongly to all sorts of different kinds of Indian music or Malaysian music, just because I grew up around it. A lot of Chinese pop and Taiwanese pop and definitely Japanese folk music, Japanese pop. But a lot of this music I feel like I can't take ownership for because I'm not from those countries. So it goes back to that thing of, like, always being a foreigner where I like these things, but I am never part of those things. I can't apply it to who I am or my identity. So all I can really say is, yeah, I listen to all these things and I really love it and it affected me but I can't say I know it." [9]

- MITSKI

Another fancy method of joining the dots is to seek the songs Mitski has covered, live or otherwise.

"I did Calvin Harris' 'How Deep Is Your Love' but a grunge rock version of it. I think it's on the internet." [7]

- MITSKI

It is! Besides "How Deep Is Your Love", Mitski has also put her twist on Personal Best's "This is What We Look Like", the Italian hymn "Bella Ciao" (but in English), and The Bleachers' "Let's Get Married", the latter of which was officially released as a split EP with Bleachers called *Terrible Thrills Vol. 3 #1*.

To summarise, there's a lot of homework to be done if you want to unpack what makes Mitski tick. And even then, you still won't get close.

"Obviously, I'm not a musicologist, so I know absolutely nothing and I probably never will. But I just like to listen to what I have access to and form my own opinions. There is a lot of comfort in quote-unquote 'world music' because my father would only really play that in the house when he'd play music at all, but also I just want to listen to music that's not dictated by the Western classical canon. It irks me when Western music theory nerds talk about how chord progressions in a song are 'wrong,' or when music from outside of the West is exoticised." [33]

- MITSKI

1.10.
MUSICAL COMPARISONS

"If someone asked me what I would rather be called, I wouldn't know the answer to it. I think the whole genre thing is more a way of organising the whole giant world of music. It doesn't really mean anything to me, but I know that iTunes needs me to put something in the genre section. I don't really think about genre, but the business world and the marketing world need me to pick a genre." [47]

- MITSKI

Journalists do what journalists do best, which is lumping artists into similar boxes, trying to make sense of a realm they often don't understand. Some of the more common names you'll find shoved next to Mitski include St. Vincent, Fiona Apple, Beabadoobee, Japanese Breakfast, Lana Del Rey, Waxahatchee, Phoebe Bridgers, Regina Spektor, and Angel Olsen.

"When I used to do piano songs, people would say 'Regina Spektor!' And I would just be like... that's not true. But now that I don't

play piano anymore, people don't say that [...] There's a lot of Angel Olsen comparisons, and I don't mind those, because I really love her music. But I also feel that everyone is saying Angel Olsen [because] she's a woman." [15]

- MITSKI

"Someone on Facebook recently said I'm, and this is a quote, 'Alex G with girl parts,' and I was just like, 'Oh no!'" [15]

- MITSKI

"It can be frustrating because that becomes your genre. It's not about the music you make, it's not about what you're trying to say. It's about what little box you fit into. And so a lot of people don't even listen to the music and immediately decide what kind of music I'm making [...] Everything I make is listened through the filter of otherness. And that can be frustrating because I actually make music to try and connect with people, and talk about how we're the same and we feel the same, when all that's heard is me being 'different'" [58]

- MITSKI

1.11.
OTHER ARTISTIC INFLUENCES

The multifacetedness of Mitski cannot be limited to music, and there are many other mediums that scooped coal into her creative train.

MOVIES

You don't have to lean far into Mitski's world to tumble into her obsession with Studio Ghibli, which goes deeper for Hayao Miyazaki's contributions, and deepest for *Princess Mononoke.*

"The first time I ever fell in love with a movie was Princes Mononoke [...] I don't have a favourite Miyazaki but that is in the top five for sure." [29]

- MITSKI

"I can't say for sure, but I think [Miyazaki's] film was the first film I ever saw. I think it was Princess Mononoke. Without even knowing it,

he's been with me my whole life. Every time I have doubts or I don't quite know how to live in the world, I watch his films, and I'm, like, 'Oh yeah, it's this simple, this is it, this is the answer.' I love how he doesn't explain a lot of things but you kind of draw your own beautiful conclusions." [27]

- MITSKI

"Everytime I think about what I would say to Miyazaki if I met him, I just start crying. He's my actual hero. Everytime I'm confused about life or don't know what to do, I watch one of his movies and I'm like [...] this is who I should be. The thing is, I've always wanted to be San from Princess Mononoke. But I think, realistically, I'm more like No Face [from Spirited Away]." [43]

- MITSKI

"It's so resolute, the way [Chihiro from Spirited Away is] looking out the window, especially because she has no return ticket. It's the face of someone who's made a decision." [33]

- MITSKI

"A lot of Hayao Miyazaki films are about lost worlds or post-apocalyptic dystopian worlds. But especially Castle in the Sky. I just love Castle in the Sky, because I love even just the idea of there being a floating island up there that's deserted and has a history that we don't know about." [25]

- MITSKI

"Castle in the Sky made me cry so hard. I was so young that I didn't understand why I was crying. It was a whole conflicting thing where

I was just crying and crying and crying. It's beautiful now that I get nostalgic about it. Because before that movie, I would cry because something sad happened, or I would laugh because something was funny. And then, at that moment, it was like it touched on an emotion that I didn't understand but just was overwhelming." [9]

- MITSKI

"I also really look up to Nausicaä from The Valley of the Wind. Love 'em all!" [43]

- MITSKI

"[Miyazaki's] movies give me the answers on how to live. I don't know, they're so kind and hopeful." [57]

- MITSKI

"I think actually more than any kind of music or anything, Hayao Miyazaki is my biggest influence." [9]

- MITSKI

With the Miyazaki spillage aside, Mitski has demonstrated a wider taste in film, some of which we will delve into later, and some we can randomly throw out now. These include *Moonstruck*...

"Nicolas Cage looks like some sort of god in that movie." [1]

- MITSKI

...and the 2017 British film *Beast*...

"I think it's my favourite movie [...] it's really beautiful. It explored a lot of things that were circling in my mind already. It felt like getting the answer to questions I didn't even know I had." [45]

- MITSKI

"That one blew my mind. Subjectively, it kind of solved a lot of problems for me that I was having creatively. It talked about a lot of things that I had been thinking about. I remember I was in L.A. and I just watched it three nights in a row—I kept going to the ArcLight Hollywood over and over again." [41]

- MITSKI

...not to mention a healthy love for horror.

"The obvious one is the Japanese film Ju-On, which became the Hollywood version The Grudge. Does not compare! I'm sorry, Hollywood! I still, to this day, have nightmares about long-haired women ghosts and small boy child ghosts." [29]

- MITSKI

"Another one that scarred me... my parents went to a party and brought me. I was ushered into the children's room, but a lot of the kids there were teenagers, or just older. They were playing this horror movie. I think it was a vampire movie. I was way too young. I wish I knew which film it was. It scarred me forever." [29]

- MITSKI

"Honestly, The Chilling Adventures of Sabrina. I know it's not a movie, but I haven't loved a TV show like this in a while." [41]

- MITSKI

BOOKS

"In my case, I focus a lot on the lyrics. So in that vein, books really influence me." [59]

- MITSKI

Mitski also reads. Of course she does.

"There was a phase freshman year where I was really obsessed with Paradise Lost. My God, what a weird fucking kid! Something about it was so dramatic and romantic, and I read it over and over and would write phrases down." [33]

- MITSKI

"My favourite story of a haunted house is Shirley Jackson's Haunting of Hill House. I think that's my favourite book of all time. I can't imagine being such a good writer." [25]

- MITSKI

"[I love] Bell Hooks, obviously [...] so many more women. I feel like we're amassing an army." [48]

- MITSKI

Apparently Mitski was also fond of reading excerpts from *The Empty Space* by Peter Brook before shows.

"He's all about minimalism: shedding everything. He's not opposed to Broadway musicals, but the crux of it is: do only what's necessary.

Sometimes what's necessary is a big production; sometimes it's one person onstage." [14]

- MITSKI

Conversely, she also finds joy in the simpler side of writing.

"Oh my god, young adult romance is the shit. I have given up on trying to pretend I'm above a good romance. I'm a songwriter, for Christ sakes! In young adult romance, there's just pure love. There isn't, like, 'Oh, honey, I would love to live with you, but I make more money than you right now, so it won't create a good situation.' Like, there's none of that adult, taxes, shit. There's just, 'I love you and you love me." [43]

- MITSKI

This begs the question: are we likely to get a book written by Mitski one day?

"I'm not a prose writer. I've done it for fun, but then I would read back what I wrote and I would understand that I'm never meant to write prose." [28]

- MITSKI

Oh well. Hopefully this book scratches that itch for the time being.

ARCHITECTURE

And finally, inspiration may strike Mitski from... buildings?

"I lived most of my life in this tunnel vision bubble, where I really was only looking at my feet. And then I became a real adult and looked around and started to appreciate architecture. I don't know anything about architecture but I appreciate buildings. I love the history of buildings. Yeah, I'm interested in buildings" [25]

- MITSKI

1.12.
PRIVACY SETTINGS

"I'm an idiot for pursuing this career because there's no going around it. When I'm writing, I'm not thinking about who's gonna listen to it. I'm just writing for myself. And then that happens to be the only thing I'm really good. So I'm, like, 'Okay, let me try to make a living off of this,' but in order to do that I have to show it to people. And the 'it' is my emotions, or myself." [51]

- MITSKI

"This is probably hard to believe, but I'm a very private person. So, just like, playing a show and then having people I don't know come up to me, talking to me about very personal things, like, 'Oh, right, because I said that...'" [51]

- MITSKI

We touched on this topic before, but as we head into the meat of Mitski's story, it's important to emphasise why certain details simply are not available, such as the truth about her dad's career or the names of her cats.

"The kids on the internet now are very savvy. They could type in the [cat] names, figure out where I live [...] they're shelter cats. Usually they have microchips where they have their information. Or someone I love could just innocuously be like, 'A and B, my favourite cats.' And if people know what their names are, they can go, 'Oh, I see.' And then they would see behind the picture of the cats, the interior of my house. And then they can pinpoint perhaps what that house is." [51]

- MITSKI

"I have developed this theory about this. When the world put me in this position, I didn't realise that I was making this deal where in exchange for giving me this platform and attention, I was supposed to give myself." [1]

- MITSKI

Nevertheless, Mitski remains a wide open book of emotional thoughts, meaning the "extra private person" label is not entirely fair.

"I have social media accounts. I answer honestly in interviews. And anyone who sees me perform can tell I'm in love with human beings. I want desperately to feel connected. Everything I do is for my love of, and yearning for, people. So press outlets nonetheless insisting I'm 'intensely private' feels vindictive, like a punishment for setting boundaries, and for not offering more of myself for content and exploitation." [1]

- MITSKI

"I'm learning to be open in certain aspects of my life to almost create a red herring so that other stuff can remain private." [33]

- MITSKI

The overall message is this: we can immerse ourselves in her music, but some personal details are Mitski's to keep, and we should respect that. This includes the topic of relationships, which comes up completely empty...

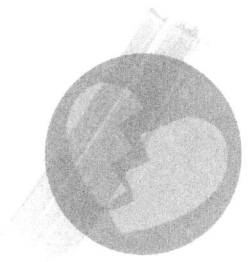

1.13.
MITSKI'S LOVE LIFE

"Oh no, I hate people. I just want my own fucking time in the morning." [52]

- MITSKI

Love life? Sex life? Sexual orientation? This is not that kind of biography. Can't help you. Nobody can.

"I take everything seriously. I don't wanna get into my sex life. A kiss means something to me." [17]

- MITSKI

"[I hate] when things are way too personal and involve my significant other, because that's none of your business. I say, 'No comment.' I understand where that question comes from, because I have very

confessional, revealing songs, but I like to keep that to my songs. I don't actually like to talk about it with people I don't know." [38]

- MITSKI

That said, we do know that astrological signs play a role.

"I'm a Libra, so my sexuality is essentially 'you can be any gender as long as you treat me like a princess.'" [60]

- MITSKI

"When I have a crush on someone, I'm casually like, 'Hey! When's your birthday? No, like, year. No, like, okay, where were you born, exactly? You don't know? Can you ask your mom real quick? I just wanna know you!' And then I make their birth-chart and then I see if we should get married and have children.'" [43]

- MITSKI

"My heart's been broken by so many Sagittariuses. When I hear someone's a Sag, I'm like, 'Oop, sorry, gotta go!'" [43]

- MITSKI

"Every Sagittarius I've been romantically involved with would not define the fucking relationship. And I need that. I need us to put our relationship in a box so I can just sleep at night. And they won't fucking do it for me!'" [11]

- MITSKI

"Controversial opinion: I love Geminis. I'm a Libra, and I guess it's an air sign thing. My sister is a Gemini, and we get along really well.

The people I've been romantically involved with who have worked out really well are Geminis. But I also hate some Geminis. There's one famous Gemini that I fucking despise, his name is Trump. So I think a good Gemini is the best sign. A bad Gemini is the worst." [11]

- MITSKI

Yet, if you pay attention, every now and then, we can catch glimpses of Mitski's relationship opinions.

"If you really love someone, you're not thinking about what it does for you." [28]

- MITSKI

"Being in romantic relationships is actually a really good learning opportunity for me. It's learning how to bring someone into your life, which I have never done. I had a really hard time wrapping my head around the concept of a relationship, because all my life I had this thing where I'd start to befriend somebody, but then we'd get into an argument, and I'd just stop talking to them. In my world it was a waste of time to try to mend a relationship, because by the time I did I would go away anyway. So just maintaining relationships is so foreign to me, it took me a while to figure it out." [6]

- MITSKI

"I honestly don't have any specific take on love and relationships, because romantic relationships are always completely different every time. There are no actual rules set out for how to conduct a relationship, and people will give you all sorts of information throughout your life. But there are actually no real rules, because the rules

are made up by the two people involved as they go along. So I would say each relationship is basically the sum of time it takes for two people to make up the rules, for a world they're trying to create for themselves to live in together. I suppose my ultimate take on love is that it's hard." [21*]

- MITSKI

And that's about all the info we have. I guess we will have to just make do with what we can forage from her songs. Which, as it turns out, is less than we thought.

"I'm revealing a big secret, but a lot of my songs are just about music and trying to pursue it, and not feeling loved by it. A lot of the 'yous' in my songs are abstract ideas about music. I will neglect everything else, including me as a person, just to get to keep making music. And even if it actually sometimes hurts, it doesn't matter as long as I get to be a musician." [6]

- MITSKI

"Music is my closest relationship. It's been my only friend sometimes growing up because I grew up moving around. But I would play music or sing music to myself, and it's like my family. So a lot of my songs are just about how much I love music. Or, you know, it's kind of hard being a musician. So sometimes when I sing about being spurned by a lover, it's actually the feeling of being spurned by music or my career in music and how it's not going well." [61]

- MITSKI

"In my music, when I'm talking about love I'm rarely talking about real love. I'm mostly talking about power and fixation and loss. Because all *those things show up in the form of love or in the form of relationships. And we're just figuring out how to be humans through each other. So I don't know if I've written many pure love songs about just being in love with someone and being in a good place about that.*" [28]

- MITSKI

"I obsess over one phrase of one line of music, over and over, and I switch out words. It ends up being my biggest relationship." [33]

- MITSKI

Be that as it may be, there is only one thing everyone truly wants to know. Does Mitski have sex to own music?

"Oh, that sounds awful! I'd be having sex, but then I'd be, like, 'Oh, shit! I should have fixed that in the production!' And then I'd be distracted." [7]

- MITSKI

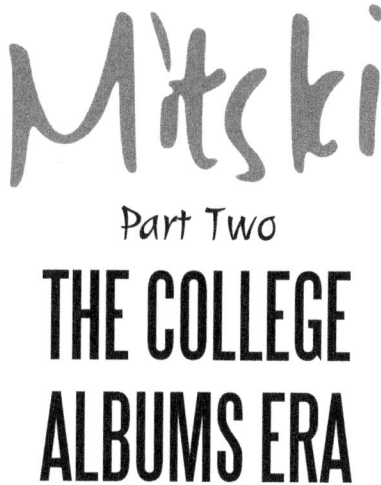

Part Two

THE COLLEGE
ALBUMS ERA

2.1.
MITSKI DOES AMERICA

"But then once I graduated early, I was, like, 'Okay, what do I do now?' Because, at that point, I wasn't writing songs. I didn't know what I wanted to do with my life. So I was kind of fucking around in Turkey for a while, and then at the very last minute, I was like, 'Oh, shit, I have to go to college!'" [9]

- MITSKI

Hi! Back on the main timeline, Mitski had just graduated in Turkey, if you remember. After that, she decided it best to locate part of her roots by moving back to America, aiming for New York City to start college.

"Although I grew up abroad, I'm still a US citizen, meaning I would ultimately have to go back to the US to get a job, because doing otherwise would either mean adopting a new nationality or forever living and working in a country as a foreigner. And getting a job in the US is generally easier with a US University education. So I came

back to the US to go to college. It's all very realistic and not very romantic. As for coming to New York, now that I think of it, I never really thought twice or questioned why it had to be New York. For some reason I just always had it in my head that I would end up living in New York City, so here I am." [21*]

- MITSKI

"Basically, the only two cities I knew were New York and L.A. I knew that if you lived in L.A, you needed a car. If you lived in New York City, you didn't need a car. So I was, like, 'Okay, I'm going to New York City." [9]

- MITSKI

"I hadn't really experienced much of the US, so in my mind, New York was America." [8]

- MITSKI

2.2.
MUSIC STUDIES

"It was the very last minute, where all the applications were already done. The place that accepted was Hunter College. I knew I wanted to go to New York City and Hunter College has, like, an all-year-round acceptance process [...] so I went to Hunter." [9]

- MITSKI

Hunter College is a public university which has several big names with which to show off. These include actor Vin Diesel, actress Cybill Shepherd, and The Strokes' bassist Nikolai Fraiture. And then there was Mitski who enrolled to study... film? Wait, what?

"I was surrounded by people who genuinely wanted to make movies, and meanwhile, I was sneaking into the music department's practice rooms every day. It was a wake-up call." [1]

- MITSKI

"I went to Hunter because I knew I needed to go to college. Hunter was in New York City which was important to me [...] and it seemed like it had a big arts program or, I guess, technical arts program. I was part of the film program, and then I just realised that wasn't what I wanted to do. I was just avoiding doing music because I thought it was a dead end, but then halfway through I was like, you know, I actually shouldn't avoid what I'm thinking about doing every day all the time. So I just sucked it up and applied to Conservatory." [9]

- MITSKI

Whew! Thankfully, Mitski's musician calling overrode her choice and she transferred to State University of New York at Purchase College's Conservatory of Music.

"I decided to go to music school, and [my parents] were, like, 'Okay! Do your thing.'" [26]

- MITSKI

"I studied studio composition. I went to SUNY Purchase, not because it's an incredibly great school, I hate to say, but they had a specific program called 'studio composition' that not only taught you music composition, but also taught you how to work in studios." [44]

- MITSKI

State University of New York at Purchase is more commonly known as Purchase College or SUNY Purchase. It's a public liberal arts college in Purchase, a hamlet in Westchester County, New York state. Zoë Kravitz, Wesley Snipes, and Regina Spektor attended this establishment.

"Purchase has a unique program. They have a classical composition program, but the one I was in was called studio composition, where you obviously study classical composition, but you also learn how to

work in studios, and you study quote-unquote 'pop music,' whatever
that means. And there's more technology incorporated in the program.
A lot of people who go into studio comp want to do film scoring or
want to do production, but want to learn how to compose
and so on." [16]

- MITSKI

"Maybe it's different now, but when I was there, it was a very free
program where you got to forge your own path. You got to take what
classes you wanted to take. And some years, to be honest, I took
as little classes as I possibly could so I could record my own music
[...] I think at the end of the day, they kind of realised they couldn't
stop me. They learned to step back and let me do it, because
if they didn't, I would find a way to do it. They really encouraged
finding your own voice." [26]

- MITSKI

2.3.
DISCOMFORT AND JOY
HOLIDAY SONGS

Only those who crawl the deepest spaces of Mitski's history will know about these little gems. Discomfort and Joy are a collaborative team of musicians from SUNY Purchase who record holiday songs usually in the space of one day. On December 17th, 2010, they released *Have Yourself A Merry Little Half-Assed Christmas* which featured our heroine. This is surely one of her oldest official recordings, as she is credited as Mitsuki Miyawaki, not to mention the Xmas classic she covered was renamed as "Have Yourself a Mitsuki Little Christmas".

The aforementioned song must have been recorded just as she joined college. And then, as she was just leaving college two years later, she appeared on another Discomfort and Joy compilation called *It's ValenTIME! Vol. 2: 14 Ways To Say I Love You*. Fittingly released on Valentine's Day, 2013, here Mitski duetted with another Purchase singer, Sean McVerry, covering the song "Tonight You Belong to Me". This time, Mitski was credited as Mitski. If you're willing to scour the Xwitter page @mitskithoughts you may even discover a video of them rehearsing the song together.

2.4.
ALBUM: LUSH (2014)

1. Liquid Smooth (2:49)
2. Wife (2:39)
3. Abbey (2:49)
4. Brand New City (2:12)
5. Eric (3:17)
6. Bag of Bones (4:36)
7. Door (2:12)
8. Pearl Diver (2:44)
9. Real Men (2:41)

TOTAL RUNTIME: 26:01

Please note: *the above track listing reflects what you'll currently find on streaming services such as Spotify. However, the original arrangement was different, while "Real Men" has since been removed from Bandcamp.*

"LUSH is my very first album. I'd never produced an album before, meaning I'd never asked and organised people to do things for me in order to make ideas in my head audible. I recorded the album using the studios available in my music conservatory, with my musician friends who were passionate about good music and who cared enough to take time out of their lives to help me produce something good, not to mention meet and embrace the anal-retentive obsessive perfectionist-Mitski that I've learned I become in the studio. So far, the bond between people born out of making music together has been better than any great sex I've ever had." [21*]

- MITSKI

Mitski's debut album, *LUSH* (all caps), was recorded as a junior in college and self-released on January 31st, 2012. Fellow student Scot Moriarty produced and mixed the record.

"I remember being in the rehearsal room at Purchase. She was, like, 'Hey, how are you?' when we met, and then she plays me these two songs, 'Liquid Smooth' and 'Pearl Diver', and [I was] like... holy shit, you know? It's so apparent how crazy talented she is and how good her voice is. So I was like, yeah, absolutely, let's work together if you're down for it." [4]

- SCOT MORIARTY

"I don't remember when I started saying it, but at some point, I was just, like, 'I think she's going to be as big as Amy Winehouse' [...] She never cancelled a session. She was never late for a session. And she always showed up and wanted to get shit done. So I felt like if anyone was going to be successful that I knew from school, it was going to be her. Mainly because of the combination of her talent and her drive." [4]

- SCOT MORIARTY

Credits thank another Scott—Scott Interrante—for organising and conducting the orchestral arrangements.

"A lot of these bands that are coming up started out when they were 13 in garages, whereas I started out as someone who looked at a sheet of music and wrote out the parts. So the way I think about music and composition and recording music isn't, like, the band is gonna sound this way. It's more the layers are going to sound this way." [5]

- MITSKI

LUSH is yet to find life in physical form, but it's streaming everywhere. It's also worth quickly mentioning that this is Mitski's only album that did not feature another SUNY student named Patrick Hyland, but we will get to him soon in a big big way.

"I think she was a little bit mysterious, because she didn't hang out on the campus too much. So, speaking just in the peer community of that school, there was something mythic that she had made this very mature sounding album and wasn't with the in-crowd of the other bands that were popular at our school. People were very impressed by the sophistication on that record, even though it was made by a student." [42]

- PATRICK HYLAND

SOUND

"I don't feel like I can do that ever again. I think it's an especially first-album kind of thing, not just for me but for any artist. Because, for your first album ever, you put together all the songs that you wrote over a long period of time when you were changing as a person constantly. Right now, I'm living the kind of life where I just have a period of time when I write for the next record, and then that's it." [16]

- MITSKI

Mitski introduced herself to the world through a mix of genres, which have been called lo-fi chamber pop, art pop, piano rock, punk rock, and vocal jazz.

"I haven't thought about that record for a long time. I think that record is all about me trying different things. It's the most varied in terms of genre or style, because it was my first album, and I took all these different songs I wrote at different times and put them in one record, as opposed to having focused time to write for it and just

writing 'an album'. I think for the first record, I was trying out all the different things I might want to do in the future." [16]

- MITSKI

ARTWORK

LUSH's photoshoot was taken by Htat Htut, who has since gone on to work with Olivia Rodrigo, Sam Smith, and James Blake, as well as tackling commercial work with Range Rover and Whatsapp.

THEMES

Referring to herself in third person, Mitski has reflected:

"She was someone who simply wrote her feelings, and didn't think about how her narrative was being conveyed [...] She was ambitious and single-minded about getting to be a musician. But maybe she didn't quite understand what that meant... what the price was at the door." [50]

- MITSKI

CHARTS AND CRITICAL

Well, of course, no one knew who Mitski was at this point, so *LUSH* did not chart and slipped through everyone's cracks. But fan opinion has not only held the record in high regard, but its accolades only appear to rise each year passing. You may even occasionally come across those who swear this is their favourite Mitski.

NOTEWORTHY SONGS

Information is scarce as Mitski has raced far from this point in her career, but here are some small crumb trails she left behind.

• Liquid Smooth

"Liquid Smooth" features the Japanese line *"Kuzurete yuku maeni"* which translates to *"Before I crumble"*. There are only two Mitski songs that feature her mother tongue, but you'll have to wait for the next one.

This song can also be found on the *Audiotree.tv Free 2015 Compilation*.

• Brand New City

"I'd say 'Brand New City' was, I guess, a precursor to the current stuff I'm working on." [16]

- MITSKI

• Eric

Those hardcore fans over on Mitski Wiki connected that "Eric" mentions a "blue light" which is the title of a later song on *Be the Cowboy*.

• Bag of Bones

As we already know, "Bag of Bones" is somehow the first official song Mitski ever wrote in her life. How is that possible? It's also the longest track on the record.

• Pearl Diver

"I was just thinking about death and dying. It's about death, sorry. But also whatever you want." [11]

- MITSKI

• Real Men

As stated earlier, *LUSH*'s track listing has shuffled like mad, with "Real Men" leaping in the most confusing of ways. Originally the fourth track on the album, it was later shoved right to the end while Bandcamp dropped the song completely.

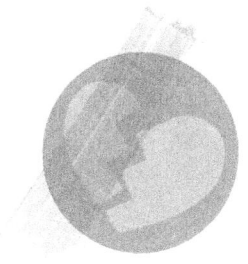

2.5.
LUSH TOUR

"[The] first tour I went on was mostly just an excuse to go on a road trip with my friends from Conservatory. And it was the best tour ever. But it also wasn't a real professional lucrative thing. It was just, like, 'Let's go jump into rivers in Upstate New York!'" [11]

- MITSKI

Hardly anyone knows about Mitski's first tour. But it did happen!

"Oh my goodness, touring was so much fun! It was the first time I toured for my own music, and I think it was a good first tour because I went with two other bands who were my friends. It almost felt like an elaborate excuse to road-trip along the east coast. None of us were well-known and we had very little money, so we basically limited our shows to venues in each of our hometowns or places we had friends, stopping by only a few big cities just to say that we did, and we slept over our family's/friends' houses. Since most of

the members were from areas where there's a lot of nature, we ended up jumping into rivers and seas, we walked in woods and had campfires, and then every night we got to play music together. It was grand." [36]

- MITSKI

Although, maybe you can't exactly refer to it as a proper tour.

"The first time I went on tour was not a real tour, let's be truthful here. It was like a GoFundMe glorified college trip with other bands from my school. It was really nice, actually. We stayed at everyone's parents' house. It was a lot of beautiful upstate areas [in like] Pennsylvania." [29]

- MITSKI

It was important nevertheless. You may even credit these shows for nudging Mitski in the direction for which she has become better known.

"The tour did wake me up to the fact that people fundamentally react better to bands than solo piano/guitar acts, and that no matter how carefully one may craft a song, if it came down to a quiet act and a loud act playing a live show, the louder act would usually grab the attention of the audience more easily. Of course, I'm not saying that's a bad thing. I just realised the fact after playing a lot of shows. So now I'm [specifically writing and arranging] for live sets. I'm not abandoning the slow piano stuff or the big orchestral stuff by any means, but I want to be able to rock out on stage for a change!" [36]

- MITSKI

"The whole live band aspect of it scares me on a trust level. I'm kind of a control freak, so I like to make sure that my hands are on every layer. With live bands, it's so hard for every single instrument to sound good in one take unless you're a very tight band. So I think my work style will always be layer-by-layer so that I can edit each one. But maybe that will change, maybe I'll feel inspired to do a band thing, but it hasn't happened yet." [5]

- MITSKI

"Everyone prefers bands because it's louder. It's fuller. More dynamics. But I tend to like playing solo, only because I don't have to worry about other people. When I'm playing with a band, I have to think about multiple things at once. But when it's solo, it's just me in my own world. Granted, if I mess up and I'm playing solo, I'm effed... I don't know if I'm allowed to swear? I'm FUCKED! Because the music stops if I fuck up. But I think I'm fundamentally a masochist where I just like seek out those like chances to really fuck up in front of people." [51]

- MITSKI

"With solo shows, you have complete control over the set list. If you feel like you want to do something different or do a new song, you can just work it in. You can talk to the audience or not talk to the audience. There's nothing that's set. It's been really good for me to learn how to work an audience or see what's going on and do that with the freedom of not being responsible for other band members. Because when you have other band members, you have to go with a set list or you have to go as planned. But I really like solo shows because I can throw in whatever I want. And if it doesn't work, there's that much more pressure. If you fail on your own up there, you're completely alone, but that's the biggest thrill. I think I'm kind of a masochist. I love the potential of being completely embarrassed. I feel like now is the time for me to take risks because I have a small audience. I feel like I should learn what I can right now while I'm still growing. With this kind of stuff, no one actually tells you how to do things. You just have to figure it out for yourself." [62]

- MITSKI

2.6.
ALBUM: RETIRED FROM SAD, NEW CAREER IN BUSINESS (2013)

1. Goodbye, My Danish Sweetheart (2:17)
(video shot by Ryan Galloway)
2. Square (3:10)
(video shot by Heather Barcelo and Alan Wertz)
3. Strawberry Blond (1:54)
(video shot by Heather Barcelo and Jovon Outlaw)
4. Humpty (3:21)
(video shot by Heather Barcelo and Jovon Outlaw)
5. I Want You (3:03)
(video shot by Jovon Outlaw)
6. Shame (2:24)
(video shot by Alan Wertz)
7. Because Dreaming Costs Money, My Dear (3:05)
(video shot by Heather Barcelo)
8. Circle (2:51)
(video shot by Alan Wertz)
9. Class of 2013 (1:49)
(video shot by Jovon Outlaw)

TOTAL RUNTIME: 23:54

"I didn't suffer any sophomoric album grief or anxiety actually, because my second album felt like such a completely different beast. My first album is more a collection of songs I'd compiled over a long period of time, while the songs on my second album were written over a more focused period of time, with the intention of putting them together into one album. My first album was also all about me learning how to arrange simple melodies and harmonies for various instruments, and about me getting used to the recording process itself. By my second album, I was secure enough in my recording processes and techniques to focus more on writing for an orchestra, as well as on actually being a producer, organising 60+ people and getting everyone on the same page, which was pretty hellish." [36]

- MITSKI

On August 1st, 2013, Mitski self-released her second album as her senior year project. And by all accounts, she took her work to the next level. First of all, every song came with a music video accompaniment piece. And secondly, she made use of the Purchase College's student orchestra. This means there is a 60-person band behind the lady, who herself was already credited for the vocals, piano, and drums.

"Maybe [it was] fun in retrospect. Like, when you're a college student and you have to direct 30 people, and they all have stuff to do that's not your music, it's very difficult to try and get everyone together. So I'm very grateful for their help... and I'm glad I'm not doing that anymore, or for a while. Maybe I'll want to in the future, but right now I'm into the minimalism of my setup." [26]

- MITSKI

You can find the full list of credits on her Bandcamp (which also curiously thanks Avant Garde artist John Zorn), but there are three names which stand taller than the rest. The first name is Sean McVerry, who previously collaborated with Mitski on the "Tonight You Belong To Me" cover, now providing "gang vocals" on her album. The second name is Scott Interrante who dealt with the orchestral arrangements on tracks 1, 2, 3, 4, 6, and 8 from *Retired from Sad, New Career in Business*. He played the same role on *LUSH*.

"I mean, I had all these classical musicians who were willing to play for free for me. And, well, you know, it was a tit-for-tat situation. A lot of it was bartering where they would play on my record. So I'd be in their recital, blah, blah, blah. And the great thing about being in school is that my job was to make music without any limitations. My job was to experiment. And so I looked around and said, 'What can I use?' And I'm going to use all of it. Because college is expensive." [11]

- MITSKI

The third (and most important) name is Patrick Hyland who produced, engineered, mixed, and mastered every track on this album. Patrick then went on to produce her next record, and her next one, and her next one right until this very day. If you are dying to know more, skip ahead a few chapters, where we'll dive deeper into the man. Or exercise a bit of patience, and you'll get there eventually.

"We were both in the same studio program at SUNY Purchase. It's a quite small program, so you get to know everybody, and that's how we crossed paths." [63]

- PATRICK HYLAND

"Just as we were about to start recording, the producer we were supposed to work with suddenly couldn't make it. So we were thinking, 'Who should we record with?' and [Patrick] happened to be there. We knew each other at university, but I didn't know what kind of music he liked. He was one of those people we barely even talked to. He was just being talked to by a professor in the hallway, so I said, 'Come on over!' and forcefully invited him." [12]

- MITSKI

"I didn't work on the first record, and I sort of came in in the middle of the second record. But as with pretty much everything we've done, it was all done on a lot of borrowed equipment and improvised recording setups. Often on a laptop running Pro Tools versions 10 and 11. That's been the case with all of our records." [63]

- PATRICK HYLAND

Like the *LUSH* debut, *Retired from Sad, New Career in Business* is yet to appear as a physical release. But it is streaming everywhere for everyone.

TITLE

"It represents the overall mentality I had in creating this album. I was a sad and angsty child/teenager, so I made a sad and angsty first album. For the second album, I basically told myself, 'Alright, you're a grown-up now, quit your bitching and get down to business.'" [36]

- MITSKI

SOUND

"Recording has a different kind of tension than a live performance, but even if I make a mistake, I can try again as many times as I want." [12]

- MITSKI

A slightly more coherent affair than her first record, *Retired from Sad, New Career in Business* has been called art pop, baroque pop, folk, classical, and indie rock. Or as Mitski calls it...

"Orchestral pop for excited young people." [64]

- MITSKI

ARTWORK

Emily Grigsby (for whom I can find zero usable information) designed the cover art. Meanwhile, photographer Jade Greene has a much bigger digital footprint. He's' since gone on to work with Louis Vuitton, Sony Pictures, and Vogue, to name not many.

"Thank you to the badass beauty on said cover photo." [65]

- MITSKI

The cover model is Pixel the Drag Jester (credited as Pixie Doll), a drag performer who was putting on a show at Purchase College's campus when this shot was snapped. Talk about being in the right place at the right time! What's more, Pixel has dedicated a lot of online energy to dishing out information about the snapshot that swept her up into Mitski's world.

"I am the drag performer on the cover of this album! Then everyone knew me as 'Trixie Doll,' but Trixie Mattel became famous and I couldn't bear to share the same name as a more famous drag queen. I have since evolved to be better known as 'Pixel the Drag Jester.' At the time, Mitski and I were going to the same college, SUNY Purchase. I believe this was taken in 2012. SUNY Purchase has a very strong LGBTQ and drag queen community. We were doing a drag show in the outdoor theatre and Jade Green was there taking pictures." [66]

- PIXEL THE DRAG JESTER

You can follow Pixel the Drag Jester on Instagram *@thedragjester*

CHARTS AND CRITICAL

As Mitski was still in college, her sophomore was critically received in much the same manner as her debut: not whatsoever. However, around this time Mitski's official website claimed that she was once described as "a little ball of angry efficiency" and that someone once told her that she "only know[s] how to have big feelings".

In retrospect, *Retired from Sad, New Career in Business* was cherished as much as or even more than *LUSH*, people praising Mitski's huge ambition and crushing emotional weight.

Nevertheless, one can only imagine how frustrating it was for Mitski to be so ignored in the mainstream press. Luckily for her, this album was the last time that would ever be the case.

SINGLES

Every song on *Retired from Sad, New Career in Business* got the single treatment with a video attached to each, building an ongoing storyline as Mitski's only visual album.

"I guess I realised people don't really sit down and listen to albums anymore. It just doesn't sync up to how we lead our daily lives these days, unless you're a music aficionado who makes a point to do so. Meanwhile, I also noticed that people do spend hours and hours watching YouTube videos. So I figured I should put my album into a medium that is easier for people nowadays to absorb, and make a simple video for each song. It was hard, though, I have to admit. It wasn't the act of filming itself that was necessarily difficult, but because I did it while I was recording this impossible album, and I was filming with the help of filmmaker friends who were already incredibly busy but doing this as a great favour to me, I compromised a lot of what I initially wanted in the videos out of pure exhaustion and lack of time, and the videos didn't quite turn out the way I envisioned they would. But this only motivates me to try to make more videos and films, if only to right past wrongs." [36]

- MITSKI

In the fastest manner possible, here is a brief overview of the visual experience:

An animated outline of Mitski ("Goodbye, My Danish Sweetheart") leads to a (mostly) black and white story. Here ("Square"), Mitski is falling out of love with her partner (played by Kevin Hillocks). After a drive with a new romantic interest (played by Peter Olynciw), she appears to break up with her first boyfriend ("Strawberry Blond"). Ambling around the house, a clothed Mitski gets into an empty bath and her new boyfriend joins her, while her old boyfriend films them which appears more metaphorical than creepy ("Humpty"). Mitski is then absent for two songs as a female (played by Angelina Torreano) smokes a cigarette in front of stage lighting ("I Want You"), and then the original boyfriend goes for a swim ("Shame") as shots of a forest intercept... with some colour! Mitski returns to play piano ("Because Dreaming Costs Money, My Dear") and then artsy mirrored split screen footage of houses move by in full colour ("Circle"). Finally, Mitski sits with her back to the camera staring out of a window ("Class of 2013").

Four directors took on this project: Ryan Galloway, Alan Wertz, Jovon Outlaw (whose CV now boasts work with Marvel Entertainment), and Heather Barcelo (who has gone on to direct further independent shorts, such as 2015's *Six of Swords* and 2024's *Unsinkable Mac*). The acting talent was carried by three individuals: Kevin Hillocks (who recently wrote and starred in the short film *OOBER Diarrhea*), Peter Olynciw (who is more focused on his musicianship, having actually played upright bass on this album!), and Angelina Torreano (who is also primarily a musician, most notably as part of the band CITRIS).

One cannot understate the significance of this project's visual side as Mitski has since become well known for hiring the right people for her music videos. This is something we shall visit often throughout this book.

"I just find an artist who I think is good, and say, 'Here's the budget, do what you want.' I tend to gravitate toward artists who already know what they want and know what they like, so they're able to handle that kind of pressure. It is a kind of pressure to be told, 'Do whatever you want.' But with really good artists, I find that they work best when you trust in them, and when you let them make what they want to make. Then they actually put in the work to try to make something they like, and it ends up being a really good piece of work. Also, I think of the music video not as a representation of the music, but just a different aspect of it. I don't really expect it to represent me. I more want it to represent that artist who made it. Same with a shirt. It might have my name on it, but I want it

to represent the artist who made it. Just because it has my name, doesn't mean that it's what I'm all about. With artists, what's best is when they're given freedom and space. At the end of the day, I just want something good." [44]

- MITSKI

OTHER NOTEWORTHY SONGS

• Square

"Square" was the first *Retired from Sad, New Career in Business* song to be heard in public. Reportedly sometime before the release of her debut, Mitski performed the track along with *LUSH*'s "Pearl Diver" at SUNY Purchase with an orchestra. There are video clips around the web, but the full performance is yet to surface.

• Strawberry Blonde

"I was on my first tour of my life [...] it wasn't a real tour. It was more like a road trip. It was in the summer, and we were driving, and it was a lot of, like, upstate New York. It was just pretty and sunny and I think that's where it comes from." [11]

- MITSKI

Many years later, in 2020, "Strawberry Blond" became Mitski's earliest (but not only) track to blow up on TikTok. The source of its viral juice was the cottagecore community, where those people found the song suited their rural farm aesthetic. You do you!

• Shame

"Shame" was originally written for the dance film, *Dalliance*. Put together by a group of artists named Big Evil Collective, the plot tells of a 100-year-old house that has seen the love affairs of seven couples. Footage of the performers dancing in freeform is available online, complete with Mitski singing live, just search YouTube for *"Mitski with dancers in a Victorian Mansion film (2013)"*. An Indiegogo campaign raised 137% of its $2000 goal in 2013, but there doesn't seem to be much info on a release.

• Circle

Kind of pointless info here, but the street sign for Arrowwood Circle is seen in the "Circle" video if you want to go get a selfie. It's in Rye Brook, New York, 10573.

BONUS TRACKS

The track listing can be confusing, so here is why you may remember *Retired from Sad, New Career in Business* having bonus tracks, and why it no longer does. In 2020, the album was rereleased with a different song ordering and with two additional versions of already included songs. Those were "Square (solo piano version)" and "Shame (Jammin' Out Solo version)." However, around July 2022, Mitski signed a deal with a music management company named Good Harbor who republished her first two albums with their original listing, meaning the bonus tracks that appeared, disappeared just as fast.

2.7.
COLLEGE CONCLUSIONS

*"While I was in college, I hated college, but once I graduated,
I realised that it was fine."* [67]

- MITSKI

Naturally, Mitski finished college with jaws dropping in her wake. As Peter Denenberg, the head of the studio production and studio composition programs at Purchase, tells us:

*"I was just floored with her work ethic and her ability to get things
done. Then once I started hearing the music, I remember on one
occasion inviting her to come talk to get a sense of who she is and
what she's doing to see if I could help. But, frankly, she didn't need
any help. She was already kicking ass and getting stuff done [...]
A lot of the changes in the curriculum and the [faculty] hirings
and knocking down of walls, a lot of it was based on inspiration
from Mitski."* [42]

- PETER DENENBERG

"My going to music school and learning the craft has helped the music come out. Because otherwise, if I didn't have all the tools in my toolbox to make music... if I didn't learn about music theory, if I didn't learn how to play an instrument, if I didn't think about song form, and yada yada, then I would just have this vague abstract idea that was spinning around me that I may not be able to express." [68]

- MITSKI

"I went to a music college and studied composition, but rather than studying how to compose, I learned about the origins of music itself and how to use the tools at school. And when I get inspired, I'm able to use what I learned to create a song. No one teaches me how to compose a song, but I was taught how to play instruments, how to record, and other methods at school. I think that teachers who try to teach you how to compose a song itself are not good teachers because there is a possibility that your originality will be taken away." [12]

- MITSKI

On reflection, Mitski associates *Retired from Sad, New Career in Business* with a burnout coming on fast.

"The album wasn't impossible in that the music was difficult to write or play. It was impossible because it required things that were beyond my means. I was a college senior with no connections in the industry and certainly no money, yet I foolishly decided I needed a full orchestra and a music video for every song on an album that will get no promotional support from a label! So I did a lot of creative manoeuvring on no sleep for a year, while also holding a job to pay

the rent and going to classes and trying to graduate from college. Looking back, it was fucking impossible." [36]

- MITSKI

"I was really, really exhausted. I was in school, and working to pay my rent, and working on the two projects and trying to graduate from college and by the end of it, I was so tired." [8]

- MITSKI

Sorry, Mitski. No time for rest. You have a world to conquer.

2.8.
INTRODUCING PATRICK HYLAND

"Making an album is a vulnerable process for me. I have to allow myself to be weak and ugly, and I find it hard to do that in front of just anyone. But I've done it enough with Patrick that I trust him." [1]

- MITSKI

While at SUNY Purchase, Mitski met fellow student Patrick Hyland, and they struck up a musical partnership to last a lifetime. He may not have produced *LUSH*, but he has produced every single album since then.

"Patrick Hyland is my long-time producer. We met in college. We met because I needed a production student for some for a project. I did it fast. I didn't really know him, but I was, like, 'You! Come with me!' We just work well together and I keep going back to working with him because now there's a trust most of the time. We don't even have to talk. We just understand. When you're making an album, you have

to allow yourself to be so vulnerable and ugly. I have a hard time being that in front of people I don't know very well." [69]

- MITSKI

"He's the only person I actually trust with my music. I've become very insular in terms of my recording process. He works at this studio called Acme Recording Studios, which is actually owned by my former professor from college." [16]

- MITSKI

"Maybe I also have trust issues." [27]

- MITSKI

"You know the Drake song 'No New Friends'? It's like that. The more I do this, the more I close-mindedly stick to the people I know." [70]

- MITSKI

If you love Mitski albums (and I know you do) then, in so many ways, you must recognise you are equally a fan of Patrick. Every album sounds like it does because of him and Mitski, plus he plays guitar with her on tour.

"Patrick's an engineer at heart. I could talk all I want about abstract ideas, like, 'No, I want it like this and I want it like that,' and use colours and shapes and sizes to describe what I want. But at the end of the day, he actually knows how to do it. I realised through meeting him and getting to know him that I don't have the engineer's brain, you know? He just thinks of things in different ways, so he really is a godsend." [16]

- MITSKI

"I've had to teach myself to let go. When it comes to the actual creation of my music, I get a little more neurotic, and a little more controlling. But again, I've taught myself to trust in Patrick, and trust in the people I've worked with. It's important in that process to make clear what your intentions are and what you want so there's no confusion about it. For example, in the studio, if I don't make clear what I want, and let Patrick do whatever he wants, if I don't like the result, I can't tell whether it's because it's not what I wanted, or because it's not good work—you know what I'm saying? But if I'm decisive and make my intentions clear in the beginning, and the result is not good or not what I wanted, then I can say, 'Oh, this isn't what I like, and this isn't what I want, because these are my intentions.' It's just another example of giving someone space to make good work. People don't really make good work when they're smothered, but you also have to make clear what your intentions are and what you want." [44]

- MITSKI

"[Patrick and I have] worked together so much that we get our rhythms and we don't have to explain a lot. We are just, like, 'Okay you do that, I'll do this, you do that, I'll do this.' but without words [...] I feel like I've just become so dependent on him that I can't record with anyone else now." [23]

- MITSKI

"It's become somewhat of a crutch because we've worked together so long that there's this sort of non-verbal communication at this point. He can anticipate how I'm gonna act and I can anticipate what he's gonna do. I know how long he takes to do things and vice versa

for him. It's much more efficient, so once you get used to that kind of efficiency, it's really hard to break away from it and try and find another producer. I think I've sort of fallen into that habit of working with him because he makes it so easy." [71]

- MITSKI

"He is someone I can rely on and feel at ease with. It's quite difficult to express myself in the studio, and I have a hard time doing it, but when I'm with him, I feel at ease, I can make mistakes, or rather, I can move forward without fear of failure. I know what I'll get in return if I say this, and there are no barriers to communication with him, so recording goes smoothly. We've been working on music together for a long time, and even if I get annoyed because I'm too enthusiastic about how much time he needs, he understands and forgives me." [12]

- MITSKI

Unsurprisingly, Hyland is spread all across this book with his thoughts on Mitski and her music...

"Mitski is very compositionally minded, and I have much more of an ear for arrangement and aesthetics. I often feel like, if she wrote something, you could turn it into a bossa-nova song or a country song or a punk song and there's a small part of her that wouldn't even care. She's much more interested in the actual substance of writing." [33]

- PATRICK HYLAND

"There's a lot of moral absolutism among her fans that I think is totally alien to Mitski as a person. I hope I'm not alienating anyone

who takes meaning from our work together, but Mitski is not someone who views the world in black and white." [60]

- PATRICK HYLAND

...but without a doubt, this is the best story about the man:

"That was so boss. So what [Patrick] did was, he'd just graduated from college SUNY Purchase [as] a studio production major. And for his final project, instead of writing a paper or something, he just walked into the office, handed my Rolling Stone review and walked out." [23]

- MITSKI

2.9.
GRADUATING TO SHOWS
IN BROOKLYN

"I don't really have plans to tour this album, as much as I'd like to. The songs on this album aren't 'band' songs. Half of them need a full orchestra to fully realise them. And as much as I enjoyed my last tour, I didn't want to resort to doing the 'solo piano girl' thing again." [36]

- MITSKI

After graduating from SUNY, Mitski took the most logical next step and started to push her music out into the NYC gig scene.

"I graduated class of 2013. I started playing shows actively in NYC once I graduated. Before that I wasn't much of a band person. I was more a composition person. I had recital

in my conservatory, [but] I wasn't really in the whole
'going to shows' mentality."[15]

- MITSKI

"I like the immediacy of basement shows. You can see everybody
and that's a very direct interaction. What happens in the room
is largely under your control as a performer. And also, the sound
is almost never good, so it allows you to become creative with
performance. You can't rely on good sound or flashy effects. To
mold people's attention it has to be good. You have to really learn
how to perform."[18]

- MITSKI

"There was a month, two-month period where I was just starting out
and I needed to train myself to get better at performing. This was in
New York City. I played a different dive bar like four times a week
or something. And I would just play deliberately to people who don't
want to hear me, and everyone in the bar would just look like Charles
Bukowski [...] and one time I was playing and this obviously coked-
out woman was looking up at me like she wanted to kick me [...] I
just kept playing. That's the thing. You just gotta keep playing even if
there's a coked-out lady yelling at you."[7]

- MITSKI

"I went through a phase when I [was] playing four shows a week
[...] deliberately just places where I knew people did not want to hear
me because I realised [...] I had to toughen up."[37]

- MITSKI

"The craziest show I ever played was at Ella Lounge in New York City, 2012/2013. Zero people. I had one keyboard, singing. The sound guy was yelling at me for not bringing any people in the audience as I was singing. He was, like, 'What am I even here for!' and then halfway through the set he just turned off the sound because no one was there. Except there were two Russian guys at the bar who are cheering for me. And I was, like, 'Yes thank you!' But then I realised they're the people playing after me."[37]

- MITSKI

2.10.
MITSKI VS. NYC

*"Goth Mist recently said that Ridgewood is the next new
neighbourhood, and I was, like, noooo!"* [59]

- MITSKI

Around this point, Mitski lived in Ridgewood, Brooklyn. Over the years, she has had a lot to say about New York City and the Brooklyn borough in which she lived. Here is a fat collection of those quotes:

"The music community that I'm in right now is closely tied to SUNY Purchase, so it almost feels like I drifted from SUNY Purchase to Brooklyn with a kind of organic ease. But obviously Brooklyn just has more bands and more venues and more people coming to your shows, and more people to talk to and more people to collaborate with. But SUNY Purchase is distinct in that, despite its pretty small community, it's very active. Everyone works with each other and everyone encourages each other. I actually find that Purchase is a little weirder

than Brooklyn and I think that's a really healthy environment to be in as a growing artist." [59]

- MITSKI

"There's so much to do. So much energy. So many different people, and I'm very impatient, so you get everything on time, which is nice. I love how in New York you can almost be nobody. You can just not exist. There are so many people and I like how anonymous you can be." [20]

- MITSKI

"I came to New York because it was really all I knew about America. If anyone's lived abroad, you know America is either New York or Los Angeles. So I didn't know much about it. I just knew that I had to go somewhere, and it was New York. I'm glad I came here. I feel at home here which is very strange for me to say. Every kind of person is here and you can be anonymous which is comforting for me as someone who was always very much noticed in a bad way. I was very different. I stuck out. People would talk about me. I did everything I could to not be noticed. So here I can just be a human and live my life and not be noticed. It sounds bad but it's very comforting for me. So that's why I stay here." [11]

- MITSKI

"For me, personally, the people I'm around more directly influence what I write. The people I've gotten to know in NY are probably the only aspect of NY keeping me here, because otherwise it can be a pretty crappy place to try to get by when you're not making or inheriting a lot of money. The great thing about NY, despite all of its craziness, is that it is filled to the brim with creative and ambitious people. And right now I've made enough connections that I know who to call when I want a bassist, or when I want to play a show at a certain venue, or where I can find a few violinists, or who I can call to record on the fly, etc. etc. If I moved away I would have to start from scratch, and that would probably keep me from writing/producing as much stuff as I'd like to." [36]

- MITSKI

"What does 'making it' mean anymore? New York, with all the stories and romance and hype around it, is still a city... albeit huge... where people live and work, just like any other city. The two main things that set it apart from the rest is that there are so many different kinds of people and ways of life, and that it is probably the most convenient place in the world when it comes to getting information and gaining exposure on a global scale. So I could say that, yes, it's a city that's more open to different styles of music. But I've also found that, because there are so many different kinds of music and people, you end up kind of blending in with the crazy technicoloured crowd and ultimately evening out to become just average, or not special. The only way you really 'make it' in NYC is by working really hard to become really good at your instrument or your craft, instead of trying to be new or different, because everything and everyone around you is new or different. Novelty is dead in New York City." [21*]

- MITSKI

"New York being so gentrified and expensive will create an environment where money comes first. Or music that makes money is the focus. And that's a world in itself. That's the whole other industry. So I think the environment will just change. I don't think the music will go away, but I am thinking of moving out of Brooklyn, because, admittedly, I'm part of the gentrifying force. I'm not from here. I'm from elsewhere. So I feel like I don't want to participate in that. And also, it's just so expensive." [23]

- MITSKI

"To become an uncompromising artist in Brooklyn, you have to basically be rich already. When I lived in New York, I was persistently distracted by how expensive everything was. To such an extent that I could never really enjoy myself. Maybe that's why I missed out on a lot of things I could've otherwise enjoyed." [18]

- MITSKI

"It's just so disheartening because being here also makes me think about money all the time. And everything I do has to do with money, and that's depressing. Like, the amount of rent I pay for the amount of space I have is ridiculous. And I still have a really good deal. And just to get anywhere or do anything, I need money. So I'm always thinking about it. So that's dangerous because then it affects my career decisions, where I make choices based on money instead of other things that should be more important to me." [23]

- MITSKI

"There's no space, so I had to learn to write with other people in the room. There's no sense of privacy, you can't really go away. I'm a reserved, private person, so just learning how to get in the zone and be in my own world and write while there's a party going on in the living room was an adjustment but you kind of have to. I think that's the main struggle, lack of space and lack of time." [56]

- MITSKI

"I can't say I'm a Brooklynite or a New Yorker, because I'm not. I'm not from there. I haven't been there long enough to call myself that, and I don't think I've contributed to the community or the health of the community long enough to call myself that—especially because, at the end of the day, I am part of the gentrifying force [...] it's tricky, because on one hand it's very easy to make it seem like it's an individual thing. Like, oh, these individual white people are bringing in their baby strollers and cupcake shops—oh, here they come! But we keep forgetting that that's a scapegoat, and it's actually more a deeply embedded thing. It's a systemic thing. Talking about, 'Oh, I won't go to that coffee shop because it's part of the gentrifying force', I mean, I guess that is true in a sense, but it's also bigger than that. Focusing on that takes the focus away from the systemic issue and why it's happening and the whole history of New York and the displacement of communities. It's one of those things that I don't even know how to talk about, because I don't feel educated enough. I think a lot of people in New York aren't even educated enough about it—no one actually knows what's going on." [16]

- MITSKI

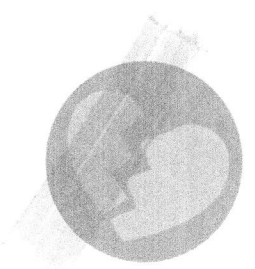

2.11.
JUST ANOTHER STRUGGLING MUSICIAN

"I do think I pay a price for what I do, but then again everyone pays some kind of price. In my case, I don't have the time or energy to pursue other interests. A hobby is out of the question. And my social life is confined to hanging out with people I'm working with at that moment, and people in the same industry. A lot of people I graduated high school with have since started pursuing lucrative and stable careers, with full-time jobs in established companies, so sometimes when I'm living gig-by-gig and taking odd jobs to get by just so I can put out a few silly songs, I wonder whether I'm doing it right. My family certainly gets worried. But a 'real job' would take time away from my doing music, for which I need a flexible schedule, and ultimately I don't think I'd be very happy at all working a job that keeps me from making music the way I want to. So yes, I think I pay a very high toll considering it's just to make some nice sounds,

and frankly I've gotten used to feeling spent in a way that's probably not healthy, but right now I don't think I'd have it any other way. If recharging means stopping, then I'd rather not recharge." [36]

- MITSKI

There was no doubt that Mitski was struggling with many factors in her life. But she was determined to make it as a musician and was willing to try new things, or anything.

"I freelance a lot and with the music industry it really is all about who you know. A lot of freelance gigs aren't advertised. You just have to know someone and someone has to recommend you [...] sometimes I teach, too. It's just, like, anything I can get my hands on." [9]

- MITSKI

"[I used to sleep] three hours. I was waiting tables all day, for twelve hours, and then I would do whatever music thing I could fit in after that." [10]

- MITSKI

"I have no energy, it's just that I'm very good at rationing it. I have no social life, I don't have fun, ever. It's just all work." [10]

- MITSKI

One thing Mitski got her hands on was a collaboration with indie-rock outfit M. Roosevelt, providing vocals for the song "Ego" as well as a cover of Kavinsky's "Nightcall" which can be listened to on their Bandcamp.

And then there was that weird short period where she fronted a prog-metal band...

2.12.
EP: HEAVEN'S SENSE
(VOICE COILS, 2015)

01. Heaven's Sense (1:45)
02. An Atrium (4:45)
03. You in a Place for a While by Yourself (5:11)
(first and only single)
04. Black is the Color of My True Love's Hair (3:14)

TOTAL RUNTIME: 14:55

"At first I was hired by Sam Garrett, who writes the music [...] we had mutual friends. I think someone recommended me as the vocalist. He just wanted a vocalist for these songs he was writing, so he hired me to sing for it and that turned into, like, 'Let's just have this be a band!' So, yeah, I was in the band for a while." [9]

- MITSKI

In 2013, Voice Coils came together in Brooklyn. It was constructed from different members of other assorted bands, such as Sam Garrett on guitars (Roomrunner), Caley Monahon-Ward on guitars (Extra Life/Feast of the Epiphany), Kelly Moran on synthesisers (Cellular Chaos), Kevin Wunderlich on bass (Epistasis/Couch Slut), and Cameron Wisch on drums (Porches/Feast of the Epiphany). And, of course, to top it all off, Mitski took the mic. Together, they released two songs on September 7th, 2014, namely "Sixths" (2:56), and "Field and Border" (4:58). Then, the following year on June 30th, 2015, the above four-track EP of new material surfaced.

Named *Heaven's Sense*, the EP was released through the label Shatter Your Leaves. It was produced by Caley Monahon-Ward and Sam Garrett, and engineered by Caley Monahon-Ward. A 2-minute 39-second version of "You in a Place for a While by Yourself" was released as a single.

An interesting side fact is that Mitski did not write the lyrics for this project. Sam Garrett took control of that role even if Mitski is said to have contributed.

"I don't write for it, but I sing in this very rigorous style, so it's a really good outlet for me to just 'be the singer' and focus on performing as a singer." [72*]

- MITSKI

Nevertheless, this project remains an absolute treat for Mitski fans, one which is largely unknown outside of her closest circle. If you're interested, every song mentioned remains on their Bandcamp page for your listening pleasure.

"The Voice Coils trajectory has kind of accelerated [...] it's obviously a good band, so a lot is happening for it that I just can't do [...] so I've amicably left." [9]

- MITSKI

Mitski exited Voice Coils shortly following the EP. It is unknown what exactly is happening with the band, but it seems they continued for a short time without her. A latter-day live performance of "An Atrium" can be found on YouTube but it's an instrumental with no Mitski. Her name is notably absent from their Facebook page, which I find admirable, as they are not cashing in on her now-famous stature.

We can debate the reasons why Mitski left Voice Coils, but one reason appears more obvious than the others. A year before the EP, she'd released another album under her name. And unlike her previous records, this one was picking up steam, then picking up fire, and then nothing was ever the same again...

Part Three

BURY ME AT
MAKEOUT CREEK ERA

3.1.
ALBUM: BURY ME AT
MAKEOUT CREEK (2014)

1. Texas Reznikoff (2:12)
2. Townie (3:25)
(second single)
3. First Love / Late Spring (4:38)
(first single)
4. Francis Forever (2:29)
5. I Don't Smoke (3:18)
(third single)
6. Jobless Monday (2:06)
7. Drunk Walk Home (2:35)
8. I Will (2:54)
(fourth single)
9. Carry Me Out (3:53)
10. Last Words of a Shooting Star (2:44)

TOTAL RUNTIME: 30:14

"I had just graduated from music conservatory and I was living in Brooklyn slash Queens slash wherever I could. I had no money, no resources, and I just had a few friends in bands who had guitars and drums and stuff. So I made that album in makeshift studios and people's houses, anywhere I could. And that was the spirit of the album. Where instead of going out and trying to find ways to um realise my vision, I just kind of looked around at what I had and said, 'what can I do with what I have?'" [13]

- MITSKI

On November 11th, 2014, a new Mitski album dropped. It was her third record and the third year in a row this had happened. Producer Patrick Hyland was rehired (obviously) as was Will Prinzi, the guitarist/bassist from *Retired from Sad, New Career in Business*. Mitski wrote every track.

"Actually, I tracked them all by instrument individually. Because I didn't have the resources or space. I didn't really record them in studios—it

was just in houses or in random makeshift places with Patrick. And
I got whoever was around who could play that instrument to just play
that one part, you know? If there were parts where me or Patrick
couldn't play them as well, because neither of us are professional
musicians at a specific instrument. It's more, like, I can usually play
what I wrote, and then he's kind of good at everything but not,
you know, a guitarist or a drummer or whatever. So I don't think
any of it was tracked live in terms of, like, having a band. It was
all on click." [16]

- MITSKI

Without access to college studios and orchestral armies, there was none of the
shiny production or stringy arrangements we may have come to expect.

"It was made in such little bits and pieces. I didn't have a studio or
anything. One day, I would just track guitar for one song and then
my time would be up in that certain place. Or I would just do vocals
for certain songs and everything was so broken up into little pieces.
I didn't really have a moment to think about the bigger picture. I was
just so focused on getting each little thing done. While going to work
and trying to be an adult and pay rent and stuff. So I don't think I
actually had the space in my brain to think." [38]

- MITSKI

And yet, that seemed to work! On May 15th, 2014, several months before the
release, Double Double Whammy announced that they had signed Mitski.

Granted, Double Double Whammy is a small label founded in 2011
by Dave Benton and Mike Caridi, both of whom attended the same SUNY
Purchase college. Nevertheless, they have more successes than just Mitski. This
same year, Frankie Cosmos' acclaimed debut *Zentropy* was released through the
label, and they have since been involved with Hatchie, LVL UP, and Great
Grandpa.

TITLE

The title is taken from the eleventh episode of the eleventh season of The Simpsons, "Faith Off." After Milhouse is hit by a truck, he utters his dying wishes, *"Bury Me at Makeout Creek!"*

"It really was just a flash of inspiration. Honestly, I just had The Simpsons on, I didn't even care, and then Millhouse said that line, and in that moment, I was just, like, that's it. Something about that line, I guess. Most of my big decisions were made on impulse without thought." [67]

- MITSKI

The title is presented in all lowercase on the album cover.

SOUND

Completing her degree, working outside jobs, and trying to afford NYC's extortionate cost of living all piled upon Mitski's exhaustion. But instead of breaking, she did what Mitski did best: used her turmoil as creative fodder. Nevertheless, her lack of resources did force a change in style far away from her former classical orchestral piano training.

"I make indie rock music right now, but I come from a composition background." [59]

- MITSKI

"I had been studying composition, so I had all these resources. I had all these student musicians willing to play; I had an orchestra at my disposal, so I would be dumb to not use it. But as I was graduating,

I realised, 'Oh, fuck, I'm not going to have an orchestra once I leave school.' I figured, okay, I have to adjust to my environment, and my environment was all these guys I knew from Purchase who were in bands. I realised my place in the scene. I wanted to play basement shows, and I wanted to make music that would sound good in those environments. Before I went to Purchase, I didn't realise that I could be in a band. Then I got to Purchase, and it was like, 'Oh, music doesn't have to be this academic, difficult thing.' I could just play with all my friends and have these catchy songs and have fun." [62]

- MITSKI

"I'm very much influenced by my environment. I think it's out of laziness where I'm not the kind of person who goes out and tries to find resources that I don't see around me. For my first two records, I was in Conservatory. I had those resources, I had musician friends playing orchestral instruments, able to record with me. Third album came about, and I was no longer in college. I had to find what was available around me, which were people who play guitar and bass and drums. So I just used that and made music. I feel like music can be made whatever you have." [51]

- MITSKI

"So I started all right. And then I went downhill to a shitty punk band." [46]

- MITSKI

Needless to say, *Bury Me at Makeout Creek* marked a gigantic leap from where we were, and a lot of that had to do with Mitski picking up and learning the guitar.

"I don't remember the first time I ever played a guitar, but I do remember why I switched from piano to guitar. I was going to another gig where I was playing keyboard and I was in NY. I was lugging this huge keyboard on the subway and everyone was just giving me death stares. And I was, like, I need a more portable instrument. This is not sustainable." [29]

- MITSKI

"I picked up a guitar purely for practical reasons. I was playing piano. I was writing songs on piano and then it came time for me to start playing live. I lived in New York City and I didn't have a car. I was playing solo, I was going to gigs alone, and I just couldn't carry a keyboard. So I picked up a guitar and I switched gears, like, 'Okay I'm gonna write songs for guitar just so I can play live, so I can go out there and pick up a guitar and play solo and go home.' I think guitar is one of those deep instruments where it's very easy to pick it up and start playing. You can be a complete amateur like me and just play. Have it accompany your voice or whatever. But it's deep in that if you actually pursue it, it's very difficult to get good, you know? It's like learning a new language, where the first two years you feel like you can already speak the language. Like when I was learning Spanish, I remember the first year or two, I was, like, 'Oh, I can speak Spanish, I can go to Spain, and I can survive.' But then my third year of learning Spanish, I realised, oh my gosh, I actually know nothing! I couldn't hold an intelligent conversation in Spanish. So I think guitar is kind of like that too, where it's very easy to pick it up and start playing, but once you actually start trying to advance, it goes really deep." [73]

- MITSKI

"That's why [the album is] kind of punky. It's kind of grungy. It's very distorted. A lot of the distortion comes from the fact that instrumentation is sparse, so it's a way to fill it up a little bit. It's very logistically distorted." [13]

- MITSKI

"Then I moved on to bass guitar because the bassist that I had employed for my band just stopped showing up to rehearsals. And so I was, like, 'Well, we have a show! I'm going to learn bass now!' And that's how I started bass." [11]

- MITSKI

Genre-wise, people have referred to *Bury Me* as rock, indie rock, folk, punk rock, slacker rock, noise pop, and noise rock.

"I wanted something that I could use to let out this rage and work on in a more solitary setting, on my own terms, on a much lower scale." [8]

- MITSKI

"I wrote them all really quickly. I didn't play guitar before this record. I'd always been playing piano and some drums. I took on a new instrument because I wanted a fresh start, so all those songs were written when I was just figuring out guitar. They were all written pretty close together really quickly [...] I realised I should play songs that I wrote on guitar. It would just sound forced if I had chords made out for piano and I played them on guitar." [62]

- MITSKI

"I could change my environment, but certain things come naturally to me. It would actually feel forced or unnatural to try to do a different singing style or to try to change my sound completely. It would be counter-punk if I was trying to do something as opposed to just letting something happen. So I figured, okay, if I fake this, it's just going to sound like I'm faking it." [62]

- MITSKI

"I've found my current voice. I'm always changing as a person and so my art changes. I don't think my first two albums weren't my voice and, probably, in a few years when I make other music I'll no longer feel like Bury Me at Makeout Creek is my voice either." [51]

- MITSKI

That's great, but would she ever consider going back to orchestral strings?

"I'm definitely going to revisit it. I just can't right now. Like, if I wrote for strings, great, it's just going to sit on a desk. I don't have string players. Maybe in the future if I'm not dead by then I'll have like resources, and just be like, 'I have a string quartet I can record.'" [46]

- MITSKI

I have a feeling you'll get those resources, Mitski.

ARTWORK

Mitski is credited for the album art, but the photo is by Chris Downer (even if he is not attributed anywhere on the album).

For super fans, you can visit the building in the UK at 20-28 Cotlands Rd, Bournemouth BH1 3NJ. And once you take your photo, don't forget to add the text using the Microsoft Himalaya font, double-spaced.

The 10th-anniversary version of the vinyl had the title space cut out so that listeners could change it to read whatever they liked.

THEMES

"I think it's about giving a shit. Honestly, in the music business, it's all about being cool or being the newest thing, or being the 'It' person. I've tried really hard to be what is expected of me or what would be advantageous to my career, and I just reached the point where I said 'No, I'm an emotional loser, I can't pretend to not care.' I can't pretend to be a cool person who doesn't care about things. I care a lot. I think with this third record, I finally just let go of wanting to impress people and just did what I wanted to do." [74]

- MITSKI

"I'd always been fascinated by death, which sounds so morbid. Especially being a woman trying to make music, I think there's a sense that you're never young enough, or your career is going to end soon. So there's that element of 'I'm going to die soon.' Maybe not physically, but I'm going to run out of time very soon. It's always on my mind. I have to do things now. The humor aspect comes from... the first two records, I put my heart and soul into, and they just weren't really heard. It was my fault, because I didn't know how to promote. But I had also become kind of... not cynical, but to kind of have a dark sense of humor about it. Like, these are my songs, I'm putting my heart into them, but people might not listen to it, so whatever, let's just have fun. The first two records were very serious because I was very serious-minded. But by the third one, I was like, 'Okay, let's just have fun.' It might not get heard, but whatever.

I think it's those two elements combining. I always had a real focus on death and then with the third record I had a better sense of humor about it." [62]

- MITSKI

CHARTS

"I made it for purely selfish reasons. I wasn't thinking of who would listen to it while I was writing or recording it, I just needed to write those songs, I was desperate, there was no real practical reason." [48]

- MITSKI

The initial 500 print run of *Bury Me at Makeout Creek* sold out after a month, so the momentum was there from the get-go. And while it certainly wasn't a smash hit of a record, Mitski's name started to prod around, hitting number 40 on the UK Independent Albums and 20 on the US Top Tastemaker Albums.

CRITICAL

Big name publications could no longer ignore Mitski either, and what's more, their reception was always warm. With a 9/10 score, Allmusic appreciated how the album was *"grungy, impulsive, and with memorably acerbic, vulnerable lyrics."* Pitchfork's 7.7/10 review showered compliments such as *"impressive"*, *"inventive"* and *"resourceful"* while calling it a *"breakthrough"*. Consequence of Sound graded it a B, noting how the record *"delicately balances on a thin line between polished, academic pop music and unhinged punk rock,"* while also noting, *"her courage as a musician distinguishes her more than any amount of training."* Finally, Rolling Stone gave the lowest score, with a still respectable 7/10, stating, *"It's Mitski's talent for penning deep-cutting lyrics that makes this album soar"*.

SINGLES

• First Love / Late Spring

"I got the inspiration from real life. I was falling in love with someone when I seriously could not afford to, considering where my life was at the moment. But it happened anyway because you can't control that shit." [48]

- MITSKI

Considered the genuine debut single from Mitski's career, "First Love / Late Spring" was released on May 15th, 2024, to coincide with Double Double Whammy's signing announcement.

"When I wrote this song, I was experiencing the kind of vulnerable first love, and experiencing that kind of love [that makes] you realise how much of a weenie you are. I felt like I was in love for the first time when I was writing that song, like a kid. I was, like, man, my body is like a grown person, but inside I'm a child. But it's not just with love. When you're doing something you're not used to, you kind of realise that you're still a kid, even though the whole world around you sees you as an adult and you're expected to act like an adult, you still haven't actually grown up." [74]

- MITSKI

"First Love / Late Spring" was certified Silver in the UK (200,000 sales) and Gold in the USA (500,000 sales). Part of its appeal was surely the lyrics, which included the line *"Lately, I've been crying like a tall child"*.

"Talking to older people, I realise that everyone is still a child even as a 40, 50 year old." [56]

- MITSKI

"I'm aware of it now, but I'm still unable to control my impulses the way that would be advantageous to me. I wish I were smart enough or controlled enough to be conniving. But at the end of the day, I'm just like an impulsive child who cries the moment she wants to cry." [9]

- MITSKI

If you've been paying attention, then you'll know that the line *"Mune ga ha-chikire-sōde"* makes for the second Mitski song to feature Japanese.

"It roughly means 'my chest is about to burst.'" [48]

- MITSKI

A video was shot for this song! Yay! But it was never released! Boo! But you can find it anyway! Yay! In it, Mitksi and a band are performing the track in a room, while she plays her famous pink bass, which really pops out within the otherwise blue grading. There's also a mannequin and subtitles that get quite playful. It was directed by Tymon Brown at Purchase College. We'll hear more from him a little later.

"I made a music video for 'First Love / Late Spring'. Even though we finished the video and were both happy with it, it ended up getting shelved due to some record label shakeup." [75]

- TYMON BROWN

• Townie

"It's about being a girl with a feeling like she should be going somewhere, doing something, taking something big for herself, but

always ending up just going to the same parties and doing stupid things over and over because that's the only way she knows how to find release, and the only role she knows how to fill. It's about being stuck, being impatient, being bored to death, being angry with what you've been given, and being young and soft and defiant inside and not knowing what to do with that." [76]

- MITSKI

When the album was announced on September 16th, 2014, the second single "Townie" dropped with it, bringing that super hype.

"I had just come out of music conservatory. I spent a couple of years surrounded by contemporary classical douchebags, and I was just, like, fuck it, here's a simple song, and I think it's pretty good. You know? Like, fuck tonality, here's just a simple chord progression that's been used over and over and over again. But I wanted that also to parallel the idea of like the teenager in a suburb or in a town where it's just, like, 'This is what they know, and it's repetitive, and it's been done before, and they don't know what to do with it, but it's there." [77]

- MITSKI

"I was a young girl partying, and I was bored of it. But I didn't know what to do with myself. I had all this energy, but I didn't know where to put it. I felt like my life wasn't going anywhere. I felt like I didn't have any talent. I loved music but I didn't see myself being a musician [...] so this is just an image of a person partying in despair." [13]

- MITSKI

"Townie" remains a big favourite, by fans and even Mitski.

"One person on Twitter covered it, posted it online. I was really genuinely happy. I realised the song was pretty good because for a long time I kept thinking that I'm a better singer than a writer, and so I keep feeling like I'm almost cheating as a writer, like, 'Oh, this song is only working because my voice is pulling it off.' So when I hear someone else cover it and it's still a good song, in my opinion, I'm like, 'Oh shit!' It worked. I am a writer. And it's weird I still have this complex where I think I'm not a writer." [13]

- MITSKI

Mitski has expressed additional fondness for the lyrics.

"'I wanna love that falls as fast as a body from the balcony.' I was really proud of that. I like it when lyrics are very physical. Like, really physical metaphors." [7]

- MITSKI

So, the good news is that there are not one but two videos for "Townie"! The bad news is that there is only really one after all, because the first video has been pulled off the internet and is nowhere to be found. What we do know, however, is that it was directed by Allyssa Yohana and premiered on Rookie on November 9th, 2014. The lo-fi content showed Mitski lying on bed as glitter and tinsel were poured over her.

Perhaps Mitski's growing reputation made her or her label feel that the video was not professional enough for the up-and-coming star or that the song deserved more. Whatever the case, a new video premiered on The Fader on March 9th, 2015. Directed by Faye Orlove, it was an animated piece where random cartoons matched the lyrics until the screen begins to fuzz out like an old TV set. Here's what Orlove had to say about it:

"The lyric 'I'm not what my daddy wants me to be' inspired the whole video for me. Those words resonated really deeply within my own

life and brought back a lot of visual memories. I drew tiny scenes of pizza boxes and tampons and balloons blowing in the wind. Things that remind me of moments growing up. Moments letting people down. Moments figuring myself out. The video was an honour to work on. It's one of my absolute favourite songs and to this day the one thing I've created that I'm most proud of. "[76]

- FAYE ORLOVE

• Other Singles

"I Don't Smoke" became a single on September 29th, 2014. "I Will" became a single on October 21st, 2014. There was no video treatment for either.

OTHER NOTEWORTHY SINGS

• Texas Reznikoff

The "Reznikoff" part of the title comes from Charles Reznikoff. He was a New York poet who wrote *Testimony: The United States (1885–1915)* which used court records to illustrate the American experience of the poor, the immigrants, and black people.

As for the "Texas", the lyrics will tell you that *"Texas is a land-locked state"*. Which, of course, it absolutely isn't.

"I know it's not landlocked. And I've gotten so many Tumblr messages and tweets like, 'Um, excuse me, Mitski, it's actually not landlocked,' and I'm like, 'Yes, I know. It's a song. It's a message to someone, and that someone understands what I mean' [...] I'm still regretting writing that, because I didn't think that I would get so many smart-ass teenagers telling me I'm wrong. I'm just like, 'I don't care, that's not the point.' "[16]

- MITSKI

"Regardless of audience, my songwriting has just evolved as I continue to do it. As an artist, I don't want to keep talking about the same things. I change as a person, I grow up, I experience more things, and so my songwriting has become less about very specific details. Like 'Texas is a landlocked state.' That doesn't make sense in the context of the song. It just makes sense to me. I've started to do less of that, only because I'm branching out into storytelling." [44]

- MITSKI

• Francis Forever

"Francis is the middle name of the person I wrote this song for. I was just very much in love and I'm a musician. I go out into the world and perform. I'm everywhere and I'm out here trying to get the world's acceptance. But when I wrote it, I was thinking none of that matters if that one person isn't watching." [73]

- MITSKI

On a 2022 list from Consequence of Sound, "Francis Forever" was deemed Mitski's 5th best song, higher than any other on *Bury Me*. But such an accolade meant nothing compared to what happened next...

"[I've] been waiting to tell [you] this for a long while [...] my music is going to be in tonight's Adventure Time." [78]

- MITSKI

That's right! In *Adventure Time*, Season 8, Episode 10, "The Music Hole", Marceline the Vampire Queen covered "Francis Forever". Now you've made it!

"One of the illustrators... or storyboarders... I don't actually know the terminology in the animation world... but one of them were already listening to my music and they emailed me. They were like, 'Hey, can I use this song?' It's funny, it wasn't through any licensing channels. It was just someone from the show emailed me. And it's funny because the fan base is so strong that people identify with the characters as if they were real people. So people think, 'Oh, that song Marceline wrote! It's like that Marceline song! You're singing it, too!' And I'm, like, 'Oh, yeah, sure, if that keeps the dream alive, then, please, right, yeah, believe that.' We're both quite sad and moody. It does work very well." [27]

- MITSKI

"A while ago I just casually looked at comments under me performing 'Francis Forever'. A lot of Adventure Time fans seem to very much genuinely believe that that's Marceline's song that I'm covering. Most of the comments under the song are, like, 'She's covering Adventure Time!' or 'Marceline did it better!' It's so funny and I actually enjoy it. I love the fact that people feel so close to it in a way that I never would have allowed people to feel with just my name on it. Because Marceline sang it, it's part of people's world now. But it's also funny to see so many comments, like 'The original was better!' and secretly I'm on the other side of the screen like 'Ahaha, if you only knew." [71]

- MITSKI

• Drunk Walk Home

Besides being a great song, "Drunk Walk Home" lands hardest on the map due to Mitski's metal scream.

*"I'd never screamed in the studio before doing 'Drunk Walk Home,'
but it just felt right for the song. I remember I did an initial take of
screams and they were pretty tame because I was shy, and then
the recording engineer stood up and said, 'Let me try,' and did a set
of screams that were better, and I was like, 'Oh, okay, fucker, watch
this,' and did the screams on the record. I'm easily coerced
by competition"* [53]

- MITSKI

*"I'm a violent person, just by my human nature. I think we all are. But
none of us really have an outlet for it. And I think I'm also a good
person. I don't want to hurt anybody or I don't want to hurt myself as
I did when I was a teenager. So it's a negotiation where you face
that violence in you and try to express it [...] I'm attracted to violence
but not even violence towards anything or anyone. That's the thing
that's most complicated. It's just this scream. I don't know what the
scream is about. I don't know what it's for. But it's there and I guess
I'm just trying to express it in the best way possible. It's not violence
towards anything or anyone, it's just violence. And I guess I'm trying
to express that. I don't know. I'll probably go home after this and be,
like, 'You know what? There was a much better way to say this.'"* [11]

- MITSKI

Lyrically, there are only two songs in Mitski's discography that have been
marked *Explicit* on streaming services. This is one of them. Even more terrifying
is where Mitski states she would retire at age 23.

*"Well, I'm already 24, so it's too late. I wrote it when I was 23. I just
felt done, you know? I just felt like there was nothing more I could do*

or nothing I could contribute. I just wanted to go somewhere quiet and wait to die." [16]

- MITSKI

• Last Words of a Shooting Star

"Fun fact: I wrote 'Last Words' on an airplane when there was turbulence and I thought I was going to die. I didn't die, obviously. But it's still probably not the best in-flight entertainment." [79*]

- MITSKI

Ever wonder about the lo-fi hissing at the end of "Last Words of a Shooting Star"? Wonder no more!

"'Last Words' was recorded in Patrick's kitchen, actually. A lot of people think, 'Is that, like, tape fuzz or hiss or something?' But actually we left the windows open and it was raining outside, so that's the hiss you hear." [16]

- MITSKI

• Bonus Tracks
On April 7th, 2015, Don Giovanni Records re-released the album with four new bonus tracks. As follows:

11. Square (live solo piano version) (3:10)
12. I Want You (live at WNYU The Sound Between) (3:05)
13. Francis Forever (live at WNYU The Sound Between) (2:51)
14. Last Words of a Shooting Star (live at WNYU
The Sound Between) (2:47)

UPDATED TOTAL RUNTIME: 42:07

In 2016, Dead Oceans quietly re-released the album again with those bonus tracks removed. Easy come, easy go!

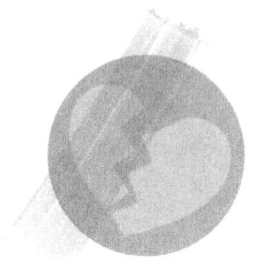

3.2.
MITSKI ON GEAR

"I just needed a way to get the lyrics and my songs out there, and it takes a lot of guts to go out and sing your songs without an accompanying instrument. Most people don't listen, so I quickly learned that I needed something to play in the background. For me, it started with piano, and I found the guitar later on." [44]

- MITSKI

One of Mitski's challenges as she rose up the ranks was how many people wanted to flex about gear on her, a topic in which she had little interest.

"So I should preface this with, like, I'm not a producer. I'm not an engineer. My mentality has always been: use what's around you and make the best of what you have. And I think when it comes to production, I'm not so much looking for the best gear. I'm not looking for the best instruments, the best players. I'm just looking at what is

available to me and trying to find what makes that thing good or what the best thing about that is and then trying to draw that out."[11]

- MITSKI

"I'm not much of a gear person, not much of a production person. I emphasise the composition because I grew up not having things or losing things. A lot of my music is still made that way. I make it so that there are as few musicians as possible."[80]

- MITSKI

"You know, instruments—no offence to all of the instrumentalists out there—are not as important to me as the core composition, which is, to me, the words and the main vocal melody. I grew up moving around, where I didn't know what I would have. I'd be in one place and have a piano, but then I would move to another place and I wouldn't have a piano. I learned not to rely on the instruments in order to make music. It's secondary to me. They're interchangeable. A song could be played on the piano, or the guitar. I want the songs to be able to stand on their own. But it depends on the artist. That's the way I work, but for a lot of people the instrument is the integral part of the composition."[44]

- MITSKI

"The really familiar feeling is asking questions, checking my knowledge. Are you using this gear? Have you heard about this gear? What does this gear do? And you can tell that they know the answer, but they're just asking you anyway and that's such a pointless penis competition. This is how big my dick is. You have a dick now? It's so pointless. At the end of the day, I'm playing the songs, it's not about the gear. The gear helps. Knowing about the gear and knowing how to manipulate the instruments help convey the message of the song, but at the end of the day it's about the song itself." [44]

- MITSKI

One can only imagine that those who confronted Mitski back then feel really stupid now.

"Gear nerd boys always made me feel like a sub-par musician for not knowing gear. Until one day, I turned around and said, 'Can you write the music I write?'" [38]

- MITSKI

"I've started to respond, 'Oh, I don't know. Sorry, I have to go play MY show.' It's totally okay to not know any of this shit because the information that they highly value isn't the information that is the most valued. Just because they think it's important doesn't mean it is the most important thing. You know things that they don't know and that is valuable to you." [38]

- MITSKI

"It's interesting when that happens at my shows because you're here to see me play music. You even paid to see it, and yet you're talking to me like I don't know anything. It's kind of wild sometimes when that happens." [38]

- MITSKI

"I never learned about gear growing up. Moving without a home or access to it, unlike you 16 year old pieces of $uburban shit. So I'm learning now. So what." [38]

- MITSKI

Okay, but for those who *are* interested in her gear...

"What I record with and what I tour with is very different. I'm much more familiar with what I tour with, which is my Reverend Justice bass and then a tuner pedal, obviously, and then a little pedal our friend John made that's basically like a fuzz/distortion. I also use a SansAmp as my bass DI and then I've come to prefer the Ampeg B-15." [63]

- MITSKI

"I tried to use a Voodoo [pedal] but maybe I just don't know how to use it. It just took out all the low end, so I stopped using it. I could just work on it, but realistically, no. And I use an overdrive that's yellow. I forgot what it's called." [46]

- MITSKI

"I'm not really picky about gear. I'm not much of a gearhead, I'm so sorry. This is why I have Patrick on the line. I basically go into the studio, see what's available, and use what's there. On tour, I have to be more conscious about what I bring, so that's when I get a little more specific." [63]

- MITSKI

"I'm so sick of heavy guitars. While I was recording I was using a Gibson or something. And I was just... 'Why is it so heavy?' I don't want to be carrying this weight. I already have my heart. That's heavy!" [46]

- MITSKI

"I'm so enamoured with the low-slung look. I'm really into it. It's probably not really conducive to actually playing well, but I don't give a shit. Obviously it's not good for your playing. That's not the point, though." [46]

- MITSKI

According to Equipboard, some of Mitski's equipment includes the Reverend Justice Bass, Gibson EB Bass, Ibanez Jet King JTKB200 Bass, Gibson Les Paul Custom Electric Guitar, Gibson ES-335 Dot Guitar, Gibson SG Special 2014 Guitar, 1977 Kay Les Paul Guitar, Fender Blacktop Stratocaster HH Guitar, Harmony Bobkat Guitar, Fender California Series Malibu Classic 2018 - 2019 Guitar, Ampeg Reverbrocket Trans Am Combo Amp, Fender FM 212DSP 100 Watt 2x12" Frontman Combo Amp with DSP Effects, Boss MT-2 Metal Zone Pedal, Boss RE-20 Space Echo Pedal, Fulltone OCD Obsessive Compulsive Drive Pedal, Electro-Harmonix Big Muff Pi Pedal, and Boss SD-1 Super OverDrive pedal. However, none became such a signature Mitski piece as her bright pink Dean Custom Zone bass.

"I have to say it wasn't conscious, in that I didn't buy it. It was a gift. But I chose to keep using it because of all the comments." [38]

- MITSKI

"I don't have my own electric guitar, actually. I just have that bass that every live show review just comes down to, 'She had a bright pink bass.'" [46]

- MITSKI

"I started to receive fan art, where the biggest thing was that I was holding a pink bass, and it wasn't about my face. That's when I was like, 'Oh, okay, I have to change guitars.'" [63]

- MITSKI

"So, here's the thing: the infamous hot pink bass was actually a gift. One of my professors was goofing around with his son at a guitar store and then just dropped this bass and had to buy it, but he didn't actually need the bass, so he just kind of gave it to me. I've been using that, but it was just so pink, and I wanted a new guitar. I was shown the Reverend Justice bass and immediately loved it. I've never really felt emotion toward an instrument before owning this Reverend Justice. I just really enjoy the tone. No matter how much I travel with it and fuck it up and treat it badly, it still basically stays in tune. I haven't had to tune up yet." [63]

- MITSKI

3.3.
BURY ME TOUR

"I want to go to places that, not only I haven't been, but that are just part of, you know, the whole American consciousness of what these places are supposed to be like. Like the south, or the west coast [to] see for myself whether the mythology is true. I want to see all the American landscapes. I did one cross country tour where I went through Colorado and Wyoming and stuff. And that was tear-inducingly beautiful. So I'm really looking forward to seeing the nooks and crannies of America." [23]

- MITSKI

Leading up to the *Bury Me* release, and during the *Bury Me* release, and after the *Bury Me* release, Mitski played tons of shows around the States.

"When I went to Miami on tour, I was actually like, 'I love this place.' It was everything Pitbull said it would be." [55]

- MITSKI

Some of the bands she performed with include LVL UP (search for footage of them and Mitski walking around a scenic field), Johanna Warren, Joyce Manor, Hundred Waters, Screaming Females, Elvis Depressedly, Eskimeaux, and Speedy Oritz. Speaking of Speedy Ortiz. Mitski thought their time together was:

"...too short, in my opinion. But while it lasted, it was very beautiful. Me and Sadie were internet friends for a while. We'd be at the same shows but wouldn't really get to hang out, so that gave us the chance to get to know each other." [74]

- MITSKI

On the day of Halloween 2015, Mitski adventured abroad to play a show in Leeds, UK, with Metz, Protomartyr, Junk, and Crows. She then continued around the country before performing in Iceland at their Airwaves Festival 2015 (with Hinds, Father John Misty, Perfume Genius, Aurora, and Beach House). She returned to finish 2015 in the USA, joined by PWR BTTM and Palehound.

"I don't regret touring a lot. It's just a lot of work and sleeping on friends' and friends of friends' floors. Like, punk houses and haunted houses. I've only recently started to stay in hotels, but before that it was, like, 'My friend's friend's Aunt has a living room that you can crash in.'" [7]

- MITSKI

Impressively, during this tour, Mitksi found enough breaks to write and record her next album.

"I actually recorded the fourth album a while ago, in January. I just got a focused amount of time in the studio—two weeks at Acme Studios—and banged it all out, because I knew that I wouldn't really have any other time to record with touring. I tend to work with my environment

rather than against it. Now we're at the point where I'm on the road a lot, whenever I'm back we mix together little by little, and kind of step away and come back to it so I can actually hear it with fresh ears." [38]

- MITSKI

But let's not get too ahead of ourselves! Instead, we should hang around the touring topic for a while and see how Mitski feels about it.

3.4.
MITSKI ON TOURING

"You can go to shows alone! You can go alone, talk to no one, feel the music, then go home. Abolish the notion of going to shows to be seen!" [38]

- MITSKI

As it turns out, Mitski really loves playing shows! Who would've thought!

"When I play a show I finally become myself and my regular day everyday Mitski is just not quite there. When I'm on stage, I'm, like, 'Oh cool, this is me!' And then when I'm off stage, just like, 'I'm sorry that I'm this way. I don't like this either.'" [46]

- MITSKI

"They're the best part of my days." [33]

- MITSKI

"It's my everything. It's my whole life. It's all I wanna do. I'll take anything just to get to perform. I feel like myself. In my daily life, my head is just crowded with thoughts, my past, the future. But when I'm onstage, it's just that moment, and I feel so connected to other people and to the world and to myself. That's when I know what I'm doing. That's when I'm the creator of a world. I am God. It's a combination of being in control, but also being free to not be in control. You're just existing and Being with a capital B onstage." [22]

- MITSKI

"Sometimes I feel more like myself onstage as a performer than I do offstage." [80]

- MITSKI

"The weird and unhealthy thing for me is that when I'm on stage [that] is who I really am at my raw being." [11]

- MITSKI

"Performing is like an ocean I can keep diving deeper and deeper into. And the deeper I go, the more magic it reveals." [50]

- MITSKI

Still, there are some things you may want to consider before attending a Mitski show.

"People in the audience, they have a 'watching TV effect'. You're right in front of them, but for some reason, people think that you can't see them. Audience members feel like they're looking at a TV

*screen or something. It's so weird. Their faces are like...
they look so stupid."* [7]

- MITSKI

*"I'm just not into moshing. One time, I was playing a show in San
Diego and it was in the US, and I wasn't the headliner so I was just
playing for another demographic and people started moshing. I straight
up just stopped playing, and they fucking hated me for it. But the
thing about it is, like, [there are] people who are bouncing around
are having a good time but all I can see are the people around the
pit who are just like, 'ahhhh' and being bounced on."* [33]

- MITSKI

*"I'm very careful to nurture that. I wanna make sure that people who
come to my show are comfortable. You know when you have firsthand experience of being at a show and not feeling like you should
be there? I don't want that to ever happen to anyone."* [56]

- MITSKI

*"My little secret is that I need glasses and I take my glasses off for
the show so that I can't see anyone. It's all a blur and I feel less
nervous [...] I have inner ear mics so I'm partially deaf and blind."* [22]

- MITSKI

Another notable aspect of Mitski's shows is that she tends not to address the
audience between songs.

*"Who I am right now, talking to you as candid as it seems, is my
social self, or the person I become in order to function in society.*

Whereas on stage, I'm truly who I am. And who I am is not someone who's verbal. I don't go back to where I was when I was writing the music because it's hard to revisit that every single night, 365 days a year. But I do go to a different plane. I want to hold a different space. I don't want my performance to be everyday life. I want it to be a place a little underneath the surface." [11]

- MITSKI

All this considered, her non-stop recording/performing schedule only increases as this book goes on. For this reason, it's no shocker that her tours weren't always a honeymoon.

"I think the pressure gets to me when I play shows and there's more people in the audience than I'm used to. Playing Bowery Ballroom [later this month], which will be the biggest room I've ever headlined. I think the physicality and reality of actually having people in front of me gets to me more." [5]

- MITSKI

"I wish I had a ritual the way baseball players do, you know? Just to get in the zone, but I haven't figured that out yet. So sometimes, you really hit home and you're on top of the world and you don't know why. And other times, you just... eff up. I'm trying not to swear right now. I'm really just trying to figure out how I can get to that point every night. I think it's just a matter of, for better or for worse, trusting the audience, trusting that they're people and they understand and they're here to listen. And, sometimes, opening yourself up is really exhausting or really hard because you're making yourself

vulnerable. But when you do get something it's truly, truly validating. So, it's a gamble, I guess." [67]

- MITSKI

"This might get a bit esoteric but it's kind of like judo or aikido. Those martial arts where, instead of trying to exert force, you take the energy of your opponent and use it for yourself. I feel like I'm learning to do that in terms of performing. Just feeding off what I'm given and giving it back. It's more like recycling energy rather than me trying to push myself onto the audience." [30]

- MITSKI

"I try to inhabit more of a swagger than I have in real life. Kim Gordon has a quote. You should probably look it up because I'm paraphrasing: 'People pay to see somebody be confident onstage.' You have thousands of people looking at you. But they're not looking at you. You're a performer." [17]

- MITSKI

"People pay money to see others believe in themselves." [82]

- KIM GORDON

"I do encores often, just because audience members feel like they've been cheated if you don't do an encore. But, sometimes, I'm really not feeling the whole shtick of, like, 'Okay, I'm going off stage!' but everyone knows I'm coming back on. Let's not do that, you know? But I still do that sometimes. When the audience keep clapping and they start booing if you don't do an encore, And that's when you gotta do [one]. But otherwise, I just don't want to do it." [7]

- MITSKI

Still, these years of hard work finally paid of, as this is about the point in the Mitski story where she leapt up several notches into higher public consciousness.

3.5.
SIGNING TO DEAD OCEANS

"Dead Oceans is a very small label, so actually it didn't really change my circumstances much. But I did get to record in a recording studio as opposed to, as Patrick said, creating makeshift studios with borrowed equipment." [63]

- MITSKI

With bigger fish comes bigger frying pans. It was inevitable that a label more equipped to deal with Mitski's rising stardom would come along and snap up the lady. That happened on December 22nd, 2015, with Mitski putting her pen to Dead Oceans' contract. Let's hear from that label's founder, Phil Waldorf.

"It's the rarest of things. I have seen it only a couple times before. I remember seeing a band like Neutral Milk Hotel in the '90s, and the way people just felt this connection with the songs and the writing and the mystery and the persona—all that. I see a lot of that

with Mitski. With her, it's a little different because she's not only connecting through songs and shows but through social media and this overarching message. It's incredibly authentic. It's something that you find an incredibly talented artist and you give the best advice you can [as a record label]. You're kind of following their instincts, because their instincts are so good. That has always been in the case with Mitski." [42]

- PHIL WALDORF

The parent company of the label is Secretly Group, and their vice-president of A&R, Jon Coombs, has sent many a glowing quote Mitski's way, including:

"She's always had a very engaged fanbase that is pretty singular. I think it has to do with how her writing really strikes to the heart of her fans." [83]

- JON COOMBS

"We're just seeing this groundswell of people connecting with [her] across the board, regardless of how they're first hearing [her]. I wish I had something to point to because then it would be easier to repeat." [83]

- JON COOMBS

Dead Oceans has worked with numerous talented names, such as Bright Eyes, Japanese Breakfast, Phoebe Bridgers, Shame, and Slowdive.

"I've expanded really gradually, but I've always been indie [...] I'm on Dead Oceans, which is an indie label." [7]

- MITSKI

Mitski remains signed to Dead Oceans right up until the publication of this book and assumedly beyond!

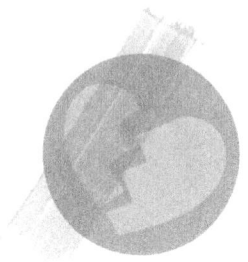

3.6.
MITSKI ON THE INDUSTRY

"Music is not the music business. I wouldn't write a love song to the music business." [28]

- MITSKI

"I couldn't take any criticism from the business people. I'd be like, 'Who the fuck are you? What do you do? Show me your work.'" [2]

- MITSKI

Now that Mitski's name is scrawled on a much larger card, she suddenly found herself with a new career in business.

"85% of my time is spent not making art. A lot of it is logistics and writing emails." [58]

- MITSKI

"I thought that if I worked really hard at this, then eventually I'd get to the point where I can just spend all my time making music. But I've found that the more I do this, the less time I get to spend on music. Around 10% of my time—less than that—I'm actually making music or playing music. Most of my time it's press and travel and admin stuff: answering emails and just being a business person, putting out fires. It's just being a working adult. No one gets to just do what they like to do all day. We have to make a living first, and then maybe in our spare time we get to do the thing that we love. I'm not complaining, I know that's just reality. But for some reason I had some fantasy in my mind that, 'Well, if I work really hard at this, then eventually I'll get to make music the way I want to, all the time.' I'm finding that's not the case." [45]

- MITSKI

Part of her struggles came with her feeling like a product rather than a person.

"It's the foundation of the entire industry to exploit the artist. The music industry was built on the backs of black musicians. It's the basis of how the system works. It's funny. People keep telling me that I'm the boss. But I don't feel like the boss." [50]

- MITSKI

"Every day, all the time, is exploitation. You can't be a human being. You have to be a product that's being bought and sold and consumed, and you have to perceive yourself that way in order to function. Everything in the world has a cost. If I truly want the greatest magic in the world, the highest euphoria, the best thing, if I want to do that, I'm going to have to pay an equivalent price." [2]

- MITSKI

"You have to accept that in the eyes of the world, you're not a person, you're a consumer product. That's just really difficult for my brain to accept." [60]

- MITSKI

"It's very hard. I'm constantly not in balance. The thing about it is the music industry is not a place where balanced people survive. You really need to want it and you need to sacrifice your well-being to a large extent in order to survive it, or you need to shape your identity around what is needed of you as a musician. So I think the pursuit of a career in music in and of itself is not balanced, at least not as long as we have the music industry as it currently is." [84]

- MITSKI

"I had found that in order to survive the music industry, I had numbed my heart and disconnected from myself. And then, after a while of actively disconnecting from myself, day after day, you really do become disconnected. Suddenly I found that I really was numb, like the way I wanted to be, but I then couldn't write music, because you can't write music from a place of being completely detached from yourself." [60]

- MITSKI

3.7.
MITSKI ON SUCCESSFULLY BREAKING OUT

"There's almost something egotistical about assuming you're the underdog. Like, you're supposed to be the champion, but everyone is bringing you down." [28]

- MITSKI

As we've seen, Mitski's success story was a slow-burning flame.

"Change is gradual. It's never been overnight for me." [28]

- MITSKI

"It's so weird to be called a breakout star because I've been alive for 24 years and I've had to deal with my own shit for 24 years. I'm actually done, I don't want me anymore. I'm old news. I still don't relate [Bury Me at Makeout Creek] to a breakout record because it's been

a very gradual process. I wouldn't have known how to promote my music and be a professional artist if I didn't have those little baby steps that those first two records helped me take. But I understand, to the public, this is the first time that a lot of people are seeing me." [38]

- MITSKI

But it goes without saying that a gradual flame is easier to manage.

"If I were asked to play Music Hall of Williamsburg right after I put out my first record, I would not have handled that situation well, even if I got through the show. I probably would not known how to perform, or fill the space. I'm glad that I had that time to grow without anyone pressuring me to be bigger than I actually am." [38]

- MITSKI

"Both are fundamentally performative, and it's good that I've done both to broaden my range. What a small DIY space requires of an artist is different than a big space. I don't think I would've been able to play the bigger spaces effectively without coming up through smaller spaces." [5]

- MITSKI

"The way we express it in Japan and America might be different, but if you put a frog in water and gradually increase the temperature of the water, the frog won't be surprised when the water reaches boiling temperature. In the same way, I've gradually gotten used to the situation, so I don't get nervous so much." [12]

- MITSKI

With the gradual expansion of fire, Mitski could keep an eye on the growing validation of her career choice.

"It's really life-affirming that other people understand these things I was going through. I feel like a lot of people who want to be weird or deliberately say they're weird aren't weird because really weird people try desperately not to be weird. I spent my whole life feeling like I was really weird or really alone or the only person feeling something. I put my heart on the line for the songs, so whenever people catch it and say they got it, it's like, 'Oh thank goodness, thank you for understanding.'" [8]

- MITSKI

"I'm glad people are crying. I was crying the whole time I was writing it, so it means that people get where I was coming from, and I'm glad I got to access that part of people." [8]

- MITSKI

"I don't want to be a musician's musician. I want to be an everyone's musician." [5]

- MITSKI

A little bit of money started coming in.

"I can afford to take a taxi now if I need to." [28]

- MITSKI

"[I'm] finally at a level where I can afford to go out to eat, I can afford health care, I can afford to turn down jobs to rest or take care of life." [33]

- MITSKI

"I can pay for my health insurance. I can eat. I can drink clean water. I can pay for a roof above my head. I've done it. Now my goal is to only make music that I feel is necessary for me to make." [6]

- MITSKI

"I put my most intimate feelings in a song and sold it." [2]

- MITSKI

"Sometimes, I think the true purpose of my working hard to make money is just so I can finally be left alone." [25]

- MITSKI

"What I see as success has nothing to do with material shit. I want freedom; the freedom to do as I please and be left alone, finally. I think I'm working this hard so that maybe in ten years I'll be left alone to just make the music I want to make at my own pace. I think that's very ambitious because no adult gets left to do what they want to do and my ultimate ambition is to do what I want to do, when I want to do it." [10]

- MITSKI

The concept of surviving as a full-time musician was looking like a reality.

"The person I am today, that person could never have imagined. I mean, simply continuing to be able to write and release music, that's miraculous to me. Because I really didn't see it as a viable option. I was doing it mostly because I couldn't see myself doing anything else, honestly." [50]

- MITSKI

"I'm not in this to be quote-unquote famous, but I want to be able to only make music as my job and make a middle-class living. That has always been the goal. I mean, it's too late now. I have no other skills. My only résumé is all the waitressing jobs that I did, oh, ten years ago. So this has to work out." [34]

- MITSKI

"It might just be ego. It might just be that I want to make a connection. I want to be known. I want to reach people. I want to be bigger than I am. I don't mean famous; I mean I want my existence to matter. I want to be recognised so that my life doesn't just disappear when I die. And that sort of thought process drove in the direction of 'Okay, how do I make something that is understood? How do I make something that people actually care about, that might mean something to someone other than myself?' I think that's what drove me to keep refining my craft as a songwriter. Just wanting to matter." [42]

- MITSKI

"Everyone wants to be remembered. That's why half the people who have children have children, because they want to pass on something of themselves, they don't want to pass into the ether." [85]

- MITSKI

To what she owed her success seemed obvious to her.

"The easy answer is it's rock band instruments. It's guitar songs, so more people relate to that. But, honestly? The third record is the first one I actually promoted. The first two records were my junior and senior projects in college. I made them, but I just put them on Bandcamp and didn't do anything about them. I didn't play live. They were just sitting on the internet. Whereas the third one, I put out after I graduated college and I decided to pursue it because I realised [attention] wasn't just going to come to me. So, I went out and played a shit ton of shows and told people about it and sent it to blogs. I actively worked for it." [38]

- MITSKI

"There's this impression that I just came out of nowhere and kind of lucked out and was suddenly 'discovered,' but I think the reality is just that I've been building and working at it little by little. So, it's been nice finally seeing some recognition." [49]

- MITSKI

But, of course, this sudden rise came with a unique set of problems.

"I'm in a scene [where I] play with a lot of the same bands or similar venues. And so now that I'm branching out or trying different things, a lot of those people have expressed that they feel betrayed, or, I don't know, used in a way. Like I used the scene to get ahead. And that's so hurtful because the fact is I would have been doing this music thing regardless of any scene. But I found this scene and I really liked it so I immersed myself in it. And now I'm trying to do

something different, and so... I'm still in the thick of it so it's hard for me to explain, but a lot of people have assumed that people are listening to my music because I'm in a certain scene. And, in my mind, I've been making music regardless of any scene. And even if I wasn't in this quote-unquote 'scene', I still would have been doing music."[15]

- MITSKI

"A lot of people have turned around and made it seem like I've gone 'corporate greed' and that's insane because I'm still not making any money. And I've actively been turning down all these different offers even though it would be nice to have money, just because I don't align with whatever those companies or whatever those projects stood for. I've actually been fighting off opportunities to make money. So being told that I'm abandoning the scene for money is so enraging to me because [...] I see other people in my 'scene' having their music in commercials and I'm, like, that's great for them! And I never take it upon myself to condemn them for that because every musician is on their own path. It's just, I don't want to have my music in commercials, so it's bewildering to think that other musicians or other people in the scene would condemn me for doing what I feel is right for my career. And I'm not even doing any of the things that they're accusing me of! It's all high school. It's all just like words flying around that aren't true."[15]

- MITSKI

"I'm very wary of [money] affecting my art because I've listened to so much music where you can tell the point of it was money, and there's something so sad about it. I don't want to create that kind of music, but I understand now how you get to that point, because you just get caught up in it until you just start making that music because it's your job and you need to get that next paycheck. And I'm very afraid of that, because I'm such a gullible person and no better than anyone. I still have problems with my ego and have that thing where I need everyone to love me and need to be validated. It's very scary—the thought that that will affect and maybe taint my music. I want to make sure that what I make is necessary and not frivolous." [42]

- MITSKI

Nevertheless, Mitski's heart remains with her fellow musicians.

"It used to be that you had to have major label representation to actually be heard because there was no internet. It was really about access [...] but now [...] everything is accessible which means that people or artists who would not have been represented can just put out their music and that's why DIY flourishes more. But, on the other hand, no one's making money. Everyone has to have other jobs and everyone's just very sad." [9]

- MITSKI

"The utopian ideal for me is that musicians are all paid the same living wage, no matter what type of music they make. I'd take commerce completely out of it. Everyone would be paid the same comfortable living wage. That way, everyone's worries would melt away and we could just focus on making music. I think we'd all make much better music and would be able to provide our service much better if we weren't constantly thinking: 'How do I make this into a product? How do I brand myself? What compromises do I have to make in order for this to make money?'" [50]

- MITSKI

"I think it's important for people who love music to stick together, because we save each other." [91]

- MITSKI

Be that as it may, Mitski's insecurities only grew with her fame which was quickly turning into a bonfire burning down the entire indie world.

"I had the notion that [success] was something that was happening to me while I was young, and that I may not be allowed to do it once I aged out." [50]

- MITSKI

"[I'm waiting] for the tide to turn and everyone to just decide to hate me. When you're happy for too long, you're kind of waiting for something bad to happen. People decided they wanted to hate Anne Hathaway after she was so popular. For no reason. That's a cycle that repeats itself everywhere." [88]

- MITSKI

This rapidly culminated into an unhealthy relationship with the media which threatened her privacy. It's a matter we shall explore often throughout this book, but for this specific period of her career, it's heartbreaking to watch the strong personality of Mitski suddenly feel overburdened by the limelight. It is in sharp contrast to when she was a child, and she would fiercely stand her ground.

"When I was a kid I used to always start every sentence with 'no!' Even when I was agreeing with you, I'd be like, 'No! Yeah!' I would start with a no so maybe that counts as me standing up for myself." [29]

- MITSKI

*"You'd be like, 'Do you like apples?' I'd be like, 'No! I like apples.'
I guess that's an easy way to get someone's attention, or assert
yourself immediately."* [1]

- MITSKI

But as she became part of the music machine, it wore her down, and she forgot
her strength of refusal.

*"In terms of press out in the world, there's no notion of consent,
like the way that there's consent in sexual situations. Once you say
something, it's public record. Anyone can ask you about it and demand
an answer about it at any time. I remember my first press trip to
Europe. I'm still traumatised by it. I was nobody, had no power. And
because I was nobody, and also because I was an Asian woman,
almost all white men, one after the other, would say the most racist,
sexist things I have ever heard to this day. I got a lot of sexual
harassment. And it wasn't just one person. I felt like a toilet stall,
where I just had to sit there and take shit. Just for another dude
to come in and give me shit again. That's a situation where I kept
saying 'yes' because I didn't know that I could say 'no.' The traumatic
part wasn't just having things said and done to me. The traumatic
part was me sitting there allowing it, over and over."* [2]

- MITSKI

*"More than anything I'm tired of questions that mine my trauma.
There would be press days where I would have ten interviews in a
row, and each interviewer would just try to just cut me open and poke
at my trauma each time. That was annoying and exhausting, because
I don't want to have to keep talking to you about how hurt I am all
day everyday. They end up just becoming struggle-porn, and trauma-*

porn, and it stops being about the music—it just starts being about, 'Look at how in pain this Asian girl is, let's ogle at it.' And it's very gendered and kind of race related, too. I'm open to talking about the songs, but I don't want it to get into the territory of just, 'Tell me exactly how you hurt, and describe it in detail.'" [41]

- MITSKI

Because of this, her already complex identity came under additional pressure. Mitski had to relearn who she was in this new world.

"When you answer one question in one interview, then all interviewers after that just asked the same question. And if it's a pretty personal question about something that happened in your life that you don't want to repeat over and over again to new people... like relive your trauma or whatever for a new audience... it can be taxing. But, I mean, I put myself in that position." [51]

- MITSKI

"I wish I could say it was done with intention but it was more, like, I didn't quite register the fact that what I was saying to that interviewer would actually be broadcasted. I would just be having a conversation and be talking about what I think. And then later, I'd see it on the internet and be, like, oh right, that's what that whole conversation was for." [51]

- MITSKI

"It's really complicated, because you do this press stuff so that people will listen to your music and come to your shows and have an interest in what you're doing. It's important to do and I gladly do it, but at the end of the day, I don't matter. I just want people to hear my songs, and to relate to the songs, and to the experiences behind the songs, and I'm not doing this to become a—what's the word?—like a thing at the carnival that you ogle at. I don't want the attention personally, I just want you to listen to my songs." [41]

- MITSKI

"There was one review by a guy in Europe... I forgot where he was from or what his name was. But he said, I'm paraphrasing, 'She's probably so anxious about trying to get a good grade in her studies or maybe the pressures from parents,' and I was just like... really? You listen to all my music, and that's what you got? I've gotten every kind of interpretation that I've just stopped feeling anything about it." [11]

- MITSKI

These challenges were frequently aggravated through two specific topics that the press appeared most thirsty for: being Asian and being a woman. To hopefully unpick the fascination, we will address those two subjects separately.

"I don't have a self. I have a million selves, and they're all me, and I inhabit them, and they all live inside me" [89]

- MITSKI

3.8.
MITSKI ON BEING ASIAN

*"In the US, I'm the Asian girl.
In Japan, I'm the white girl.
I can't win."* [7]

- MITSKI

Firstly, it's essential we illustrate how Mitski is proud of her Japanese heritage and what it culturally means to her, even if she is the sum of so much more.

"There's a big sense of community, because in Japan, it's such a small country with little space and a lot of people, so there's this emphasis of, 'If we don't work together, we really can't do this,' especially after the war. And there are a lot of earthquakes, and a lot of natural disasters happen. But I don't know if the way I am, my personality or whatever, can be attributed to any one culture. It's one of those lifelong questions of whether it's nature or nurture. I grew up a little bit in Japan, and I am Japanese by nationality, but I

also grew up in a lot of other countries. It's hard for me to think about where I got what, or where I'm from, or what can be attributed to where." [16]

- MITSKI

"Western architecture is, like, columns and squares; everything is even. In Japan, there'll be a painting with one dot on one end—that's beauty. My sense of balance isn't quite symmetrical." [14]

- MITSKI

When asked about her ethnicity, Mitski will often refer to herself as Asian American, even if it didn't initially feel right. She did so...

"...for the benefit of other people to explain who I am." [2]

- MITSKI

"[I'm] half Japanese, half American, but not fully either." [90]

- MITSKI

"I didn't fit in anywhere when I grew up, but I was always American, so to survive I created this 'ideal America'. Finally I came to the US and realised, 'Oh, I don't belong here, either.'" [32]

- MITSKI

"When I came to the US, I didn't know I was Asian. I just got here and everyone treated me like an Asian person. And I was, like, 'Oh.' And now I identify as Asian American, but it's been a process. Because outside of the US, I wasn't Asian American. I was just American. Or I was just this anomaly. This person who looks like

everyone else and yet is definitely not from here and everyone can tell." [11]

- MITSKI

"My whole life, I had been told by everybody that I was American and then I got to America and I felt so outside of it. So it's just been a constant process of trying to figure out what it is to be American. And I have a feeling a lot of Americans actually feel the same way. It's a very interesting diverse place. It's so big. It's so hard to identify yourself with a giant country with so many cultures and so many landscapes. So it's very interesting. I'm still figuring it out." [92]

- MITSKI

"At least when I was abroad, there was a sense that, 'She's weird because she's from a different culture'. When I got here it was just, 'She, as an individual, is weird.' It was me, as a person: I was flawed." [32]

- MITSKI

Especially earlier in her career, it seemed like a go-to fascination of the press to layer on just how Asian she was.

"I got one once where the writer was very much stuck on the fact that I was [...] a studious Asian girl. I don't know how they got that from the music, but they managed it." [58]

- MITSKI

"I'm not writing as an Asian woman. I'm writing as a person. I'm not making music to be a politician and I'm kind of being dressed up as that." [10]

- MITSKI

"It almost doesn't matter what music I write and put out into the world. At the end of the day, I'm a woman in public, allowing myself to be consumed. I put out songs, but really what people are buying is the product that is me. Even completely private citizens who are Asian women are more objectified, fetishised, and expected to be submissive. There's more a feeling of ownership towards people of my identity, in general. My being in public has made that assumption more extreme." [93]

- MITSKI

"With my appearance, it's always surprising more than annoying. It's always like, 'Oh, I just remembered that I'm being judged for my appearance. I had very blissfully forgotten for a second, but you wouldn't let me forget.' There was an article that said, 'famously underdressed Mitski,' and I did not realise that I was famously underdressed. I was wearing a shirt and pants." [38]

- MITSKI

Her sense of belonging does not get any easier when publications praise her on "musician women of colour" lists

"It almost feels like including me in that list is like, 'Look, here's a pale person.'" [2]

- MITSKI

Mitski felt a sudden weight of representing the entire Asian culture.

"Most public people who aren't white feel this pressure and are asked to represent everybody. I know for a fact that I'm problematic. I shouldn't be looked to for any kind of guidance. I have to go out and consciously say, 'I'm a person, I can't be a role model, I'm not a representative of anything.' I have to consciously go out and do that, or else it's gonna be put upon me." [80]

- MITSKI

"I never set out to be a girl power artist, you know? My lyrics are about being fucked up. I'm not a Power Ranger. I've been stronger than I'm expected to be because I'm a woman. I'm weak and I'm not allowed to be, because then I lose my ability to control my destiny or whatever. Also, I'm Asian so suddenly I also have to be every single Asian woman. Which is half the world. If you actually listened to my music you would never make me a role model." [17]

- MITSKI

"I'm less talking about fame in the crude sense, and more [about how] I'm someone who goes on stage and becomes a symbol. People project onto me. Internally, [I'm trying] to understand that dynamic. I think that's something that everyone thinks about. Even in day-to-day conversation, we're projecting onto each other. And [there's] a weird dissatisfaction either way: you want people to project onto you and see you as something bigger than you are, but when people actually do that, it's not what you want. You want people to know you for who you are, but when they actually know you for who you are, you're like, 'No, I want you to think I'm great.'" [45]

- MITSKI

"There's the loneliness of being a symbol and a projection, but I think that loneliness [says a lot about] being a woman, or being another kind of identity that has a lot of symbols attached to it. And there's also just touring. Touring is a very... it isolates. The longer musicians tour, the more isolated they become from the rest of society, because the way you live is so incredibly different. And no one can really relate to your experiences, so you can't talk to anybody about it and you go deeper and deeper inside." [45]

- MITSKI

"On the one hand, it's really cool that we're talking about these things, but it's turning me into a trope, even if the intentions are good. I didn't go into this thinking, 'Let me subvert something,' or as an activist. I'm in it because I love music and that's what I do. I'm a musician." [32]

- MITSKI

"It's like racism masked in progressive thought. At the end of the day, therefore, I'm not a person. I'm a symbol. And then people start talking about how I'm not representing it properly." [10]

- MITSKI

"White privilege is deciding to not think about America's racism anymore because it makes you feel bad, then getting to live your life without it affecting you." [94]

- MITSKI

That noted, Mitski does recognise how crucial representation is, in both music and the media.

"Sometimes it's helpful when there are other East Asian girls who message me and they say, 'Oh my gosh, there aren't any other East Asian women. I didn't realise I was missing that figure until I saw you.' That's always encouraging." [10]

- MITSKI

"What's satisfying is that there's this feeling of being able to talk to my younger self, or reach my younger self. In a way, redo my life through other people. Sometimes, when I meet a young half Asian girl [who says], 'I'm so glad you exist! It makes me want to cry!' I mean, no offence, it's not even about her. I feel like I'm talking to my former self and I'm able to turn back time and have that which I never had when I was younger. It's a satisfying thing. But it's also sad because you can never redo your life. But it's second best. Where you get to be that for someone else and feel like you are living better or you had a better life just through other people. It's very selfish..." [11]

- MITSKI

"That's something that other people deal with as well. Other Asian people or people of colour. When you can't imagine yourself being there, it's hard to get there. And, also, when you can't imagine another artist of colour being in a certain position, you almost can't believe that they're there, or you can't believe that they'll get there, and so you tend to underestimate them, if that makes any sense." [11]

- MITSKI

"That's one of the reasons it took me so long to start my career. Before I couldn't even visualise my face doing what I do. That's why representation is important. The first step is being able to imagine yourself doing it, and if you can't imagine yourself doing it, you can't begin to start doing it." [74]

- MITSKI

"I was an Asian girl who wasn't hot. Who wanted to write my own music and didn't want to do anything that I was seeing. It's so strange how when you don't see an example of something it's very hard to imagine it." [37]

- MITSKI

"I always loved music. But for a long time, I didn't believe I could be a musician. I just didn't see anyone like me doing what I wanted to do. Just to understand that it was possible for me took a long time." [37]

- MITSKI

"My whole life I have been told I am both pretty and ugly at the same time. This would have been less confusing if I wasn't convinced that whether I was pretty or ugly determined whether I was good or bad. This wouldn't be such a big deal to me if I didn't want so badly to be good." [8]

- MITSKI

It couldn't have been easy, but thankfully, Mitski shattered through her doubts and we are all more blessed for it.

"I try to remember that fear of failure or self-doubt are actually very egotistical feelings, because they imply that you think you're meant to look good or impressive and you're scared of not appearing so, or that it would matter to the world or other people if you reveal yourself to be a failure. I'm just a flawed human and artist, I don't need to look good or be impressive because it's not about me. My function is to allow people the space to feel things, and give people a release. Whenever I start to feel doubtful or scared about performing or putting my music out there, I remind myself that it's not about me, it's about the audience, and once I'm no longer thinking about myself or how I'd do, everything becomes easier." [95]

- MITSKI

"You don't have to like my face for me to be good at what I do." [38]

- MITSKI

"If you're a younger listener, take pictures of yourself. Because when I was younger I thought I was ugly and I refused to have pictures of me taken. But now I wish I had that to look at. So even if you think you're ugly, take pictures of yourself, because you're gonna enjoy it, like, ten years from now." [9]

- MITSKI

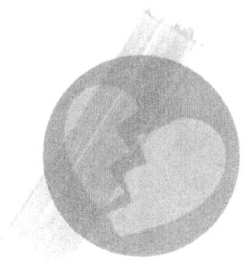

3.9.
MITSKI ON BEING A WOMAN

"Being a woman is part of it as well. As a woman of colour, I always have to be at 150 percent and better than everybody in the room to be considered competent. A white male can write mediocre songs and be in a band and still be cool. I need to be the best, and not just the best, but know everything and be on top of everything and walk in and be assertive, or else the power will be taken from me so quickly. That's the hard thing on the day-to-day, having to be better than perfect. I can't relax." [74]

- MITSKI

Like every woman in music, a lot of attention is placed on Mitski's gender.

"I have to make a really deliberate effort not to be emotive in any way because any sign of emotion is seen as 'hysterical' or weakness.

No matter what kind of crazy shit happens and no matter how I'm treated, just completely be 'business' and rational and icy cold." [58]

- MITSKI

"Women are required to be actors. Women have to be whoever their man desires. Be a dream! Be an ideal! We're trained to mould ourselves into a character just to fit the person you're with. 'I'm a dragon, you're a whore.' Even though none of us would sing that, we relate to Lana Del Rey. She's a character but in some parts of our lives we've become her." [17]

- MITSKI

Note: *The above lyric is taken from Lana Del Rey's song, "Fucked My Way Up To The Top".*

Mitski had often identified herself as a feminist.

"I don't run into any of the male-female dynamic problems with [male colleagues] because they know my stance. They know I'm a feminist. They're totally supportive of that. I think more in the past when I was struggling to find my voice and I was trying to find people to work with who I didn't know, [that] was when I had more trouble standing my ground and trying to make sure my voice is heard among males." [59]

- MITSKI

"In the '70s, free love got twisted. Getting to have sex whenever you want is important. But not having to have any sex is just as important. Somehow it's been turned around on women. You're not truly feminist if you don't feel like you can have sex at any moment. A guy can be like, 'Are you a prude? Are you really a feminist?' Then you have something to prove." [17]

- MITSKI

"I wish we could get to a point where we could call... men, women, trans people, everybody... just musicians, you know? But we're not there yet. And if we decided today we're just not gonna talk about people's genders then very slowly we're gonna notice that everyone who's successful is just white and male. Because those are the people who are in power. And they choose other people like them, even subconsciously. So I think we're at a point still where we have to celebrate non-cis men." [51]

- MITSKI

One annoyance that Mitski often circles back to is how lazy journalists compare her to a vessel.

"It's not like it just pours out. It's not like I'm a vessel." [96]

- MITSKI

"[People] really need to imagine me as some sort of vessel for emotion or vehicle for music instead of the creator." [97]

- MITSKI

"People cannot fathom the fact that maybe a woman created something from nothing, and that she has control over what she makes. People have worked so hard to try to make me seem like I don't know what I'm doing. But I know exactly what I'm doing." [88]

- MITSKI

"People work really hard to take autonomy and authority away from a woman artist. They don't want to have to acknowledge and understand that a woman is in control of her process and creating something. The work that goes into it—it doesn't just happen." [58]

- MITSKI

"It's interesting because, even as I write my own material and I'm the one singing, and it's my voice, and I'm the one controlling it, there's still this perception that it comes from somewhere else. It is my voice! I am controlling it! And dictating what it does! And yet there's this perception that I am this fevered priestess. Like, this vessel through which a voice comes and I have no real control over it. I get comments like that on Twitter. A lot of interview questions are like that [...] based on the assumption that I don't know what I'm doing when it is my voice! It's so fascinating to try to unravel that because it speaks to the fact that women, or female-identifying people, truly are seen as not having any autonomy or authority. I can write it and sing it and record it and present it and still have it perceived as, like, 'Oh, you're so lucky to have this, it's such a gift!' And I'm just, like, 'I made it from scratch, so...'" [98]

- MITSKI

"I still encounter roadblocks where I see other people walk straight, but then when I try to walk beside them, there are so many walls that I have to first break down. And I've accepted that. I understand that those are walls that are part of the basket of things that I got. Just like everyone is born with their basket of things that they have to deal with. It's hard, but I see what I do as what I'm meant to do with my life. So I will endure anything in order to get to do what I'm *doing [...] Yes, there are hurdles but they're just in your basket of things that you have to deal with. And it's really sad and unproductive to compare yourself to other people. You just have to do what you have to do in order to get to where you want to go."* [11]

- MITSKI

With that out of the way, everyone must appreciate Mitski for maintaining a sense of optimism about the future of women artists.

"We still have a long way to go, but it's something, it's a beginning, things aren't gonna change overnight. What's that phrase? The first steps to overcoming addiction is recognising it or becoming aware of it, and it's somewhat of an addiction globally to keep men in power and keep women repressed." [71]

- MITSKI

"It's really, really great to have... I don't know if I should say 'community' because, realistically, we don't see each other often, but I think it keeps us all going to have the knowledge that there are other women around, trying to do a similar thing. But at the same time, I love that while we're all trying to do our own thing and make own music, we're all supportive of another. There's this myth that women are supposed to compete with each other or something, or we're supposed to hate each other, and that's totally not productive. We've created this environment of supporting each other, loving each other, trying to get each other on our own bills, or trying to get each other gigs. We really want to see each other succeed." [74]

- MITSKI

"I think a lot of women understand the give and take of communication more. I think because they've been on the other end of being talked at or being directed so they understand that it's a collaboration." [59]

- MITSKI

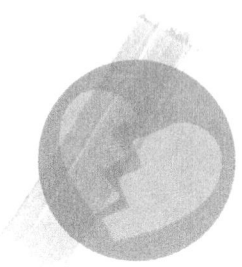

3.10.
MITSKI SESSIONS

Over the course of 2015, Mitski pushed her name everywhere she could including through various live sessions across various platforms, all of which remain available today. Seek out the following:

MITSKI'S DAYTROTTER SESSION

RELEASED: April 29th, 2015
RECORDED: Rock Island, Illinois (probably)

1. Welcome to Daytrotter (0:05)
2. Townie (3:07)
3. I Don't Smoke (3:03)
4. Francis Forever (2:35)
5. Last Words of a Shooting Star (2:52)

TOTAL RUNTIME: 11:48

MITSKI ON AUDIOTREE LIVE

RELEASED: July 1st, 2015
RECORDED: Audiotree, Chicago, Illinois

1. I Don't Smoke (02:53)
(featuring Casey Weissbuch on drums)
2. Class of 2013 (02:11)
3. Last Words of a Shooting Star (02:57)
4. Liquid Smooth (02:51)
5. Pearl Diver (02:52)

TOTAL RUNTIME: 13:44

MITSKI NPR MUSIC TINY DESK CONCERT

RELEASED: August 31st, 2015
RECORDED: NPR Music headquarters, Washington DC

1. Townie (2:16)
2. Class of 2013 (2:13)
3. Last Words of a Shooting (4:03)

TOTAL RUNTIME: 8:32

Her NPR performance for "Class of 2013" was a strong talking point for her early reputation, the iconic vision of Mitski screaming into her guitar pick-ups becoming a fixed association with her live presence.

3.11.
HIRED GUN, PART 1

Welcome to the first in our Hired Gun chapter series, where we look at some of the work Mitski has done outside of the Mitski album sphere. For this round, we have Gabby's World's second album, *O.K.*, released on May 12th, 2015. Known then as Eskimeaux, she and Mitski were so tight that Mitski contributed writing and/or vocals to not one but *four* songs on the record. These were "Broken Necks", "Pocket Full of Posies", "Folly", and "Sparrow".

Another largely unknown Mitski project is her work on the short film *Hoof* (2017). It was directed by Tymon Brown, remember him? The guy who shot the unreleased video for "First Love / Late Spring"? Turns out, that was a trade of skills, because, for payment, Mitski provided the score to his mini-flick. You can watch (or listen to) it on YouTube.

"To clarify: Mitski did the opening/closing theme, sung in French, based off a poem she liked. She also composed and performed the cello, piano, and droning tracks used throughout the movie. There are a few other tracks by other artists peppered throughout as well. We stayed in touch for a little while after school but it's been a

long time since we've talked. Mitski, If you ever see this, really hope you're doing well, pal!"[75]

- TYMON BROWN

That's it for now, see you at the next one!

Part Four
PUBERTY 2 ERA

4.1.
ALBUM: PUBERTY 2 (2016)

1. Happy (3:40)
(second single)
2. Dan the Dancer (2:25)
3. Once More to See You (3:01)
4. Fireworks (2:37)
5. Your Best American Girl (3:32)
(first single)
6. I Bet on Losing Dogs (2:50)
7. My Body's Made of Crushed Little Stars (1:56)
8. Thursday Girl (3:08)
9. A Loving Feeling (1:32)
10. Crack Baby (4:52)
11. A Burning Hill (1:49)

TOTAL RUNTIME: 31:25

"By my fourth album, I felt like I knew how to record an album. For my first and second ones, at least I was still a student in college, in music conservatory. A lot of that recording process was just about learning how to even record an album, learning how to direct people, learning how to give good performances in-studio which is very different from live and different from playing privately. So by the fourth one I think I got the hang of it and I could actually focus on the music, which I guess doesn't make much sense because the whole point of recording an album is to make the music. I think for my first three albums, a lot of the recording wasn't... I shouldn't say wasn't about the music... but I was really caught up in just doing the thing and I wasn't thinking about the thing itself as much." [54]

- MITSKI

On June 17th, 2016, Dead Oceans released *Puberty 2*, and it exploded across the musical landscape, obliterating everything 2016 knew. The album had been recorded in the (now closed) Acme Studios in Westchester, New York.

"I went to this place called Acme Studios in Westchester, NY. It's defunct now, but it was run by my former professor at SUNY Purchase, Peter Denenberg, who produced the Spin Doctors and also the Space Jam soundtrack. He teaches now. He's the head of the department and I stayed close with him, as did Patrick [Hyland], who produced the record. So he let us use the studio for a reduced price, and we just booked two straight weeks and stayed in there and got it done." [5]

- MITSKI

Let's hear from Professor Peter Denenberg on that one.

"Mitski and Patrick actually lived in the studio for several weeks, sleeping on the floor. Every few days, they'd walk to my house and take showers." [33]

- PETER DENENBERG

"It was just, wake up, do the thing until you're too tired to keep doing it." [63]

- PATRICK HYLAND

"The studio was running Pro Tools HD, so that's what I was using. I also happened to work at that studio, so it felt very much like home for me. It was kind of my home base at that time." [63]

- PATRICK HYLAND

As far as credits, Mitski wrote the songs, Patrick Hyland recorded the songs. They split the instrumental duties between them.

"Just [Patrick] and me." [80]

- MITSKI

Yup, you read that right. The mighty *Puberty 2* was just Mitski and Patrick Hyland. Nobody else.

"I recorded Puberty 2 in the span of two weeks, and I think that was only possible because it was just the two of us and we'd worked together before, so we knew each other's rhythms. You know, while I was working on something, he could be working on something, and it just freed me up totally to work much more efficiently." [26]

- MITSKI

"I really enjoyed it. It's our third record working together so we know our rhythms. A lot of times, we wouldn't have to discuss things, we'd just understand. I know when to give him space and when to jump in. That's what made it so quick. It only took two weeks because we were able to work really fast. While he was working on something, I could trust him to do it and go work on something else." [5]

- MITSKI

"I used to work with a lot more musicians. Lately, it's just me and [Patrick]. We switch off on instrumentation and I think that's why a lot of my records have a lot of amateur playing because it's either me playing or the producer Patrick Hyland playing. Neither of us are virtuosos. When I used to have musicians come in they would almost get frustrated with how simple it is because you don't get to really show off with my melodic lines. A guitarist would come in for a solo and they'd try to embellish it and I'd be, like, 'No! Do it

how I wrote it!' I think it would be frustrating. That said, I do think that really great musicians can make the simplest lines make you cry. There's that line, 'There are no small parts, only small actors.' I think it's the same way with music. It's very difficult to write something simple and good." [13]

- MITSKI

<u>TITLE</u>

When you come up with a title that says so much with so little, you have to expect a million questions. Mitski has addressed the concept of *Puberty 2* over and over. Here are only some of her responses:

"I get this question a lot. But, actually, it started out as just a joke between me and Patrick. We were riffing on what the title should be. He said, "oh, Puberty 2," like, you know, Puberty 2, like a blockbuster movie. [It] just sounds like the worst thing. Puberty again. But I latched on to it. Maybe in five, ten years, I'll look back and be, like, 'Oh, that's the deep Freudian reason why I named it Puberty 2,' but, right now, it just sprung from a joke." [27]

- MITSKI

"Literally, it's like Puberty 2. I had come out of college. I was expected to be an adult. But I hadn't quite figured it out yet. I still felt like a child. But then I also had to really figure out my taxes. It's just that feeling of knowing you're not a child anymore, but also not quite being ready to let it go yet, because the alternative is facing adulthood." [13]

- MITSKI

"Most things that are important, I deliberately don't think about. So maybe it has loads of meaning and that's why I gravitated towards it. But how it happened was that me and the producer were just riffing on what the album title should be, just joking around and I latched on to it. Maybe I latched on to it for deeper meanings but I try not to get too existential!" [10]

- MITSKI

"I actually had a ridiculously long argument whether it should be the number 2 or a Roman numeral." [70]

- MITSKI

<u>SOUND</u>

"I'm impressed by how scrappy it is. It's very young, in that it has the resilience of youth. I didn't have resources, but I made it happen, and I used whatever was around me to try to express myself. I try to remember that feeling of needing to create. I'm still an indie artist, so I'm still often in a position where I don't have access to things. But I'm glad that I went through [making] my first four records, because they taught me that you can make it work. I don't get discouraged when I hear 'no'. I just think, okay, how do I make it work?" [45]

- MITSKI

Expanding on *Bury Me*'s rocky centre, *Puberty 2* has been called indie rock, punk rock, noise pop, art pop, and slacker rock.

"I went into this record—for the first time—very confident in knowing what I wanted out of it, knowing how to get it, and then getting it and confident enough to take risks. But at the same time, I always want to be a pop artist. Not that I want to be Top 40, but in that I always want to be for the populace. I don't want to be elitist. I don't want to deliberately say anything that people wouldn't understand. I think music is supposed to be shared. I took a lot of risks but at the same time my stance is that I always want to be understood." [99]

- MITSKI

"When I record, it's this very precious and insular thing. And so after doing the whole 'Bury Me' thing, recording this album became even more of an escape. So instead of feeling pressure or feeling like I had to make something that everyone would like, it became this very juicy time where I finally could get to do music again. Because I felt that, with promoting Bury Me, I was so out of touch with music. So, yeah, I wasn't thinking as far ahead as, 'Oh god, I have to put it out and is it going to be as good as the last one?'" [5]

- MITSKI

"I do like recording with tracks as opposed to with the live band. I don't think I've ever done a live band recording for my records before. Like I said, I'm not a production-based artist. And a lot of people talk about how my records jump through so many genres. But I think if the main melody is there, the arrangement almost doesn't matter to me. Or if it turns out that the guitarist can't come in for a studio session, then I'll just play a keyboard part, or I'll do it myself somehow." [27]

- MITSKI

Hyland first made the observation that Mitski's albums seem to work in twos. Mitski doesn't disagree.

"LUSH was in college, like, 'Oh, my gosh, there are studios! There are other instrumentalists!' And then Retired From Sad, New Career in Business was taking orchestral instruments and refining piano music. Bury Me at Makeout Creek was very DIY, punk-influenced, and guitar-driven because I had left school. I didn't have any more of those resources. I just had a guitar that I was learning how to play." [1]

- MITSKI

"It's kind of a two parter. It's similar in sound, but a direct growth from that record. I had a certain confidence this time. I knew what I wanted, knew what I was doing and wasn't afraid to do things that some people may not like." [103]

- MITSKI

"[Bury Me] was like 'I'm angryyyyy' or 'I'm saaaaaaad,' and that was the world. But then I grew up a little." [80]

- MITSKI

The most notable difference was *Bury Me*'s energetic live feel, oven-ready for shows. *Puberty 2* leaned into the strengths of the studio without concern of concert translation.

"I quote-unquote 'went back to my roots' a little bit. With Bury Me, my focus was that I would be able to play specifically for these small DIY spaces with the equipment that was there. I didn't want to make all these grand compositions and then not be able to realise them in

my reality, which, at that time, was Brooklyn and spaces like the Silent Barn. But when I was making this fourth record, I wasn't thinking so much about whether I could play it live anymore. I was thinking more about how I could make these recordings good for what they are, and I knew that I could always just recreate a different version live." [5]

- MITSKI

"For Bury Me At Makeout Creek, I was very conscious of making sure I recorded everything that I could recreate live and that's why it's very fixed on guitar, drums, and bass. For this new record, there are a lot of other sounds and I think I was less concerned with being able to recreate it live or I wasn't thinking about it so much. I was just focused on recording something in the studio and worrying about this, the live thing, later. So we'll see how it goes." [56]

- MITSKI

"For this record, I wasn't so concerned about playing it live because I realised that I could just have a different live version. I just wanted the record to sound good, to go into the studio and do what served each song regardless of how I would play it later, live." [10]

- MITSKI

"The impulse of the album was [that] I had two weeks between years of tour to start and finish an album. So it was good because I had to be very decisive before I even went into the studio. I couldn't dawdle. I couldn't improvise in the studio. I had to write everything beforehand and then make quick decisions. And I think it was helpful.

But, yeah, it's kind of like a growth from Bury Me. I had more resources, less time." [13]

- MITSKI

"For Bury Me, I was so focused on putting myself out there that everything I made was filtered towards how can I get people's attention? How can I reach people? And maybe it was more abrasive because I was like... listen!!! Whereas for this fourth record, it was more centered around, 'I'm gonna do what I want.' Like, I would still be able to play the songs off the new record in smaller spaces, but there was more of a sense of safety. It wasn't that I thought that I would be able to play bigger spaces, it was just more like, I'll be okay if I can't play these live, or I'll be okay if I have to figure out a different way to perform these later, or I'll be okay if people don't like it." [5]

- MITSKI

ARTWORK

Keeping the work in the family, even the album photo was shot by Patrick Hyland.

"I went to a place in upstate New York. There's like just open fields everywhere. The thing is, the image just popped in my head and it took me a while to know whether I should just go with it, go with what I imagined, but I'm thinking, like, I'm painting my face white because, in Japan, you do the whiteface and make-up and whenever you're like an artist or performer or group of that traditional art. There's this tradition of painting your face white with makeup on. And

I think I was just trying to express how I want to be a part of that or that's part of my heritage. But it's all blotchy and I'm not doing it well. I'm not quite doing it, but I want to. I want to be a part of it and it's part of my history, but I'm never going to be a part of it or belong to it." [56]

- MITSKI

The cover font is Edwardian Script ITC.

<u>THEMES</u>

"I think it's just that I've grown up a little bit. When you're a teenager and you're sad, the world is ending. But when you're an adult, you can be sad and still go to work. Or your life can be fucked up, but as an adult you understand that your life isn't the world, and the world goes on and you just deal with it in your own way privately, or talk to a friend. In The Breakfast Club, there's this quote that goes, 'When you grow up, your heart dies,' and that's such a teenage perspective of what I'm talking about. I used to be afraid of that, but now that I'm older, I'm just like, no, your perspective grows and you realise that your one intense sadness isn't everything." [56]

- MITSKI

Puberty 2 explores the complex themes Mitski is famous for: love, longing for that love, the alienation that comes from a lack of identity, and how happiness can be as dangerous as sadness.

"Happiness is up, sadness is down, but one's almost more destructive than the other. When you realise you can't have one without the other, it's possible to spend periods of happiness just waiting for that other wave." [104]

- MITSKI

"There's a sort of cynicism, too. A little bit of cynicism can be healthy. It's also just self-awareness. In previous records, what worked was that I was so in-the-moment and in my feelings, and on this record, there's more of a perspective and objectivity to my emotions. And that's why I feel, lyrically, I used a lot more metaphors and a lot more characters than I did before. I feel this way, this is what happened—there's less of that." [5]

- MITSKI

Puberty 2's themes also dabbled in realms of fiction, which is a technique Mitski ploughed deeper into the further her career moved on, as we shall pick apart later.

"The perspectives are still mine, but I think I'm just becoming more aware of the layers of who I am. No one is just one person, no one is just one feeling. Just like with writing fiction—even though this isn't fiction—sometimes the best way to convey an emotion isn't just to straightforwardly describe it, but to imply it through metaphor or use characters. There's a quote that goes, like, 'Fiction is closer to truth than nonfiction.' With this record, I focused more on finding the essence of whatever I'm feeling and describing it so that it's more about that essential emotion rather than my personal one." [5]

- MITSKI

CHARTS

Bury Me at Makeout Creek set up Mitski's name to take the shot. On *Puberty 2*, she sank every basket. The album charted well across the board, hitting the top 20 on the US Top Alternative Albums (19), the US Independent Albums (18), and the US Heatseekers Albums (5).

But these positions meant nothing next to the critical acclaim...

CRITICAL

What is still considered her defining work by many, *Puberty 2* was not called a bad name by anyone. Awarding it full marks, The A.V. Club said Mitski was *"an exceptionally keen observer of the human condition, and Puberty 2 marks a triumphant new step in her evolution."* Consequence of Sound, Allmusic, and Spin gave it 90+, with the latter stating, *"It's a high-watermark of post-irony indie, a cracked safe of perspectives previously unheard in lump-throated punk."* With 8.5/10, Pitchfork stamped the album with its revered Best New Music badge, saying, *"She might be an 'indie rock' artist, she currently stands apart from—and above—much of the genre."*

Many reviewers noted how its troubled themes were its primary weapon, including DIY Magazine (*"[it makes] grim tales seem even worse than you could possibly imagine. It's a brutally tough shock to the system, one that will leave its trace for years to come."*) and The Guardian (*"It may have been exhausting and painful to put down on record, but listening to it is anything but."*). Both gave it 4 out of 5 stars.

The worst major review came from Rolling Stone who offered some backhanded compliments with, *"Puberty 2 shows Miyawaki indulging her whims with a devil-may-care attitude—the result is an incendiary self-portrait,"* yet even they could not go lower than a 75% score. All in all, according to review aggregate site Metacritic, *Puberty 2* reached universal acclaim with an 87% total.

"There's been good press, which I'm thankful for. But the reality is that I'm just on tour. I'm in the van, I go to the show, I play the show and that's my life. So all that stuff outside, I don't even really notice it. My life itself, my personal life, just hasn't changed. It's just everything around me has changed." [27]

- MITSKI

One thing that didn't change was the accolades as the End of Year 2016 Album lists rolled around. *Puberty 2* was included in the top 20 more often than not, including Pitchfork (18), The Skinny (15), The A.V. Club (8), Stereogum (8), Paste (5), and Time (3). Pitchfork later dubbed it the 30th Best Album of the 2010s. And despite their previous sniffs, Rolling Stone called it the 49th Best Album of the 21st Century So Far.

To what do we owe such successes? Mitski has a theory.

"I figured out what to do. I was touring more, doing more press—just learning how to be a working musician. That was it. I honestly don't know if it was anything related to music. I'd done three albums by then, and I was like, 'Oh, okay, if I don't do press, then no one hears about it. If I don't tour, then no one cares.' When I was writing it, it was still a very sincere process of wanting and needing to make music. I don't make music in order to make a living. But I do make music, and I have to figure out how to make a living." [45]

- MITSKI

SINGLES

• Your Best American Girl

"I wanted to use those white-American-guy stereotypes as a Japanese girl who can't fit in, who can never be an American girl." [90]

- MITSKI

Talk about coming out swinging, the announcement for *Puberty 2* on March 1st, 2016, was accompanied by the first single, "Your Best American Girl". Annoyingly, the song did not come with any separate artwork, but all was forgiven when it was the best song anyone had ever heard.

"'Your Best American Girl' is a love song. A lot of reviews have agreed on a narrative that 'she wrote this song to stick it to 'the white boy indie rock world!'' But I wasn't thinking about any of that when I was writing it. I wasn't trying to send a message. I was in love. I loved somebody so much, but I also realised I can never be what would fit into their life." [33]

- MITSKI

With her constant grappling with national identity, Mitski had never hit the theme quite as poignantly than on this song, which expresses itself through cultural differences within a relationship context. Sadly, it was based on real-life experience.

"I didn't grow up in the US. It came from wanting to just fit into this very American person's life, and simply not being able to." [105]

- MITSKI

"It's just a feeling of loving someone so much, and yet being from completely different backgrounds and not being able to do anything about it. You watch movies where the couple loves each other so much but can't be together because of their fate or whatever, and when I was younger I thought that was so stupid. I just thought, 'They love each other, why can't they be together? This is ridiculous.' But then as I got older, it's, like, 'Oh, I see.' Sometimes life or your backgrounds just kind of get in the way, and there's nothing you can really do about it." [26]

- MITSKI

"I don't think I have the kind of creativity to write fiction. [This is] the first album where I kind of stretched outside of my own experience and used more metaphors. I don't know if I would go as far as to say I tell other people's stories. They're still my stories, but I just use characters or use metaphors to describe better what I'm feeling at the moment. But this song is quite autobiographical because I didn't grow up in the US. I am half Japanese, and it came from wanting to just fit into this very American person's life and simply not being able to. Just fundamentally being from a different place and feeling like I would just get in the way of their progression in their life, because I could just never get to wherever they're naturally going." [19]

- MITSKI

"Yes, in the musical composition I used tropes from 'white indie rock' of my adolescence. But I used those tropes to accentuate the point that I would never ever fit [in]." [106]

- MITSKI

A lot of publications spoke about its political undertones.

"Just the fact that it's me who is expressing my thoughts in itself is political. Like, my existence is political so I almost can't help it even if I'm not intending to make it political. It just becomes political, because I am a political being." [20]

- MITSKI

"Here's the thing: Everything is an undercurrent. No woman of colour can be in love without it being political. I can't walk through the world without being a political entity just by being who I am. So when I fall in love, it is political. When I'm in a relationship, everything is political. The personal is political and the political is personal. I wanted to make a distinction that when I wrote this song, it wasn't a rallying fight song. It wasn't me attempting to be political. It was more just like me writing something that is truthful to me and emotional to me and obviously it has all those undertones. I kind of like that there are many interpretations of the song because I think a song is successful when it says many things at once." [54]

- MITSKI

"A song doesn't have to be one thing. 'Your Best American Girl' is so genuine for me and it's coming from a real place. But that doesn't mean I can't also be dry and cynical within it. I want all my songs to be human. And human beings contain multitudes, as they say. So, yeah, it is there but it's not the point. It's like pretty nail polish. It's not the point of the person but it makes it look nice." [11]

- MITSKI

Naturally, when a song is this good, it blasts off with a life of its own.

"It's wild that the song has become what it is to people I've never met." [95]

- MITSKI

Pitchfork observed that *"by the sounds of [this song, Mitski is] making mature choices, both musically and personally,"* awarding it the Best New Track status. The Village Voice's 44th annual Pazz & Jop critic's poll voted it as the 5th best song of 2016. Both NPR and Paste went even further, each placing it as the second best song of year, respectively calling it an *"angst-ridden anthem about an identity crisis"* and saying it *"forces us each to conjure up our 'all-American boy' and then take issue with the fact that coming up with a picture of him was so easy"*.

"Your Best American Girl" hung on for the duration of the decade, and made many Best Songs of the 2010s lists including #13 for the ever-difficult to please Rolling Stone (*"[it walks] the chasm between romantic ideals and cultural reality to make for breathtaking music"*), #7 for Pitchfork, and #2 for the Opinion Police.

What is further interesting is how the movie world snapped up the song, appearing on the soundtrack for 2018's *Hearts Beat Loud* (92% on Rotten Tomatoes) and 2019's *Someone Great* (83% on Rotten Tomatoes). It probably helped that both of these films were about music, but it does highlight how few movie soundtracks Mitski appears on. Why?

"They doth protest too much. Songs sync better if they could apply to a lot of things. I think my music is actually incredibly specific, and it's a little too individualistic; it's a little too 'listen to me.' Movies and TV shows don't want that." [45]

- MITSKI

The song found its way to television as well, heard on both *Dickinson* and *Billions*. It was also included on the compilation *Uncut: Protest Now! - 15 Modern Anthems*.

Onto the music video! It premiered on April 13th, 2016, and was directed by Zia Anger. She has also worked on music videos for Jenny Hval, Beach House, Zola Jesus, and Angel Olsen. She directed her first film in 2024, aptly titled *My First Film*. More importantly, she has provided her skills for many more Mitski projects to come, so this is not the last time you'll read her name.

According to the video press release, it *"plays on the idea of, as a Japanese girl, never quite fitting in with the genre's surplus of white American guys."* It was said to be partly inspired by PJ Harvey.

A basic summary goes like this: a sweet interaction between an Asian girl (Mitski) and an American boy (Bro played by Tyler Gardella) is interrupted as an American girl (Babe played by Candace Bryant) starts kissing Bro. Heartbroken Mitski turns to her hand and makes out with it instead. Eventually, Mitski rocks out on guitar as the couple continue kissing while wrapped up in an American flag. It's hilarious, weird, passionate, erotic, and total cinematic magic.

"I really wanted to create a scenario that first made your heart ache, then represented what one might do to deal with that heart ache. When I was trying to figure out what Mitski should do at the end of the video, I think I asked Ashley [Connor], 'What's the most don't-give-a-fuck thing she could do right now?' And Ashley said, 'Shred.'" [27]

- ZIA ANGER

Ashley Connor was the cinematographer. She has some pretty impressive credits to her name, including work on the films *Knives Out* and *The Miseducation of Cameron Post*. It's not the last time we'll hear from her in this book either.

"[It's] the sort of 'woman with guitar and nothing else in a white space'." [100]

- ASHLEY CONNOR

To present Mitski with the hand kissing idea, Zia sent a video of herself performing the scene.

"It takes a very specific performer to look at that video that [Zia] sent her and say yes. [She's] trusting, fearless, and exact." [100]

- ASHLEY CONNOR

What's more, Mitski really commits to the role! Like, really really. You have to see it for yourself.

"And at the end of the take, the entire crew, everybody just stopped and clapped for her. Zia and I just kind of looked at each other like, 'Fuck yeah, man! That's how you do it!'" [100]

- ASHLEY CONNOR

In response to the video, New York Magazine called it a satire on cutesy festival girls. Mitski did not agree and told them so:

"Don't pit me against other girls. It's not about that." [32]

- MITSKI

• Happy

"Happiness fucks you. Once it's in your hands you try to hold onto it, but the nature of happiness is that it passes through and eventually leaves, and something else—sadness, anger, a low after the high—has to follow. This song is about this exhaustive and exhausting cycle, and how sometimes one would rather not have any of it at all than be constantly thrown about by the waves of these fleeting states." [100]

- MITSKI

On May 3rd, 2016, "Happy", the second and final *Puberty 2* single, arrived. Again, there was no artwork (boooo!) but at least the composition itself made for a fascinating conversation piece.

"I wrote the verses and the choruses separately. So maybe that's why they sound disjointed [...] If you just put the melody, set it aside from the rest of what's going on in the arrangement, I think it's very bluegrassy or folky. I wrote it and I was, like, 'Oh my God, this is a fucking country song!' So I wanted to put a twist on it. I was listening to Portishead's 'Machine Gun' and there's that incessant drum sample—or maybe it might not even be a drum sample, just a sample—and was inspired by that for the initial drum sample track." [13]

- MITSKI

That intro/outro drum sample definitely catches one's attention.

"I believe it's some kind of kick sample that's repeating over and over. I wanted something that was incessant and obsessive, a little bit. I mention trains in the song, and I think I wanted to evoke that without actually using train sounds." [26]

- MITSKI

"I heard that on a train track and I was, like, 'Oh, that's good. I should make that into a drum beat." [13]

- MITSKI

The crazy sax solo is the first time Mitski has used horns since *Retired from Sad, New Career in Business*. And who could be responsible for such a thing?

"The producer, Patrick Hyland, is playing. He played [sax] in a high school jazz band. But it's going through a guitar amp and it's a little distorted." [13]

- MITSKI

Like everything *Puberty 2*, the press loved the song. It was another Best New Track from Pitchfork, who concluded that *"Mitski resists psychic death by constantly pushing forth into bolder textures, refusing to be meek and sedated even as joy feels compromised."* AllMusic called it one the album's highlights.

Which brings us to the video...

"This video is all Maegan Houang. She's in L.A., and I'm in NY, so I emailed her vague ideas about what the video should be, and she turned around and came back with a completely out-of-the-box narrative that blew us all away. So I just went, 'Right, I'm going to trust you on this and have you do what you want.' Sometimes the best thing to do is to step back and let people do what they're good at." [102]

- MITSKI

The director, Maegan Houang, has worked on various projects including music videos for Charly Bliss and Vagabon as well as the TV series *Shōgun*. She's another frequent go-to Mitski collaborator, so look out for her as we move forward. But for now, on May 23rd, 2016, 20 days after the single was released, the music video landed.

"I wanted to explore the impact other people's actions—from affairs to murdering other people—have on the ones closest to them, as we still live in a very solipsistic society." [107]

- MAEGAN HOUANG

Warning: before you read this summary, it is recommended you watch the video first!

Done? Okay, here's the summary: After finding wads of blonde hair everywhere, a woman suspects her husband is having an affair. Tensions rise until she uncovers the truth: he is murdering and cutting these women to pieces. Upon being discovered, the husband tries to kill his wife, but she escapes by knocking him out with a bone. Yikes.

"I'm a huge fan of Mitski and dreamt of doing a music video for her for a long time. Her music inspires me on a daily basis and I especially like to make work for female artists. The juxtaposition between the title of the song 'Happy' and the sober tone of the music reminded me of 1950s melodramas where things look so beautiful, but people feel so emotionally tortured and trapped... Stylistically, Douglas Sirk, particularly All That Heaven Allows, was the main inspiration for the video, as well as Wong Kar Wai's In the Mood For Love. It was important to me to cast an Asian American female as the lead as we rarely see Asian American women portrayed in the past, even though they did exist. When I was growing up I never saw anyone that looked like me—I'm half-Asian—on screen, so to see someone like Mitski, who is also half-Asian, connect with so many people is very inspiring." [108]

– MAEGAN HOUANG

Vice called the music video *"anything but happy"*. And while it does not feature Mitski, it does star Jin Maley who has credits on *Gilmore Girls*, *Grey's Anatomy*, *The Young and the Restless*, *Star Trek: Picard*, and... *Bones*. As for the ending, it is rumoured that an extended version exists where the wife smashes the walls in the basement which are full of blonde hair.

OTHER NOTEWORTHY SONGS

• Dan the Dancer

"Out of all the songs people say they like in the album, I don't get that song much. I think it's because it's not as flashy as the other ones maybe." [54]

- MITSKI

"With 'Dan the Dancer,' there is no Dan. I'm not Dan. It's a story, but it expresses an emotion I had. So, as I evolve as a songwriter, I'm starting to create narratives that serve the emotion that I'm trying to deliver without including those weird details. But it's not really about an expanding audience. It's about me as a songwriter finding that I'm growing and learning new things about how to write songs." [44]

- MITSKI

"An image came up in my head of someone hanging off a cliff, but also simultaneously living their life like it's not a dire situation, and they've always been hanging off a cliff and they're trying to pretend that it's okay." [47]

- MITSKI

"Dan is a metaphor. I just thought about someone living their life, hanging off of a cliff, and that in itself as a metaphor. And then I thought, well, what if that person wanted to fall in love and then they wanted to hold hands with somebody? What would they do when they're hanging off of a cliff? What if they let go of one hand to

hold someone's hand? Now they're hanging off of a cliff with just one hand. What do they do? I pursued that thought." [54]

- MITSKI

"Dan the Dancer" can also be found on the *Rough Trade Shops: Counter Culture 16* compilation.

• I Bet on Losing Dogs

There isn't much to note here except to highlight how this song remains a giant fan favourite, to which anyone who has attended her live shows will attest.

• My Body's Made of Crushed Little Stars

Some "Crushed Little Stars" could be heard in the superhero comedy series *Extraordinary*, season one, episode two, "Magic Bullets".

• Thursday Girl

"It relates to the other song, 'Happy', where it occurred to me that happiness is also exhausting. Happiness is an up as opposed to sadness' down and so both can equally be imbalances." [47]

- MITSKI

Some cool things happened with "Thursday Girl". The first cool thing was when a fan edited footage of Kendall Roy from *Succession* looking depressed set to this song. It made the rounds in 2021 and eventually reached Mitski.

"It's the best thing that's happened to me on the internet." [60]

- MITSKI

Another cool thing is that "Thursday Girl" featured in season 3, episode 2 of *Supergirl*, as well as in the short film *Sitting*, which we'll get deeper into a little later.

• Crack Baby

Writing a song about a crack baby as a metaphor for lost love was always going to rub some people the wrong way. Mitski responds:

"All I can really say is that I wrote it when I was a teenager and in a bad place. I guess all I can do is apologise for the insensitivity, because in order for me to actually explain myself I would have to reveal things about my life and about things that I am just not that comfortable with putting out in public. The world is a big place with many opinions. That's that." [47]

- MITSKI

• A Burning Hill

While not a single, "Burning Hill" received a video which was released on October 11th, 2016. It was directed by the creative team (and married couple) So Yong Kim and Bradley Rust Gray (aka Soandbrad). Together they have worked on many other projects, including the feature films *In Between Days* and *Lovesong*.

The quick video is mostly close-ups of Mitski's face and hands as she floats in water or watches the world pass out of windows. In some ways, it harks back to Mitski's *Retired from Sad, New Career in Business* visual project, especially "Strawberry Blond" and "Class of 2013".

• Bonus Tracks

The Japanese version of *Puberty 2* came with two bonus tracks, pushing the total album time up to 37:03.

The first bonus track was "Fireproof" (1:49), a One Direction cover.

"I like that song. Usually, I don't like covers because if it's a good song and it has good production then I don't feel like there's a need for a cover. I think a cover is just saying the same thing over and over again. But with this song, I heard it and I just immediately heard a different version of it in my head, so I felt like I could actually

contribute something by doing a cover of it. I think a lot of One Direction songs [and] a lot of those pop songs, they're good because the composition is good. And with a good composition, you can really arrange it in any way, and it would still sound good. So I wanted to show that." [27]

- MITSKI

This song was also found on *Our First 100 Days* (2017), which was a compilation album released track-by-track for the first 100 days of Donald Trump's first presidency (20 January to 29 April). Other artists on the track list include Angel Olsen, Avey Tare, Suuns, Jessica Lea Mayfield, Gold Panda, Speedy Ortiz, Kae Tempest, Julien Baker, Protomartyr, and Waxahatchee. Mitski's contribution was day number 78. Proceeds went towards organisations threatened by Trump's policies, such as those fighting climate change or standing for LGBTQ+ rights, reproductive rights, or immigrants' rights.

Interestingly, Mitski is known to have covered the song live as early as 2015, but the footage has disappeared off the face of the web. This proves Mitski as a proper One Direction fan, even if she once foolishly said this outloud:

"When One Direction broke up I didn't really feel anything. I've stopped feeling things for a long time. I almost felt like it was a matter of time... I love all of One Direction. Please don't hurt me." [43]

- MITSKI

The second bonus track was "I'm a Fool to Want You" (3:49), a Frank Sinatra cover. This pop and jazz standard has been additionally covered over 100 times, with most people convinced that Mitski used the Billie Holiday version as her blueprint.

This recording was also featured as track 10 on the *7-Inches For Planned Parenthood* compilation. Released on October 20th, 2017, other artists involved include Björk, Bon Iver, St. Vincent, Foo Fighters, Sleater-Kinney, Chvrches, and Feist.

And that's *Puberty 2!* Leaving our jaws hanging low while shooting Mitski to an even higher realm of stars, testing her ability to deal with life more than ever before.

"Realistically, I don't think we ever actually find anything. It depends not only day by day, but hour by hour. But right now, in this moment, I feel like I'm doing a job. For so long I worked towards people listening to my music. And now people are listening to my music, and I'm talking to you, and my album's coming out. I think I'm feeling pretty content. We'll see how I feel in an hour, and tomorrow, and in a year, you know?" [26]

- MITSKI

4.2.
UNFIT FOR MUSICAL STARDOM

"I'm not a star. I can say that with confidence because I have met real stars. And I have cowered before them." [21]

- MITSKI

Celebrities, they're just like us! They also like to meet other celebrities!

"One time, I was walking around near Union Square, and Benedict Cumberbatch walked in front of me. I didn't realise how tall he is! And, also, how great his posture is! So, when he walked by, I was like, 'Oh wow, a star! It's all about posture!'" [21]

- MITSKI

"My last celebrity encounter at an airport was Margaret Cho. I sat down at the gate and I realised she was sitting right across

from me. I didn't want to bother her, but I kind of wanted to say something, like, 'Hey, like I'm Asian too!' But I didn't talk to her." [7]

- MITSKI

"I'm not the kind of person who gets starstruck." [2]

- MITSKI

But with the limelight heating her own celebrity power, Mitski's anxiety heated with it. She recalls one nightmare incident of panic backstage at a benefit concert, where she was surrounded by famous faces.

"I started to get a headache and heart palpitations. My hands started to shake. I thought I was gonna throw up, I really did. I told my manager, 'I need to get out of here,' and I practically ran out." [2]

- MITSKI

"It was, like, all the people around [the celebrities] together emitted an energy that made me feel like I was on a bad high. I think you're always conscious of something when you feel you don't have it." [2]

- MITSKI

"I remember Taylor Swift talking to me, but I don't remember what I said back to her. I remember her saying, 'Well.' And then leaving."" [2]

- MITSKI

Part of the problem is that Mitski knew how the public treated women in her position. Talking about that one Esquire profile where Megan Fox was compared to a human sacrifice:

"It was ridiculed at the time, but I thought it made a good point. We have it hard-wired in our brain that we need this ritual. We prop up

a beautiful woman and then shit on her and destroy her. Thankfully, I am 31 now, so maybe I don't qualify anymore." [1]

- MITSKI

When publications asked to write a feature about *"A Day In the Life of Mitski"* she rejected them for that very reason.

"Okay. Do you want to come to a few meetings with me? Do you want to come see me rehearse? Go on tour? And they're, like, 'No, let's go out on the town, go shopping, look at vintage clothing.' And I'm, like, 'I don't do that!' They want to imagine women having fun, being sexual, lounging." [33]

- MITSKI

Pretty soon, Mitski formed a shell to protect herself while reevaluating how she slots into this new dimension.

"Putting on that guise of being a brash, confident person was a way to protect the vulnerable parts of myself that I didn't want the world to get at. The flipside was that it really hardened me, because I didn't allow myself to be soft, ever. I always had the masks on. I didn't even have time for friendships! But it affected my writing, because in writing you have to be vulnerable." [93]

- MITSKI

"I'm finding that the more I do this, the more isolated I become. And it is a weird realisation process because I make music to go, 'Hey, look, you've felt this way too, so I'm not actually that different. I'm part of you, I'm one of you, accept me.' That's what I'm saying when I'm making my music. And yet the more I put out my music,

in a weird paradox, the more I kind of get pushed out of the big group. Because I'm on stage with just a few other band members facing a whole big crowd." [41]

- MITSKI

"I wouldn't say it's an alter ego, but I have anxiety around social situations, and I don't like going to parties. As a performer, onstage I know my place. I'm sure of myself. There's no doubt. It's just existing, and it's so lovely to get to be that for an hour." [1]

- MITSKI

"I came from a DIY punk scene where there are a bunch of white-guy bands, and they got to just put out music, go on tour, and then go home. I thought that applied to me. I didn't realise that I was breaking this contract that I'd entered into. Keeping some things to myself makes people very, very angry. Because they might not be conscious of it, but they think I have not come through on my end of the deal." [1]

- MITSKI

"I guess fame is relative. There's Taylor Swift fame and then there's local-DIY-scene fame. The real struggle for me in getting bigger is, how do I maintain integrity in the performance? How do I make sure the audience experience is still intimate and emotional in this 8,000-cap room? How do I not resort to flashy pyrotechnics onstage? Because I don't want my show to be about that. I want people to enter into a place with me and have an experience, and then leave having experienced something important." [1]

- MITSKI

"The natural progression starts feeling like, 'Bigger venues, more records sold, more press, more accolades.' And I'm at a point where I've been very lucky that I can make a normal, non-musician working person's living from music, and I have to think about what will be enough now. What is the point of me doing this now that I can make a living and do what I want? Because it doesn't feel like making more money is the point to me. So I think, 'Do I want more accolades? Do I want more people to know me? Where should I go now?' is kind of the question." [42]

- MITSKI

"It's really scary, because being in this cycle, you get really caught up in it. Everyone around you is getting more and more and more, and there's this feeling that you have to progress to the next stage— do the bigger venues, do the better festivals. But I want to make sure that I'm making music because I want to make music. I want to make sure that's the priority. I'm probably being very confusing, but it's probably because I personally feel confused about it. I have to decide what is the point of it for me now and what I want out of it. It doesn't feel like playing bigger venues is the point, but it's also hard to turn it down when it's in your grasp." [42]

- MITSKI

4.3.
HAPPY?

"It's so unhealthy because I've gotten to a point where I don't trust happiness anymore. When I'm too happy, I'm just waiting for something to happen, and that ruins my happiness." [5]
- MITSKI

Mitski's raw lyrics have opened her career up to a ceaseless onslaught of questions about depression. With *Puberty 2*'s song "Happy", perhaps now it is a decent juncture to lump all of these responses in one place.

"I don't think I'm alone in this: I'm obsessed with trying to not only be happy but maintain happiness, but my definition of happiness is skewed more towards ecstasy rather than contentment. Ecstasy can't last forever, so there's the inevitable comedown from that. I think it's less the 'what,' and more the thing itself. I've been learning that I can use many different things to try to chase that feeling, but the most unhealthy thing is the chasing itself. I think in the song

['Happy'], I touch on the fact that chasing it and then coming down from it and then chasing it again is the most exhausting process. When I was writing this song, I just wanted none of it. I didn't want the happiness and I didn't want the sadness that comes after it. That's kind of what the song is about: not wanting to go up or down anymore." [26]

- MITSKI

"I've never been diagnosed as depressed, but then again I've never been to a psychiatrist, so who knows! I've come to terms with the fact that I'm always sad, though, underneath all the day-to-day emotions. And I find that whether I feel fully sad or not depends on whether I'm occupied with something at that moment, so I try to always be occupied—with making albums, for example. But I think a lot of people can relate to that. Even when everything's swell, there's always the feeling that something is not right at all. And I actually think the kind of upbeat or 'happy' songs that people really come to love are the ones which convey that mixed feeling, instead of flat-out 'I am feeling great.'" [36]

- MITSKI

It's important to note that since the above quote, Mitski has attended therapy.

"I love therapy! Having someone to talk to, who you don't feel like you're burdening, because it's their job, it really eases up all your friendships. You're saying it out loud, giving it words; it clears things up. In America, there's still this notion that you're not good until you're happy. I hope we can get away from that." [93]

- MITSKI

This naturally leads to the age-old question: does one have to be tortured to be an artist?

"I think about it all the time. Every day, I'm like: 'What if I just destroy this? Then maybe that would save me.' If the music went away and I stopped being this way and I could just be a normal healthy person with a regular job, I would do that in a heartbeat. I really would. I would love to be just happy." [80]

- MITSKI

"That myth is incredibly toxic because it demands artists to be unhappy and it keeps us from, for example, thinking about how to create a better work environment for artists. Or how to take care of artists' mental health. It keeps us from thinking about those important things because we're, like, well, artists have to be unhappy. So I don't think that's healthy. I think my being unhappy or happy or however I feel is just being human. And it's not so much being an artist. I could not be an artist and still feel the same things I feel." [28]

- MITSKI

"That kind of impulsive emotionality helps in writing. The moment inspiration strikes and just going with it. But I think I've been very bad about this." [9]

- MITSKI

"I have a very conveniently photographic memory of emotions. It's overwhelming, because things don't fade for me. But it's very good for songwriting because something could happen three years ago, and I could be in that moment and write emotively about it. It'll be there, for better or for worse." [80]

- MITSKI

"I have a lot of chaotic energy in me. Or just a confusing kind of emotion wanting to come out. And what I've been trying to do is try to hone that into a laser beam and take that intensity or whatever that's inside and focus its energy. When I put it out, it's less about just releasing, and it's more about squeezing it into one focal point." [73]

- MITSKI

As Mitski matured, so did her perspective. Watch it happen in real-time:

"I can call myself an adult now. Not everything is such a big deal to me anymore. Maybe that's a bit sad. You know when one of [The Breakfast Club] characters says: 'When you grow up your heart dies?' I believe that. Your heart has to die in order to survive the world. It's such a horrible world." [17]

- MITSKI

"I wish I were smart enough to figure out [how to improve society]. I just know that the way it is now is terrible, and I feel my soul dying every day. [At least] I still have the privilege of being able to complain about my soul, you know? Because I'm middle class, I get to talk about my existence. A lot of people don't have the room to do that. I only seem to be wired to write my little songs about my feelings. It really makes me sad how useless and unintelligent I am. It's really terrible." [93]

- MITSKI

"But when you stuff things down for a long time, they'll explode eventually." [58]

- MITSKI

244

"I'm still living day to day. I'm still a big baby. I'm still always anxious about money. I still embarrass myself every day." [48]

- MITSKI

"Now that I'm actually growing up, I'm realising that you heavily need to depend on other people to live and that doesn't change. In fact, that probably becomes more important as you get older. What I think today, and this might change tomorrow, is that being an adult is understanding you're not the centre of the world. You're just one little minnow in a big sea. And that's okay." [38]

- MITSKI

"When I was a teenager it was all about experiencing everything. I was a junkie for emotion and I wanted it all. Lately, I've found that I just want to be happy. You get a little older and you just get tired. So maybe when I was younger, I chased that and sometimes I would do it for the song. I've had a lot of relationships where I knew from the start... I was like, 'Oh, this is so juicy. This is gonna hurt!' Now I just don't have the time or energy. Honestly, if I could give all of this away for happiness, I would. I would rather be boring and happy than be fucked up and—apparently—a good artist." [10]

- MITSKI

"I'm trying to break the cycle of thinking only fraught situations bring meaningful art." [80]

- MITSKI

There is a sense of serenity that comes with age, and in latter years, there have been noticeable improvements in Mitski's innards.

"A lot makes me laugh. I make me laugh. It disturbs people. I'll make a joke and laugh forever, and people go, 'That's not funny.'" [17]

- MITSKI

"I think both happiness and sadness don't define you as an individual. They're things that just happen to you. At least that's how I see it. We tend to chase happiness, but happiness can be just as exhausting as sadness. When you're happy you feel like it's going to last forever. And I think that's scary, because when it goes away you're extra sad. Or extra empty. You feel like you should be happy but you're not anymore. I think that's exhausting, anyway. You start asking yourself: why are you not happy? But if you see happiness as something that simply passes through you, maybe it wouldn't be as exhausting." [18]

- MITSKI

"Heartbreak doesn't have to be a hard, horrible, bad thing. It's just like 'I'm so infatuated and in love that I feel myself crumbling... but in a good way!' It doesn't have to be a bad thing. It's just something very joyful and wonderful about breaking down, and kind of coming apart, there's something very delightful about that." [85]

- MITSKI

"At a certain point, the feeling of being an outsider is self-imposed. Growing up, moving around, and then also being on tour, I didn't allow myself to attach to anything, because I knew that eventually I would have to go away again. I think I've allowed myself to attach to things again, or people again, or just become attached." [60]

- MITSKI

"I'm always living in the now and that sounds very enlightened but I can only take things a day at a time." [54]

- MITSKI

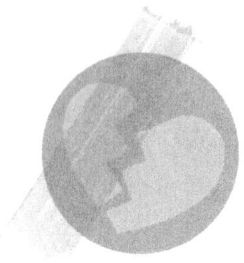

4.4.
PUBERTY TWOURS

Back on that grind! The inevitable album tour kicked off with a lot of 2016/2017 shows taking our best American girl around the USA, Canada, Belgium, UK, France, Switzerland, Czech Republic, Netherlands, Ireland, Italy, Germany, Denmark, Israel, and Australia. Bands who joined her included Japanese Breakfast, Jay Som, Fear of Men, and Weaves.

Speaking of Weaves, Mitski has shared some glowing words for that group.

"I'm gonna declare it" [Weaves are] the best live band I've ever seen, next to Downtown Boys." [27]

- MITSKI

"You know how they say you need to know the rules to break them? I think that describes [Weaves] perfectly. They are such good musicians. They know the rules, and therefore, it sounds so good when they mess it up a little. It sounds all the more tasty, because they're so tight that they can afford to be loosey-goosey,

if that makes sense. The music seems to be composed so that you can hear each person have a little solo in their own right. Every member very much brings something and it has to be the four of them. I find myself singing 'You're so coo coo!' all the time, just like in the shower, in the kitchen. That's always in my head." [109]

- MITSKI

As for Japanese Breakfast and Jay Som, some have noted with fondness how they were all Asian artists sharing the stage.

"It was me, Michelle [Japanese Breakfast], and Jay Som all on one tour. And it was really good. We're all so different. That's the thing. We are all so different. That's what needs to be highlighted. Me and Japanese Breakfast and Jay Som think in totally different ways and make different music. I want us to get to a point where our Asianness is not the point." [11]

- MITSKI

Mitski made headlines when, at a *Puberty* show in Athens, Georgia, she asked everyone who voted for Trump to leave, offering a full refund.

"This is a safe space. Voting for him was a violent act." [110]

- MITSKI

"Trump's platform is violently hateful. He incites violence at his conventions. His proposed policies will cause death and violence to millions of minorities, so voting for that is to say 'I wish violence on these people.' This is not about difference in beliefs. This is about giving the people at my show, many of them queer/people of colour, just one night of feeling safe and free of harm." [110]

- MITSKI

The *Puberty 2* act also became a festival staple, playing at (but not limited to): SXSW 2016, Coachella 2017, and Primavera Sound 2017. You may have also seen her face playing "Your Best American Girl" on Late Show With Stephen Colbert.

As if this wasn't crazy enough, while on tour, Mitski was announced as the opener for... the Pixies!! She would be supporting shows for their USA *Head Carrier* tour (6th - 21st of October, 2017).

"Yeah, that was very strange. First of all, both the guitarist in the band and I are such huge Pixies fans. When I told the guitarist... Patrick Hyland... actually, what am I saying, the guitarist? He also produced a lot of my records and he's also the guitarist in my band... he fucking cried. He was, like, 'I can't believe it.' They've been such an influence on my thinking about music and my melody writing. So it was very strange to be on a tour with people who have directly influenced me." [71]

- MITSKI

"When Patrick and I were together, our manager called us to tell us about the opening act, and we were so surprised and moved that we both cried. We've both been fans for years, and when we first heard about it, it didn't really feel real. We actually went on tour, experienced a professional scene, and learned a lot from it. Pixies' live performance is conscious of a large audience, and the performance itself is well-structured for two hours. They've spent a lot of money on everything, including the visuals, and we saw our goal of levelling up like that." [12]

- MITSKI

Not big enough? How about this: while she was playing those Pixies shows, Mitski was announced as the opener for some of Lorde's USA *Melodrama* tour shows (March 24th - April 15th, 2018).

"I realise now, having done that tour, that a lot of people in the US really never venture outside of Top 40. And the magic of Melodrama is that it gave everyone who listened to that kind of music everything they wanted, but also snuck little nuggets in there that were challenging them. I feel like it must have broadened a lot of people's perspectives on what 'pop' is." [45]

- MITSKI

"While I was playing I realised [the crowd had] never heard anything like my music. I saw so much confusion on people's faces like: 'What's happening?! What is this sound?'" [17]

- MITSKI

"It was like I was inventing punk music in front of them." [11]

- MITSKI

What made this stream of concerts even more fascinating is that hip hop duo Run the Jewels was sandwiched between Mitski and Lorde.

"It was Lorde's tour officially, but Run the Jewels were main support and I played first at 7 pm every night. I was just happy to be there! I was happy to play in an arena for the first time. Everything was new. Catering was amazing. But it's one of those things where you kind of have to realise you're not the main attraction there. You're kind of just there to play while everyone files in. And I think that's the mindset I played in. With my own shows, it's very much, like, 'Thank you for coming for me, let me give you what you came for.' But when it's somebody else's show, it's like, here, maybe you would like this. Hopefully you would like this." [112]

- MITSKI

Despite the chaos, Mitski appeared to enjoy herself on her *Puberty 2* tour, especially concerning her relationships with the songs and the fans between them.

"A lot of making an album for me is just doing what feels right and then, afterwards, psychoanalysing and realising the reasons I did things." [30]

- MITSKI

"I think they're more a part of me now, because I've played them over and over on tour. Those songs and I have passed the infatuation phase of our relationship when everything is exciting and shiny, and we've entered a new phase where we're comfortable and natural with each other, and love each other more deeply." [95]

- MITSKI

"I've come to love it. I used to think of it as this vacation from real life, that didn't count as my life. But then I found that I was on tour nine months out of the year and I can't discount nine months out of the year anymore. So I started to face it and see it as my life, and therefore regulate it. Make sure I get sleep, and make sure I eat. And that's made it better than seeing it as a vacation. But also now I enjoy it." [13]

- MITSKI

Part of the release comes with surrendering her songs, no longer in her care and now part of the world.

"It's so funny, album cycles. As soon as I'm done with an album, it's separate from me. So it's a little bit strange to go through an album cycle and have this thing that for me feels done, [is] new for other

people. The songs almost take on a completely different meaning for me once I start performing it. And that's helpful. Because it's not like I'm reliving the writing process while I'm singing every time. It's almost not mine anymore, you know? Once I put out an album, I'm giving it away. It's a gift, um, that I'm selling." [22]

- MITSKI

"I have let the interpretations of my music go. Once you make it and you put it out, it's not yours anymore. It's up to the listener to do with it what they will. I think I prefer that. I don't want people to be listening to it, imagining my experience. The whole beauty of listening to music, at least for me, is that you get to put yourself into it and hear someone else say something you felt." [19]

- MITSKI

"It doesn't matter. When you listen to an album it's yours. It's no longer the artist's, so you can do what you want with it." [85]

- MITSKI

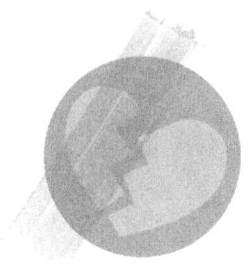

4.5.
SHOW STRUGGLES

"The thing about being on tour is that you can pretend you don't have your problems. So I can go out on the road and think I'm someone without a human being, without problems. And now I'm afraid to not be on tour anymore because I would have to come home and face my problems. So it's like a great escape from the psyche... until it all comes down." [13]

- MITSKI

As much as Mitski had aligned to her true calling, she was racing along at break-neck speed, which is why it's not surprising she hit a few road bumps.

"In my ideal, magical world, I would be able to be at home and then perform every night. But it doesn't work like that." [60]

- MITSKI

One topic that comes up a lot is her loneliness.

"If you're a suburban mom surrounded by family with a nice life you still feel alone. On tour, I'm surrounded by people all the time but it's lonely." [17]

- MITSKI

"It's not personal or individual loneliness because you're always surrounded by people on tour, right? But there's a sort of structural societal loneliness because you're always in a different time zone. You're far away from everyone you know. Your work is so different from everyone else's. None of your friends can really relate to your experiences. So, little by little, you become more and more solitary. I think that's the kind of loneliness I'm talking about or I experience on tour." [61]

- MITSKI

"Touring is my life now. It's a very isolating experience. I found that the more I do this, the more I reach out to other people doing what I do and hold on tight to them. I try to support them and get their support." [37]

- MITSKI

No doubt about it, some cracks were beginning to show.

"Lacking routine [...] your body gets so confused because you're always eating at a different time, not eating healthy, sleeping at different times, at a different altitude, on different surfaces. And your

body, at a certain point, is just, like, 'Stop. Stop doing this.' But I think actually what keeps me doing it is, like, I don't have anything else." [46]

- MITSKI

4.6.
SHOW-MADIC

"What's important to me is that my songs can exist without any material anything. It's very reflective of my ideology." [80]

- MITSKI

If Mitski was feeling the pressure of touring, one can hardly imagine how other artists manage. Because, if there was one advantage of Mitski's rootless youth, it's that the constant relocation of her position was something she grew up with and got used to.

"A lot of issues that other artists might have with touring, like missing places or feeling out of place in certain places, I don't have issues with because my life was led feeling out of place. It's nothing new to me. It's quite a familiar feeling. I don't miss anywhere. I don't feel like I belong anywhere. So that upbringing has moulded me into the perfect touring musician." [16]

- MITSKI

"People just live everywhere. You can make a life. I feel like it's the same with the idea of finding a soulmate. There's never really any one place that you're meant to be. You can just live anywhere and live your life. Also moving away to somewhere else won't change your life because you still have to deal with yourself and you still have to live with yourself." [7]

- MITSKI

For financial reasons, Mitski decided to completely give up on renting a place. It would make no sense as she would never be there.

"I don't live anywhere. I also don't have a place to live. I haven't for the past couple of years. I have money to stay at hotels, Airbnbs, and stuff, but that's because I don't pay rent. I don't have rent so instead of rent I can just pay for wherever I'm staying at that time." [7]

- MITSKI

"Because I'm on the road so much, even if I had an apartment, I would be responsible for it and not live in it. So when I'm not on the road I just stay with people." [18]

- MITSKI

"I had, whatever, an identity crisis about it a few years ago. But now I'm fine with not having a home. It's convenient for my lifestyle right now because I'm on tour all the time. Having some place to miss can be really inconvenient. But for holidays, I just go wherever my parents are at the moment, or just go to my friend's house or whatever." [15]

- MITSKI

"My friends are, like, 'You really need to find a place to live,' and I do think maybe it's a little dangerous for me to not grow roots a little bit. To go further and further out into untethered rootlessness." [33]

- MITSKI

"You're on the fringes of society. Everyone else has a place to live. Everyone else goes to work somewhere. Everybody has shit they wanna complain about. I can't complain about being a rock musician. Even if I tried, my best friends would say: 'Shut the fuck up, you get to write music.'" [17]

- MITSKI

There are pros and cons to everything, of course. And Mitski has often spoken words of appreciation for how she gets to see America in all its glory—and, indeed, the whole world.

"I've driven through a lot of real cowboy country now. America's so big I feel like half of understanding it is seeing all sides of it that aren't just LA and New York." [85]

- MITSKI

"I'm very fascinated by America because I'm supposed to be American, but I'm not really from there. I never grew up there and I've spent my adult life trying to figure out what it means." [85]

- MITSKI

"It's interesting how I am an American citizen. I have the passport but I feel like a foreigner. I feel like I'm a tourist when I'm on tour or just interacting with people. But when it comes down to actual

patriotism or just feeling like I belong or have a say in politics, it's kind of a weird dichotomy of feeling like an outsider." [9]

- MITSKI

"America is supposed to stand for something. It projects that image internationally and nationally. But then we're kind of... what's the word? Not 'hidden from,' but... it's kind of kept out of the public consciousness [...] American optimism was kind of a coping mechanism, or a survival technique, you know, during post-war, in that if you didn't think that way, then you couldn't live. But I feel like now it's actually quite detrimental because it keeps us from actually facing things. And if we don't engage, we can't change what needs to be changed." [9]

- MITSKI

"Oh honey, it's on fire! The whole country is on fire, what can I say?" [71]

- MITSKI

"I get to see the whole world, and what you realise is there's so many wonderful places that it becomes hard to choose just one place to live. There's always constant FOMO for other places." [85]

- MITSKI

I know what you're thinking. With all this moving around, sleeping in a different bed every night, surely Mitski has some ghost stories? Well, of course she does!

"I've been to one haunted Airbnb. I like to believe it's haunted [...] It's in the middle of nowhere California, we walk in, immediately something's off. There's a fucking rocking horse in the middle of the living room.

Why would you have that? It was 2 am, so we go upstairs, me and my band, and I go into the room that's supposed to be mine and immediately there's just like a fuckton of pictures of American soldiers. And I'm, like, okay, well, I'm just sleepy, I'm gonna try to go to sleep. I lie down, I turn to my right, and there's a gigantic fisheye mirror right next to me as I'm sleeping. I can't avoid it. It's terrifying. And then I look up, and there's an obviously sealed attic door. I'm, like, I'm not gonna sleep here. I go to the next room where my band members are sleeping and I'm, like, 'Can I join you guys?' I crawl into bed with one of the band members and this room is just wall-to-wall dolls. All dolls. Shelves and shelves of dolls. So my band member gets scared and she turns around a bunch of the scariest dolls so they're not facing us while we're sleeping. And then, while I'm kind of about to fall asleep, I hear people talking in the room but I just assume it's my members and I fall asleep. And in the morning, I talk to them, I'm, like, 'Were you awake talking at night?' and they were, like, 'No, why?' and I was, like, 'I just heard people talking in the room.' And they're, like, 'No, I heard it too.' There were people in our room talking! So that's our haunted Airbnb story." [7]

- MITSKI

"I was in Albany, New York, to shoot my music video for 'Working for the Knife'. And there was this beautiful stone mansion next to my hotel that just stopped me in my tracks. I didn't know anything about it. I stopped in front of it, looked at it, and I just stood in the street, staring at it. And I was, like, 'I want to live in that house. I want to be in that house. I want to be in that house.' And then I looked it up, and, sure enough, it was, like, top 10 most haunted buildings in the United States. I think it was pulling me in." [25]

- MITSKI

"I love ghost stories. I've loved them since I was a kid. I used to collect them and then I would go to my classmates and be, like, 'Do you want to hear a ghost story?' and they'd be, like, 'No.' The one that scared me the most was Toire no Hanako-san. Hanako is a Japanese girl's name. It's just about the girl in the toilet. It's never explained why there's a girl ghost in the bathroom. She just haunts the toilet and it's really scary when you're a kid and you're going to the bathroom alone. Just alone in the toilet stall and thinking there's going to be a ghost. I used to think a hand would come out of the toilet bowl and just grab my butt. I don't know what it would do once it grabbed my butt, but I was afraid of the grabbing." [25]

- MITSKI

4.7.
WORKING ON TOUR

"Well, the thing is, I don't do well chilling. I don't chill, so I have a break from tours actually coming up in August and September, but I have another project lined up for that, which I can't really talk about." [63]

- MITSKI

Despite any stresses she may have felt, Mitski can't help Mitski-ing, and she never stopped working on new stuff. By the end of her tour, she just about had another album ready to offer.

"I have to keep touring. The album cycle is, like, one to two years depending on how much you want to milk the album. And I'm really milking it. So I'm going to be on tour for a while. I have music already done and written and recorded. Don't quote me on this, but I can't put it out until, like, middle of next year because I have to be on tour for Puberty 2 for a long time." [13]

- MITSKI

How does she do it? Let's take a glimpse into how her "working on tour" procedure might go.

"Writing on the road is hard for me. On the road, I get little snippets of inspiration but I can't follow through, so I'd make a voice memo and then I'd have to go somewhere. Tour isn't good for writing, but it's good for inspiration. The record was made over a long period of time of having hundreds of snippets and putting them together into a cohesive thing in the end. But I can't write on the road because I need a space and a focus that you just don't have in that environment." [5]

- MITSKI

"On tour I can't write, but I can think of ideas. So, what I do is I make little voice memos of snippets or I write down little phrases and kind of collect little pieces of a song. And then I go off tour and go through my notebooks and my voice memos and then organise them. So that's kind of how I write right now." [11]

- MITSKI

"I am inspired on tour and I jot down ideas on tour. But I can't put them all together until I'm off tour. So when I come off tour, I have a notebook full or like a phone full of little ideas. And then it's my time to organise them." [13]

- MITSKI

4.8.
HOW TO WRITE MUSIC LIKE MITSKI

"I'm still very much an idiot about music. I still don't know enough. You could study music for a lifetime and not know enough, but I guess the tools in my toolkit come from listening to pop songs and seeing how they're structured. Or trying to read between the lines, beyond the lines, playing different instruments, making different kinds of music, and drawing from all of that. [That said], I don't think I have nearly a big enough toolkit. I'd like to learn much more about music." [28]

- MITSKI

Sorry to interrupt, but now seems like a decent enough spot to pause for a masterclass in Mitski songwriting. So, if you wish to pen music like Mitski, the first thing to remember is to start with lyric building.

"I do more sort of thinking—of a phrase here and there, or a sound there—and then writing it down in my notebook, or singing it into a Voice Memo, putting the pieces together later, like a puzzle." [33]

- MITSKI

"I have listened to a lot of lyrics where I felt underestimated as a listener. I'm not stupid, I've felt many different things in my, albeit short, life. And even though we can all be very different as people, I'm still human and made up of basically the same things as other human listeners, so it would be extremely self-involved of me to assume that I'm the only person ever to have felt the things I've felt. That's why I could go as far as say I feel patronised when lyrics are dumbed down, which is a lot of pop music. There seems to be an assumption that the audience won't 'get it'. That certain scenes or emotions the writer wishes to convey would be too specific to their experiences for listeners to relate to. So it's generalised, to be all-encompassing. But that's condescending. I want writers to trust that their audience is intelligent and is human, and that we're not so different that we can't relate to their most recent heartache. I want you to trust me." [21*]

- MITSKI

"When I experience something that I know I'm going to write about, it feels very quiet and focused. There's this almost this feeling of relief, like a feeling of purpose. A feeling of being serene with myself. Because I think my purpose in life is to write, so when I get those moments when I'm about to write I'm, like, 'Ah, this is what I'm doing,' and it's very serene. Maybe it's a coping mechanism. Maybe when I

felt these extreme sad or mad emotions, my body was, like, 'I need to turn this into something productive in order to deal with it.'" [11]

- MITSKI

"I just try to make sure each song I write has a humanity to it and takes into account the whole human. Real whole humans are both dark and light, both right and wrong, etc etc. It's less that I try to find balance, and I certainly don't want to start thinking of my songs as some sort of lesson for someone to learn, because that would make them preachy, shallow, and bad, in my opinion. It's more that I try to remain honest as I write, and if I'm honest then both the good and the bad come out naturally and, I think, become a more accurate reflection of what it means to be human." [95]

- MITSKI

"As arrogant or deluded as it sounds, I think of my purpose in life is to express whatever I'm experiencing through art. So I'm able to just see it as me doing my job. I'm talking about really emotional stuff, but in a deluded way I'm, like, 'This is what I'm supposed to do, so I don't have a choice.' So it's very easy for me to do it. I've never had reservations about bearing it all. But also, here's the thing, my music is not about specific narratives, like things as they happen to me in my life. They're about core emotions I felt through those things. So it doesn't even matter what the narrative is or what I actually experienced. My goal is to convey that emotion. So, sometimes the narrative in my song is different from the narrative that happened in my life. And that's fine, because my focus is sharing this core emotion that I believe everyone else has probably experienced. So, maybe, in your writing, instead of thinking of it as explaining what happened to you, word-for-word, you can focus on that core emotion that you felt through what happened to you, and describing that emotion, and doing what you can to let that emotion out." [11]

- MITSKI

"Often with my own music, I find out what I was actually trying to say much later on. Maybe that's what the whole process is about, too. Just sorting things out so that I understand." [45]

- MITSKI

The lyrics then dictate the vocal melody, which is equally important, if not, more so.

"[My melodies] often follow the inflections of a word or sentence as they're spoken." [33]

- MITSKI

"No offence to everyone else, but my voice is what matters. Specifically, the vocal melody is what matters to me. And I want to make sure, especially with the way I grew up, that all my songs, people can sing them regardless of whatever instruments they have or whether they have karaoke. I want all my music to be singable when there's nothing, because that's how I started music. So everything else is just, like, 'Well, I have to play a show, and they won't want just my voice. So I better get a piano and some bullshit instruments.' Or, 'Well, I guess I have to make an album and it'll be boring [with just vocals].'" [11]

- MITSKI

"I want the vocal melody to be the most important thing. I want people to be able to sing it regardless of whether they have instruments. That people [are] able to sing it to themselves in their car, in the shower. Because I didn't have instruments, or I didn't know what instruments I had." [20]

- MITSKI

"With most of my songwriting, the words and the vocal melody comes first. The chords and the arrangement almost don't matter to me or it is interchangeable. A lot of people write chord progressions first, and say, 'Okay, what vocal melody can we put on top of this?' But for me, and going back to my upbringing, I come from a background of not having resources. I don't know when I'm going to have a guitar or piano. I'm moving around. I'm usually in a car. And I'm usually alone. My upbringing is that I sang songs to myself and so in my writing, even today, I want to make sure that the vocal melody and the song can stand on its own without any backing instrument." [77]

- MITSKI

"I almost exclusively write for my voice. I find that it can be limiting, actually, because I end up writing in the same range. I know my range. I tend to write things that I'm good at, so that limits me. I might want to write something but then we discover that I can't really sing it very well and then discard it. I also find that, over the years as I sing more and more, I become a better singer. As I become a better singer, I become a better writer, because my range gets better and I can do more things." [13]

- MITSKI

When a song is written, hit that record button and sing it as best you can. But don't forget that the music is important too!

"I'm very particular about the vocals. They're done last, and I do them on days when I feel prepared, and I take them very seriously." [85]

- MITSKI

"My music is so heavily lyrics-based. So much of my intention in the songs are expressed in the lyrics. It does make me feel good that people who don't speak English still like my music because, to me anyway, it would probably mean that they genuinely enjoy the music itself, and that's an area that I'm still not very confident about. I'm more confident about my lyrics, and my actual songwriting, than my actual music. When people who don't speak English tell me they like my music, I'm like, 'Oh, wow! You really do like the music!' But it is a different dynamic, especially when we're playing shows. You can sense that people are getting something different out of it." [44]

- MITSKI

"I am a Libra. I'm always about balance. So I think it's very intriguing when there's a contrast between distorted heavy music played by, like, someone who looks like they're about to go to work. I'm all about kind of finding balance and finding a weird middle ground. I do that in my compositions. If there's a heavy, subby bass, then I want to put a little high note in there just to balance it out. I'm exploring those contrasts." [11]

- MITSKI

"If there's anything I think of most, it's proportion." [14]

- MITSKI

When you have enough songs, well done! Put them in a little pile, shuffle them into a satisfactory order, and there's your album!

"The sequencing is more based on general mood as opposed to telling a story." [85]

- MITSKI

"I hate to disappoint, but when I make an album, it's not that I have an idea behind the album. It's more like I've amassed enough songs to make an album, so I'm going to make one. I find that, naturally, since I write these songs within a time period, and I don't drastically change as a person within that time period, that they end up being themes. It's just never really as intentional." [13]

- MITSKI

"The song I write reflects who I am at that moment. I am basically a consistent person during a short period of time. I don't know about everyone, but I change as a person every year. In one month, I'm usually consistently one person. So if I write an album in one month, then all of the songs will be coming from that one person in that one stage of life. So it'll all feel cohesive." [16]

- MITSKI

"I don't write albums as full albums, I write for the songs instead of albums. I write songs individually and I try to give each of them what they need. A lot of artists write albums thematically or they have an overarching narrative, but I don't. It was just a collection of songs that I had which amounted to an album. I didn't really have a message

in mind, I think I just listened to the songs and figured out how they flowed best and used that to make the track list." [47]

- MITSKI

"When I'm writing songs, I'm not thinking about anything. I'm just doing what I feel. And then, after they're written and recorded, I face the consequences of what I've written." [9]

- MITSKI

Above all else, remember who you are writing songs for. Hint: it's not the audience. It is yourself.

"I'm a very selfish person. I'm always thinking about myself, so it's not difficult. Obviously I'm performing for an audience, but when I'm writing I'm not thinking about any kind of audience. I go back into that world I've cultivated for myself that's just mine, and when I go there I dig up something and try to express it in some abstract way." [26]

- MITSKI

"I'm kind of a selfish musician who uses music to express something I wanna express. I want to make sure that I communicate to the best of my ability what it's like for me to be alive and feel alive. That is the reason I live." [113]

- MITSKI

"I don't want to continue to make music that is protective of myself. The music I love, that has saved me, is the kind that really gets to the heart of myself and the person performing it. And so I decided that even if more harm may come to me, I would be serving *my purpose better if I actually wrote something that felt closer to my heart."* [93]

- MITSKI

"I want people to listen to music uncynically again. So much of music listening is, like, listening for brands and I hope we can get to a point where we can just enjoy songs whatever genre they are." [9]

- MITSKI

And don't stress if some days are more difficult than others, as this is just the manner in which the creative gods work.

"You know, a good song usually takes 30 minutes, tops, because it just comes. But it doesn't always happen that way, and sometimes I do it for like an hour and let it sit, maybe let it sit for a few days so I can get a fresh perspective and come back to it. It really just depends, honestly, on the song and what it needs." [67]

- MITSKI

"Sometimes, everything comes at once. Those are a blessing because you have a song done and in an hour out of nowhere. But also, sometimes, I just have a bank of lyrics and a bank of melodies and a bank of harmonies and I put them together. Sometimes I have verses and choruses and I put them together." [9]

- MITSKI

"No matter how much I think about making music, it's difficult to create a song exactly like that. There are some parts that are

out of control, and I'm not good at creating songs in a planned or intentional way." [12]

- MITSKI

Done? Then congratulations! You're now a Mitski! That is, of course, if you remember to keep up the work!

"I think being an artist is about putting your head down and doing the work. You can make something really nice, and you can be proud of it, but you can't hold onto it. People have been making nice things way before you were born, they're making nice things as we speak, and they'll continue to make nice things long after you die, so don't kid yourself. You don't hold onto your one or two nice things and feel contented with that, because that's not the point. The point is not to make something that people think is good, or to make something that people think is so good that it makes you famous, or even to make something that makes you so famous that people remember you after you die. It's not about making a shitload of money and living comfortably either, and it's not about the 'glory' of dying poor, sick, or hungry for the sake of your art. It's about the work. You keep your head down and you keep working, not because it'll bear fruit to any rewards, and not even because it makes you feel fulfilled in any way, but because that is what you do as an artist; you keeping making things. That's what I think, anyway." [36]

- MITSKI

"Maybe it just boils down to: I'm a woman who's really into her career, so I'm obsessed with the craft of my work. There's a romance in that for me." [33]

- MITSKI

4.9.
MITSKI, THE MUSIC JOURNALIST

During her brutal schedule of touring *Puberty 2* while writing a new record, Mitski somehow found the time to submit two album reviews for Talkhouse Media.

The first was Weezer's *Pacific Daydream*, for which she concluded:

"Weezer's newest album has provided unexpected clues in an examination of my own writing, too, as I inevitably age and negotiate an ever-evolving self with an enduring idolatry of youth." [114]

- MITSKI

The second was for Harry Styles' self-titled solo debut, which is worth the read for lines like these:

"Harry's vocal performances do glitter with charisma. His voice throughout the album is as precise and attractive as would be expected from someone who's performed in stadiums for his entire adult life [...] I would stand like an ant in an arena crowd just to

witness his magnetism; his expansion as a performer since his beginnings in One Direction. There's no doubt in anyone's mind that his solitary voice can fill the room just fine [...] If Harry Styles reads this, he'll probably hate it. But then, I think it's fine. It's not really about him, anyway. " [115]

- MITSKI

Finally, I don't wish to start a gang war between Swifties and Mitskies, but Mitski did previously offer her critiques on Taylor Swift's "Bad Blood" single, noting:

"It feels weird. As someone who writes lyrics, that she did 'cuuuuut'. Like the word 'cut' on three notes feels a little weird going down. But, whatever, I don't care. She can write her own songs. I remember I took a music course in junior year of high school, and some girl brought in 'Teardrops On My Guitar,' and she was like, 'Isn't this song great?' And everyone was like, 'Who's Taylor Swift?' And now every time I listen to Taylor Swift, I remember that moment. Like, wow, Taylor, you came far. Good for you, Taylor." [115]

- MITSKI

4.10.
FILM: SITTING

Once again, I am unsure how Mitski crammed everything in, but another 2017 sidequest brings us the short film *Sitting*. It was released on November 1st, 2017, and all 7 minutes 30 seconds of it can be found on YouTube. Emily Yoshida wrote and directed it. Her other credits including the TV show *Shōgun* and a music video for Speedy Ortiz's "Lucky 88".

IMDB describes the plot as "A down-and-out young woman takes a job delivering an unusual drug to high profile clients, sitting with them while they have life-altering experiences."

There are several actors involved but Mitski is the absolute centrepiece, not only as the lead but also with her song "Thursday Girl" playing a fundamental role. It was a thrill to watch, and does make one wonder: with such a competent performance, could Mitski the Movie Star fall upon our future cards?

"Well, I was a film major for a year but I quit because I realised I love music, whereas I just like watching movies. It takes so much to make a movie. Even more than making an album. So much more has to go right in order to make a decent movie. And I just don't know

if I have the leadership skills to direct such a team effort. I'd rather kind of just work solitarily and make my album and then go back to my room and not talk to anybody." [41]

- MITSKI

"I love making music videos. I just love filming. I was a film major for a year before I transferred to music. I enjoy it, but in order to actually make film, you have to be dedicated to it, and it's more something I just enjoy doing. I love films, but it's not in me to do it. My ethos is usually just to say 'yes' and see what happens, but I'm not a good actor so [they'd probably be] making a mistake." [85]

- MITSKI

"I'm not good at it and there are people who are good at it. I feel like there are a lot of jobless actors who are really good at acting. They should get the part. And also, my thing is when famous celebrities transition into music, I fucking hate it. So I don't want to do the same thing to actors. I feel like actors would hate me if I casually acted in a movie or a TV series." [7]

- MITSKI

4.11.
HIRED GUN, PART 2

Another one of these sections! Let's take a look at what Mitski has been up to outside of her own musical world.

On December 13th, 2016, the *Adult Swim Singles Program 2016* compilation was released involving many artists, including Ryan Hemsworth, whose contribution "Wait" featured Mitski alongside Keaton Henson.

"I've been working on little ideas with Keaton for a while. But once I had the chance to get Mitski involved as well it made complete sense to me. They're easily two of my favourite singers so it was really inspiring to work on this one together." [116]

- RYAN HEMSWORTH

General reaction to the song was lukewarm at best.

Zip forward to April 20th, 2018, a teensy before *Be the Cowboy*. There you may bump into "Between the Breaths", a Mitski collaboration with fellow pop weirdos Xiu Xiu. It was part of the *How to Talk to Girls at Parties* soundtrack, a scifi romcom based on a 2006 short story by Neil Gaiman. The star power of Elle Fanning, Alex Sharp, and Nicole Kidman could not save the film from mediocre reviews.

Over already? Oh well, see you next time!

4.12.
THE GIRL I USED TO KNOW

I t's difficult to know where to place this section, because the information itself is so hazy. But perhaps the most sought-after of Mitski's unreleased songs is the one fans call "The Girl I Used To Know", if it even exists.

The story largely revolves around Sterling Fox, a record producer who has worked with Lana Del Rey, Kylie Minogue, and Britney Spears, to name a few. Reportedly on an Instagram story, he posted a 12-second snippet of an unheard Mitski track which was recorded in 2017 but scrapped. It definitely sounds like her. Keen-eyed fans noticed that the demo playtime was over 4 minutes long, meaning it would be one of her lengthiest songs ever recorded.

What happened next gets even more confusing. A full-length version appeared, rumoured to have been created by Avicii, the late-record producer, but was never released due to his passing in 2018. Again, it sounds like her, which is why many believe the story to be true. Meanwhile, others suggest it's merely an AI-generated Mitski. *Puke.* Unfortunately, without her official word on the matter, it's probably safest to listen from a distance.

Nevertheless, if it was genuine, that would mean it was once in the running to be included on Mitski's next record... *Be the Cowboy.*

Part Five

BE THE COWBOY ERA

5.1.
ALBUM: BE THE COWBOY (2018)

1. Geyser (2:23)
(first single)
2. Why Didn't You Stop Me? (2:21)
3. Old Friend (1:52)
4. A Pearl (2:36)
5. Lonesome Love (1:50)
6. Remember My Name (2:15)
7. Me and My Husband (2:17)
8. Come into the Water (1:32)
9. Nobody (3:13)
(second single)
10. Pink in the Night (2:16)
11. A Horse Named Cold Air (2:03)
12. Washing Machine Heart (2:08)
13. Blue Light (1:43)
14. Two Slow Dancers (3:59)
(third single)

TOTAL RUNTIME: 32:28

"If you haven't heard Be the Cowboy, I hope that you are not wanting Puberty 3. Because you might not get that." [28]

- MITSKI

Without any prior announcement, *Be the Cowboy* abruptly roared up for preorders on May 14th, 2018. On August 17th, the album was released through Dead Oceans. It had been recorded in studios around Philadelphia (Retro City), New Jersey (Gradwell House) and Los Angeles (Red Bull). Mitski wrote the whole thing. Patrick Hyland produced the whole thing.

"I think I was the most pathetic out of all the different albums I've made. I was the most anxious, the most unsure. It's not any one moment. It's a lot of moments of me whining and yelling at Patrick, like, 'I don't know, I don't know,' just repeating the words 'I don't know' at him and poor Patrick just being like 'weeeeell, let's figure it out.' All my

past albums, I had just written what I felt, I was never fully conscious or never fully recognised the fact that there would be people listening to my music after I put it out. This album was the first one where I fully comprehended that I will have people listen to and judge the album when it comes out. That completely changed my process because it kind of filled me with doubt, I guess. I could no longer just completely turn to instinct because I was anticipating all of the interview questions I would get. So I think a lot more second guessing and thinking deeply and being more objective with the theme of this album. But yeah, it was just a lot of yelling at poor Patrick. He was just like 'I'm trying to make your album!' and I was like 'I don't know, can you just decide for me?' and he was, like, 'No, I can't just decide for you, you have to make this!'"[71]

- MITSKI

One of the most essential points of *Be the Cowboy* is that it was written during the exhausting tour detailed in the last chapter.

"It was done little by little between tours—which was challenging, because it gave me so much time to doubt and second-guess myself. Between each song's recording, I'd go on tour and be left pondering about whether I'd done it right. I don't wanna do that again. If I make another album, I'd like to do it in a limited amount of time so I can be in it and then get out of it, so that by the time I start doubting it'd be too late. It was mostly just me and [producer Patrick Hyland] in the room. We played most of the instruments except for the occasional horns—that's something you just can't fake. So we got a couple of horn players who we didn't know based on recommendation of the studio owner, but other than that it was very straightforward."[45]

- MITSKI

"It's just about leaning into it, about understanding that being an exhausted adult is also a universal experience. I was moving away from the internal pressure I put on myself of like, 'Oh, I need to write about adolescent feelings' or 'I need to write about love, I need to write about infatuation,' stepping away from that and leaning into, 'What does it mean to be an adult? What does it mean to push down your emotions in order to be responsible and fit into the working world?' Not turning away from it." [84]

- MITSKI

"I had been on the road for a long time, which is so isolating, and had to run my own business at the same time. A lot of this record was me not having any feelings, being completely spent but then trying to rally myself and wake up and get back to Mitski. I was feeling really nihilistic and trying to make pop songs." [96]

- MITSKI

"I think I was very tired and feeling existential. And because I've just been on tour... I love what I do but it kind of takes something out of you. And to try to write something while you're in that process can be difficult. So I was just feeling spent and I think that's where the music came from. Where I was very tired but I was also trying to rally myself. And so there's a lot more upbeat music [...] I guess I was thinking a little bit of like Andy Warhol's pop art where it's very colourful, very bright, very pop, but, you know, when you hear Andy Warhol explain it, he's, like, 'Well, I just made a can,' you know? It's very kind of empty, and, kind of, like... I don't know if I'm making sense." [12]

- MITSKI

The album was mastered by Ted Jensen, whose list of hundreds of classic credits is enough to make you vomit. Some include Eagles' *Hotel California*, Green Day's *American Idiot*, Norah Jones' *Come Away with Me*, Talking Heads' *Speaking in Tongues*, Bob Marley and the Wailers' *Exodus*, Madonna's *Erotica*, Glassjaw's *Everything You Ever Wanted to Know About Silence*, Hole's *Celebrity Skin*, Marilyn Manson's *Mechanical Animals*, Deftones' *Diamond Eyes*, and Huey Lewis and the News' *Sports*. Wow!

TITLE

"When I say 'cowboy' I mean the ideal swaggering Clint Eastwood cowboy. In my daily life, I tend to be the quintessential Asian woman, so I thought, 'What if I was a tough white cowboy?'" [17]

- MITSKI

Always with her thought-provoking titles, *Be The Cowboy* was one of the more abstract ideas. That means everyone asked Mitski about it, and Mitski delivered a generous amount of information.

"The cowboy, in my mind, is powerful in that he's free. Free that he's able to ride into town, wreck shit and then leave without thinking about it. There's a strange power in not caring. I'm interested in that idea of power." [85]

- MITSKI

"I think the idea of the cowboy is so American. The idea of a man riding into town, wrecking shit, and then walking out like he's the hero." [61]

- MITSKI

"They ride into town, wreak havoc and then just leave. They don't care. They don't have to live in the town. And my brain and my

conscience wouldn't allow that. There's no shame to the cowboy, and I think I will always carry shame." [85]

- MITSKI

"There was just a sort of abandon and confidence, something that I couldn't embody in my real life. Something very sure. A freeness. I think it's about freedom. I want freedom and I don't have freedom. I want to portray something that is free. There is such an idea of freedom around the cowboy." [58]

- MITSKI

"Like a white man leaning on a fence and squinting. Or, like, Clint Eastwood riding into town. That kind of cowboy. There's such an arrogance and a freedom to it that is so appealing to me especially because I'm an Asian woman. I walk into a room and feel like I have to apologise for existing. I was so attracted to that idea of freedom and arrogance and not having to apologise. So this album, its protagonist is someone like me who feels like they want to channel or embody that energy of a cowboy." [61]

- MITSKI

"I definitely wasn't thinking about the real working cowboy that exists today. I was thinking more of the Marlboro commercial cowboy, that incredibly exaggerated myth of the western cowboy. The album title kind of came from the fact that I would always kind of jokingly say to myself, 'Be the cowboy you wish to see the world' whenever I was in a situation where maybe I was acting too much like my identity, which is wanting everyone to be happy, not thinking I'm worthy, being submissive, and not asking for more. Every time I would find myself doing exactly what the world expects of me as an Asian woman, I would turn around and tell myself 'Well, what would a cowboy do?' It also came from [remembering] this guy in college who was an excellent performer because he was swaggering and confident. There was something mysterious about him; I didn't really know him as a person but he as a performer was just so charismatic. I stopped seeing him live, and I missed seeing that presence on stage. And I sort of turned around and thought, well, if that's something I want to see on stage then why don't I try to embody that which I want to see on stage?" [84]

- MITSKI

"[It's] a kind of joke. There was this artist I really loved who used to have such a cowboy swagger. They were so electric live. With a lot of the romantic infatuations I've had, when I look back, I wonder: did I want them or did I want to be them? Did I love them or did I want to absorb whatever power they had? I decided I could just be my own cowboy." [96]

- MITSKI

"It just started out as an inside joke between me and myself. I would tell myself 'be the cowboy you wish to see in the world,' somewhat like 'be the change you wish to see in the world.' And I kept telling myself that. Whenever I felt like I needed to act arrogant or confident or walk into a room like I own the place, just to push down my insecurities. That turned into the album title. It's great." [27]

- MITSKI

"There's a lot of characters in the songs that are trying to be that person. It's not so much being the cowboy, but telling yourself, 'Be the cowboy,' like, 'Do it! Be confident! You can do it! Why are you this way? Be stronger!' I think that's more the idea." [85]

- MITSKI

But before you seek too much deeper meaning within the album, remember this:

"When I was writing the songs, I wasn't thinking of the title." [85]

- MITSKI

SOUND

"I want to make sure that I'm always challenging myself or making something new. I feel like, on one hand, following the same path would be a very comfortable way to make music again, but I'm also afraid that it would end up sounding similar to what I did before. So we'll see. I'll figure it out, but there is that fear of, I don't know whether I should keep doing the same thing." [5]

- MITSKI

Be the Cowboy galloped into town with a shift in sound. The long list of genres you may come across include pop, art pop, indie pop, indie rock, chamber rock, new wave, dream pop, pop-punk, punk, electrowave, disco, alt-pop, funk, synth-pop, techno-surf, country rock, Eurodisco, and retro electric folk.

"I very much am a people pleaser. I want everybody to be happy, so what I tend to do is overcompensate by making sure I do what people might not like. But often it was hard to go in that direction, because

I'm just like everyone else and what other people like tends to be what I like as well. I'm very much a pop enthusiast. For example, my heart's desire is to just write a pop song form just like verse, pre-chorus, chorus, verse, pre-chorus, bridge, chorus. A very standard pop song form is genuinely what I like. But I pushed myself to move away from that just to challenge myself and maybe challenge the listener, too, and try to figure out ways to pace a song that wasn't reliant on classic song form." [84]

- MITSKI

"I fucked with the form, almost in ways that make me uncomfortable. It's almost like: 'Well, before this goes to shit and you stop liking me, I'm going to do something that I know you won't like, so that I'm the one who's rejecting you.'" [88]

- MITSKI

People have noted a hark back to old-timey genres, like disco or show tunes.

"There's a lot of completely un-self-aware drama in that era's music. Very uncritical, very uncynical." [45]

- MITSKI

Another markable change came with the instrumentation, Mitski's electric guitar completely thrown out the window.

"That became something people recognised me for, and I wanted to make sure I didn't repeat myself or unintentionally create a signature sound." [96]

- MITSKI

"The whole point of marketing is to distill a complex human being into an easily digestible symbol. And it's not just marketing. It's very hard for the human brain to take in everything so we just pick out the things that stand out and that is what we retain. I wanted to make sure that I was always seen as a sort of artist in a holistic sense. I didn't want to be known as the person to turn to if you want a distorted guitar. I wanted to be bigger than that. I wanted to be more complex and human than that." [84]

- MITSKI

"I tried to go against what I always fall back on. Like, whenever I want an intense emotion in the song, my instinct or my fallback plan is just to add a shitton of distortion to a guitar. Or add a lot of guitar layers. But I thought, well, I don't want to become The Distorted Guitar Artist. So how else should I express that emotion that I would otherwise express through a distorted guitar?" [28]

- MITSKI

"When arranging songs, I would think, 'Oh, a really distorted guitar would sound really good here...but I'm not going to put it in because I'm known for that.' I deliberately pushed a lot of things away." [58]

- MITSKI

"I've never had this many eyes on me before. Knowing that people are going to listen to the record and trying to make sure that I don't just try and make people happy. My instinct is to always try and make people happy, so I have to be conscious of that and fight against it." [58]

- MITSKI

"You develop this constant ticker in your mind of people's potential criticism or commentary on whatever you're making, even in the middle of making it. And that will never really go away, I don't think." [117]

- MITSKI

"When I'm writing, there is always that kind of... I forgot what it's called, but that infinite scroll on the bottom of a news broadcast... the crawl! There's kind of that when I'm writing, but of interview questions I would be asked if I wrote that, and how I'm going to explain that. But the thing I love about writing is it makes everything quiet and it gives me this focus that I can't get doing anything else." [11]

- MITSKI

Mitski largely turned back to writing on her old friend, the piano.

"My writing is a little different with guitar as opposed to piano. With piano, I'm much more focused on interesting chord progressions. With guitar, because my skill level is still elementary, I end up just going with the most simple chord progressions because that would often be what I'm able to play. Whereas with piano, I have more experience with it. So I would work in a little bit more weird stuff. I feel like I would have more freedom to explore the musicality of it outside of the vocal melody." [11]

- MITSKI

"When I'm writing on guitar, I think more in chords. Because on a guitar—at least the way I play it—when I'm composing on guitar I tend to think about the chord progressions. But when I'm writing on the

piano I can think more about counterpoint and individual notes and melodies. I think that's the main difference." [85]

- MITSKI

She also approached her vocals differently.

"I did change up how I record vocals. I've always sang right up at the mic so that my mouth touches the mic or touches the foam in front of the mic. But I've learned to step back and project more. I think it just comes from having more confidence in my vocals. I used to not be able to project as much, so I would have to be right up at the mic, but now I can step back and be confident that my voice would still reach the mic in a good way. That also translated to not doubling any vocals. Most of the music we listen to, even though it sounds like one voice singing, it's actually doubled, where there's a second layer of vocals singing the exact same thing to make the vocals sound fuller. But I didn't do that. And I have very little harmonies, which I've always done a lot of on past albums. I left it bare a little more." [84]

- MITSKI

"[It was scary, but] it's kind of similar to my change in outlook about getting my picture taken. I used to be really self-conscious about wanting to look pretty in pictures, but I realised that doesn't actually make for a good photo. It makes for a better photo if I am more focused on making an interesting photo rather than looking pretty. That also translated to my vocals. I realised it's okay if I'm a little pitchy or my voice cracks. The point isn't for me to sound pretty. The point is to express something." [84]

- MITSKI

"I have leaned into an easiness with vocals that aren't doubled. Keeping vocal flaws in there and not having harmonies, just one voice. Not soft and giving. All the sounds are sort of opinionated." [58]

- MITSKI

Another interesting element is that *Be the Cowboy* is made from short songs, as only two of the 14 tracks run over three minutes.

"[A long song] comes from privileged people who have always had an audience, no matter what they did, they always got an award. So a lot of that is jerking off. And I don't want to do that because I think I am not confident in the fact that I will always have an audience. I have a very small window within which people look at me and listen to what I'm saying. So I have to stuff everything I want to say into that. And that's why all my songs are really short. I'm aware of it." [11]

- MITSKI

"I like to say something in as little time as possible. I don't think I have the fundamental confidence necessary to write a four-minute meandering song. Number one, because I'm impatient. But number two, because I've never been someone who is listened to. No one would stop to listen to me. I'm not a white guy noodling on a guitar for 45 minutes. No one would stay for me. I learned from a young age to be concise because there's a very small window for me to grab someone's attention. With novels it's about painting a whole story, but what's beautiful about songs is that you can show one little snapshot, express one little moment. I like the idea of painting one little picture and then moving on, instead of showing the full movie." [58]

- MITSKI

"We're proponents of 'Say what you need to say and don't say anymore.' But I keep getting the criticism of, like, 'Your songs are too short! Why is it under 3 minutes?' and I'm just, like, 'Well, this is what I wanted to say and it's over. Let's not add more stuff to it.'" [118]

- MITSKI

"Someone said somewhere... I don't remember who and I'm probably very much paraphrasing, but the smartest people are the people who can take complex ideas about astrophysics and stuff like that and explain it to a six-year-old. For example, college kids who use really long words in every single sentence and don't make sense actually are the people who don't understand what they're even saying. Really smart people are the people who can explain anything to a small child. I strive towards that kind of writing. Where it's not about how complicated it is. It's not about how elaborate it is. It's about explaining these muddy things in just a couple lyrics." [11]

- MITSKI

"The key to a good ending is to depart. We have to realise that things can end when we just leave conversations. [It] can actually end if we just leave the room. Online debates can actually end if someone just stops talking." [118]

- MITSKI

Patrick rightfully adds:

"No one's ever gotten bored listening to a Buzzcocks song or something. Because you just get it really quickly." [118]

- PATRICK HYLAND

"There's so much that goes into writing a song, it's hard to think about just one thing. This is more abstract, but it's important to think about. I know this sounds very obvious, but you have to think about what you're saying, means. For example, you can describe a scene that happened in your life word for word as it happened, but you need to understand why you're describing it, and why it'll be important to the listener. What is significant to you might not be significant to the listener. What I'm trying to say is, if you're trying to express something through a scene or through a description of how things happen, you need to get to the point of the matter. I know I'm being long-winded for someone who's talking about getting to the point, but when you think about the scene you're describing, you have to think about why it's important to you, and why you want to express it to someone. Otherwise, unfortunately, everything that matters to you may not matter to the listener. That may sound really discouraging, but I'm trying to stress how important it is to be a good communicator. It's not prose. It's not, like, you have pages and pages of space to grab someone's attention. You have to make sure that everything you say matters and has a point. That's a more succinct way of saying what I'm trying to say." [44]

- MITSKI

"It goes back to that awareness that no one needs to listen to me and I have a very short amount of time. Not just where people listen to me, but... not to get too real, but a very short amount of time on Earth. I want to make sure that I communicate to the best of my ability what it's like for me to be alive and feel alive. That is the reason I live. So I guess that's why there's so much care or you hear so much care in my work. Because I am living in order to communicate these songs. Everyone has their own meaning in life and

I've decided that my songs are my meaning in life. They're my legacy, where I want to make sure I communicate it all very clearly." [11]

- MITSKI

ARTWORK

"I was thinking about movies and I was imagining this idea of a repressed woman or just a woman who has a lot of chaos inside of her, maybe a lot of feelings, a lot of desires, but is for some reason unable to express them, or doesn't allow herself to express them. I thought about, 'Okay, what kind of films have sort of expressed that?' I thought first of the film The Piano Teacher by Michael Haneke, which is based on the book The Piano Teacher by Elfriede Jelinek. I recommend both very much, by the way, if you have time. And I was thinking about that main character. I was also thinking about a lot of Hitchcock heroines and how we perceive Hitchcock's heroines is very much through Hitchcock's lens. Very literally, but also metaphorically. I started thinking that Hitchcock portrays these women as icy and cold and mysterious but I thought, well, what are those characters like when Hitchcock is not watching them? That was the inspiration behind those pictures. So I tried to play up the drama." [71]

- MITSKI

The cover art you see for *Be the Cowboy* is not even half the story. When looking at the full printed package and the singles covers, a movie poster theme weaves itself across the media. The deluxe album bundle also included 100% silk handkerchiefs, *"perfect for dabbing tears or waving goodbye to a lover on the train."*

"The photographer Bao [Ngo] very much helped me realise the overall concept. I talked with her a lot about it. There's a lot of

covering a lot of my flesh because I wanted to express that sort of conservatism and [lend] that old school Hollywood feeling to it." [71]

- MITSKI

Bao Ngo snapped the photos for this project and... another coming later. She's also worked with Billboard, Dazed, Epitaph Records, Google, The Guardian, National Geographic, The New York Times, NPR, and Rolling Stone.

The album design was taken care of by Mary Banas, who has since become such an integral fixture to Mitski's art that there's a separate section dedicated to her later.

"I designed the album art including vinyl record packaging, movie-size poster, and a pair of 100% silk handkerchiefs, as well as a CD package and art for 3 digital singles for Mitski/Dead Oceans. [The back cover features] the BTC track list and can also be read as a cute public inside joke—fans often share that the music of Mitski makes them cry." [119]

- MARY BANAS

The fonts used were Steelfish by Typodermic and Calafia by Neil Secretario.

"Calafia outlined [also] functions as a 'veil' on the cover, that the subject is looking through. I was thinking about the gaze, the viewer, the audience, and stardom itself." [87]

- MARY BANAS

Such care did not go unnoticed and it was nominated for the Best Recording Package in the 2018 Grammy Awards. It lost to St Vincent's *Masseduction*.

THEMES

"This album is about not taking responsibility for your mistakes. Just fucking up and being like, 'Whatever.' That's what a white guy would do. In cowboy movies they're destroying a town but they're the hero. I'm entitled to these things." [17]

- MITSKI

The cowboy aesthetic is obvious, but as with all things Mitski, it runs deeper. A lot of her comments wrap the record around growing older into womanhood and how that ties into a different type of femininity than what's usually peddled to the masses.

"I think it's a very feminine album. There can be something incredibly violent about being a woman and having desires as a woman. Not so nice, not so soft. And I think that's an interesting experience to draw on. When I say 'feminine album' those words make it sound soft, but I mean feminine in the real way." [58]

- MITSKI

"When I say feminine album, immediately the perception is that it must be soft and lovely, but I mean feminine in the violent sense. Desiring, but not being able to define your desire, wanting power but being powerless and blaming it on yourself, or just hurting yourself as a way to let out the aggression in you. It's a lot of pent-up anger or desire without a socially acceptable outlet." [88]

- MITSKI

"I was conscious of the fact that my previous album was represented as full of adolescent feelings. So for this record I was conscious of

representing ageing, or a love that's more complicated than just, 'I'm so infatuated with you because you're hot.'" [58]

- MITSKI

"I never set out to make a song my diary. It's hard to continue to make music people can relate to. Your experiences are what people relate to." [17]

- MITSKI

"Lean into whatever you're experiencing. I know that a lot of my musician friends have trouble as they progress in their careers to write new music because it becomes harder for people who don't live our lifestyles to understand what we're going through. And that's why there are so many rock and roll songs about the road. Like, 'I'm on the road, I'm driving down the highway,' just because that's all we do all the time. And there are only so many ways you can turn that into a metaphor. But I think I read Courtney Barnett saying in an interview, like, she was worried about how she might not be able to write music that people can relate to anymore because her life is just so isolated and far removed from how other people live. So I was just, like, you know what? I'm going to lean into this weird world that I live in and these feelings of isolation and just constant travel and being on a stage." [112]

- MITSKI

"I think this is my saddest album. I think there is, in my previous albums, a very useful romanticisation or glorification of a sadness. And there's glory in it and something incredibly brave and beautiful about my sadness. Or that's how I portray my sadness in my previous albums, wherein Be the Cowboy, there's a realisation that no one gives a shit that you're sad, and you're still sad. Your sadness is no longer profound, and you're still sad. It's that kind of growing up and realising that it's not cool anymore to be sad, but you're still sad." [42]

- MITSKI

Besides keeping it real, Mitski also kept it unreal by testing out more character-based themes.

"For this new record, I experimented in narrative and fiction." [120]

- MITSKI

"I've got a lot of, 'It must pour out of her' and, 'This is her diary'. I've read a lot of commentary and criticism where people go out of their way to make me out as this fevered priestess. And I think my going for the narrative perspective was fueled by that. Because I went to music school!" [58]

- MITSKI

"I don't really think of it as fiction because all the music comes from a very true place for me [...] Sometimes utilising a character or using a narrative that didn't exactly happen to me expresses the feeling I had better in a more saturated way than explaining word-for-word what exactly happened. Sometimes what actually happens in your life is mundane. But the feeling you get is not mundane. So I am trying to express the feeling rather than a story. I don't really think of it as personas or fiction." [112]

- MITSKI

"On one hand, most of the narratives in the songs I write are narratives that didn't happen in my real life. Sometimes fiction or made up stories is actually the best path towards speaking some sort of personal truth. So I am all of these characters. In my mind, all of these songs are true in essence. But I'm just putting it through a character that doesn't exist or a narrative that didn't happen because that happens to be the best way to express how I really feel." [121]

- MITSKI

"I never want to say my songs are fictional, because they all come from my feelings and things I've seen. It's just a matter of putting together different parts to make them tell a story and evoke a feeling. The human romantic relationship is the best metaphor, the best narrative vehicle. This album is about a feeling of ending, a feeling of resignation, and often using the narrative of the ending relationship is the easiest way to convey that emotion." [93]

- MITSKI

"I think Björk said in an interview that all of her albums are just exaggerations of a specific part of herself. I think it's like that for me. It's not like [the album's protagonist] is a fictional character, but I noticed a personality in me that was very obsessed with control and feeling like I have power—because I am powerless and don't have a lot of control. So I kind of investigated that person in me. What is the exaggerated form? Well, it's a woman who's incredibly controlled, severe, and austere. But maybe there's some kind of deep desire or emotion that's whirling around in her and trying to get out. Maybe she's losing control." [45]

- MITSKI

Be the Cowboy is not a concept album and remains as autobiographical as any Mitski offering. However, there is a discernible character that grew from her personality.

"I think the theme that I unfortunately saw—unfortunately for me—was the theme of loneliness or the idea of being alone. And the idea of being alone, not because the world is forcing you to be alone but because you are the person causing your aloneness. I mean, I say the word 'lonely' so much on this album. It's so literal. And then I just started thinking, 'Who is this person who keeps writing about loneliness? Who is the exaggerated form of this person?' And I came up with the idea of the Hitchcock blonde heroine who is mysterious and unravels throughout the film. Or the main character of the film The Piano Teacher. I just started thinking about these female solitary figures who might be repressed or might be creating a wall around herself. It's a very muddled, unclear process, but I think that's how it all came together." [42]

- MITSKI

"The image of someone alone on a stage, singing solo with a single spotlight trained on them in an otherwise dark room. For most of the tracks, we didn't layer the vocals with doubles or harmonies, to achieve that campy 'person singing alone on stage' atmosphere. We also made the music swell louder than the main vocals and left in vocal errors like when my voice breaks in 'Nobody,' right when the band goes quiet, all for a similar effect." [122]

- MITSKI

"There's just something campy about it. And in my real life I'm pouring my heart out performing, putting my all into it. But there's also a very kind of dry cynical side of me, watching myself do it and being like 'that's embarrassing.' I think in a lot of musical theatre there's a lot of that, where it's just like one spotlight on one singer theatrically performing, but there's also something very kind of funny about that." [85]

- MITSKI

"I mean, it's not even just the act of singing. It's that as a metaphor for something. Its campness and theatricality; being both fully into it and also watching yourself do it." [85]

- MITSKI

"This protagonist is a person who's in me. It's just I'm not this person all the time. It's this woman who feels powerless and overcompensates by exercising extreme control on herself and on her environment, and just trying to be powerful within her own the limits of her her body and who she is, but kind of just unraveling a little bit because the amount of control she's exercising on to herself maybe isn't healthy or isn't natural. There's something more warm and human inside that she's pushing down in order to appear strong to the world." [84]

- MITSKI

"[There's] some unifying theme in order for people to gravitate towards it and immediately be able to digest it [...] I used to not think about it. And then people started to listen to my music, and people would come to my shows and talk to me about me. And that's when I started to realise, 'Oh, this is an expression of myself.' It's weird to say that out loud, because I never thought of it that way. I always thought I was making songs because I needed to for myself. It was just something I did. Maybe I was just being naïve, but I never thought of it as introducing myself or making people see me." [42]

- MITSKI

In this narrative, the character begins to feel the pressure and come apart, which offers a deep glimpse into how Mitski was dealing with life during this era.

"[It's about] a very controlled icy repressed woman who is starting to unravel. Because women have so little power and showing emotion is seen as weakness, this 'character' clings to any amount of control she can get. Still, there is something very primordial in her that is trying to find a way to get out." [96]

- MITSKI

"I do a lot of repetition of words. Single words over and over in the album. I did that because I wanted to express a sort of mania. A sort of, like, fixation, maybe. The mental state of someone who would just repeat a word over and over and over." [28]

- MITSKI

"There's something subtly unhinged about it. There's something always a little bit off in the music." [88]

- MITSKI

"I think the character of the album is less a cowboy and more someone desperately trying to be a cowboy character and not being able to. I'm imagining, in an incredibly pitiful comedic way, someone who is obviously not okay, just red eyes, tears streaming down her face, *but being like, 'I am a fucking cowboy, so help me God.' Just the ridiculousness of this woman who doesn't look like a cowboy dressed up like one and being like, 'I'm a goddam cowboy.' It's funny to me. It's funny in a really pitiful way, that idea."* [42]

- MITSKI

"This whole album just stinks of denial, because the music itself, a lot of it is poppy and peppy. A lot of it is very clean sounding. But if you listen to the lyrics it's horrible. Just the idea of someone having this incredible sadness but putting it in a tight little box, putting a ribbon on it, and carrying it around like it's a beautiful gift. Sometimes you might pass this person and catch a whiff of the stench of the stuff inside the little box. But it's very neatly prepared, like, 'I'm completely okay. I am a cowboy. I'm confident. I'm riding into the sunset as we speak.'" [42]

- MITSKI

CHARTS

"On previous albums, I never thought anyone would think something or have an opinion on my music. It was just all about how I felt." [58]

- MITSKI

Did *Be the Cowboy* sell? Yes. Better than anything she'd done before. It was Mitski's first album to chart on the Billboard 200. Canada, Ireland, and the UK all welcomed her into their charts too. The album climbed up into the top 10 on the UK Independent Albums chart (9), the US Top Rock Albums chart (7), the US Top Alternative Albums chart (6), the Australia ARIA Hitseekers chart (4), and the US Independent Albums (3). It was certified gold in both the UK and USA with 100,000 and 500,000 sold respectively.

CRITICAL

If you thought *Puberty 2* smashed those critical chops, you'd better buckle up. *Be the Cowboy* received 100% full marks from The Guardian (*"arrangements that are rich without being precious"*), Tiny Mix Tapes (*"She's walking the divide between love and heartache, between dejection and fury. But Miyawaki has the talent to straddle that line with poise and aplomb"*), NOW Magazine (*"pop songs [that are] as loud and vibrant as they [are] quite devastating"*), and Consequence of Sound (*"...that two minutes is more than enough time to melt down emotion into a pure concentrate and nearly drown yourself in it."*). With 8.8/10, Pitchfork called it *"her greatest to date"* and *"from the music to her emotions, Mitski has the power to make the complex seem dazzlingly clear,"* earning her another Best New Music honour. The number of publications that scored her 80%+ would be too many to mention, but include NME, Q Magazine, Boston Globe, Mojo, and even Rolling Stone, finally. You'd struggle to find a reputable source rating it anything below 70%, and as a result, its Metacritic aggregate score sits at 87%, matching *Puberty 2* on the dot.

The 2018 End of Year lists were even more impressive, Mitski featured on all of them but made the top 10 for Stereogum (10), Slant Magazine (7), The Guardian (5), Entertainment Weekly (4), Time (3), NPR (2), and The New York Times (2). Not good enough? Okay, how about where *Be the Cowboy* was called the Absolute Best Album of 2018 by Vulture, Consequence of Sound, Flood Magazine, The Line of Best Fit, and Pitchfork. When the end of the 2010s came, many publications praised the album as one of the Greatest of the Decade including The Independent (34), Rolling Stone (33), and Consequence of Sound (10).

SINGLES

• Geyser

"This is one of my vaguest songs. Usually, my songs have a narrative of some sort. But this song is all feeling." [68]

- MITSKI

"I wrote it about music. As a musician, you have to keep sacrificing other things in your life. Sacrificing relationships, sacrificing other opportunities, maybe even your physical or mental health, in order to do it. Because it's not an easy thing to do. And it's not a job that people need you to do, like being a doctor or plumber. You really have to give up a lot of things to do it. And so I wrote it over a long period of time thinking about all the things I give up for it. But I gladly give it up because I love it so much and I can't imagine doing anything else." [123]

- MITSKI

"Geyser" was *Cowboy's* frontrunner, kicking down the doors on May 14th, 2018. Much like the entire album experience, the single's artwork was essential to the project. Shot by Bao Ng and designed by Mary Banas, the movie theme is clear with the *"Mitski as 'Mitski' in..."* tagline. The image shows Mitski against a wall looking like a Hollywood star.

"My instinct is always to follow a very classic pop song form, like verse, pre-chorus, chorus, etc. But I fought that instinct and tried to write songs that didn't always follow that song structure. Like with Geyser, it's just A section, B section, C section, D section." [28]

- MITSKI

Interestingly, Mitski started writing "Geyser" a long time ago. Long before *Be the Cowboy*. Long before most of her albums.

"It was the first song I started to write. I started to write it in college. It's the song I've taken the longest to write. It had become my 'White Whale'—Moby Dick reference—where I couldn't get it right. Every time I thought I'd finished it it just didn't feel right, so I kept changing it. It's gone through many iterations; probably people who went to school with me, who've been in seminars with me, are, like, 'Wait, I

heard that somewhere...' And then I finally got to a point where I was, like, 'You know what? I need to end this, I'm never gonna be happy with it so let me finish it.' So I did." [85]

- MITSKI

If you need proof, search YouTube for *"Mitski: The Red Barn @ Hampshire College - 11/24/2014 (COMPLETE PERFORMANCE)"* where she plays the song live back in 2014.

Another common and reasonable "Geyser" question is: what's up with the glitchy sound in the beginning?

"That was Patrick's idea. At first, it was, like, 'Uuuurgh, people won't like it,' but then I was, like, 'Fuck it, it's cool, it's fun.' Evan from the label, when he first heard it, he was, like, 'Is this glitch intentional?' and Patrick responded via email saying, 'You are experiencing the art.'" [85]

- MITSKI

The Fader called "Geyser" the 12th best song of the year.

On "Geyser" release day, a video appeared with it, directed by our "Best American Girl" director, Zia Anger. Here, Mitski is on a beach where she runs, rolls, and digs.

"It was New York. It looks so alien because the tide is so... uh, gosh I don't know anything about tides. But I think it's high? Or low? Very... an extreme. You don't really see it on the screen, but it was pouring rain. It was cold. There were so many physical extremes that actually really fueled my performance. And Zia is so good at capturing sentiments with physical and absurd symbols on the screen. She has such a knack for it. That whole thing was completely her idea." [68]

- MITSKI

The Japan edition of the album has a demo of "Geyser" as a bonus track.

• Nobody

"I'm actually quite proud of 'Nobody' in the fact that I got away with making a chorus that was just one word over and over." [28]

- MITSKI

Second time luckier and *Cowboy*'s next single hit the big time. Released on June 26th, 2018, the artwork adds to the Hollywood vibes with a *"Mitski stars in... NOBODY"* title. Mitski sits in a car like a frame from a film.

"I just wanted to write a four-on-the-floor dance track, because I like dancing. And there's something about being so hopelessly lonely that you're like 'all I can really do is dance. There's nothing else I can do. I can't talk this away, I can't fix these problems, I'm just going to go out... and dance.'" [85]

- MITSKI

"The lyrics are quite desolate and desperate but it's on a disco beat. I kind of wanted to express that feeling of being perhaps empty inside, but here, let's dance." [112]

- MITSKI

Mitski was kind enough to break "Nobody" down for fans, so we have a lot of information about it. The song was written on a piano bought from Toys "R" Us in Kuala Lumpur, capital of Malaysia. Mitski was there over one Christmas and decided not to go home because flights were too expensive. This proved to be a bad idea. It devastated her with loneliness. But, then again, it also was ultimately a good idea, because now she had this hit song to help purchase future flights.

"I was in Kuala Lumpur, in KLCC, which is the city centre. And I subletted a little studio apartment. So I literally just opened the windows to hear other people being alive. [124]

- MITSKI

"I always think of myself as an independent woman who doesn't need anybody. I was completely, unexpectedly crushed by the fact that I not only didn't know anyone in the country, but it was the holidays, and everyone's with their family, and I wasn't." [33]

- MITSKI

"I am too proud to be hysterical to other people, but the chorus was literally me in a semi-fugue state on my hands and knees on the floor just crying and repeating the word 'nobody'. And then I was, like, 'Let me use this pain, exploit it for money!'" [124]

- MITSKI

"I think there's something incredibly manic about it, or maybe I'm thinking more maniacal. I'm not sure, but obsessive repetition like that sort of illustrates that mindset. I don't know about other people, but I get obsessed a lot or stuck on words a lot. I think it has something to do with my brain or my psyche, so I wanted to express that feeling of like, 'Oh, is the protagonist a little off?'" [84]

- MITSKI

Another noteworthy section goes, *"Venus, planet of love, was destroyed by global warming. Did its people want too much, too?"*

"So I read an article that said that Venus at some point in its history experienced global warming, and now it's a planet that is post-global

warming. So I just imagine that if there actually was a civilisation on Venus that caused its global warming, and I thought, 'Did those people want too much too, and is that what caused their global warming?' It's all hypothetical, but the fact that it experienced global warming is real." [85]

- MITSKI

"I can't give you the exact source, but I read somewhere right about the time I was writing this song that Venus experienced global warming. So I thought, 'Oh, how interesting!' I imagined maybe there was a civilization on Venus, which we call the planet of love, but they wanted so many things the way we desire so much. They wanted so much that's out of their means and drove their planet to global warming. Like, wouldn't that be funny if that's what happened?" [112]

- MITSKI

How about the line, *"And I don't want your pity, I just want somebody near me"*?

"I don't want your fucking pity. Like, can you just sit next to me? Don't even talk. Just please don't talk. Just be next to me and I wanna feel another human being being around me." [124]

- MITSKI

Another super lyric is, *"I'm just asking for a kiss. Give me one good movie kiss"*.

"I think the movie kiss I was referring to, in my mind, the kind of kiss that wouldn't be from one particular movie. It's the kind of cinematic kiss in your mouth that your mind conjures that doesn't even exist anywhere, that can never be realised." [112]

- MITSKI

"Sometimes you don't even want words. Like... You just wanna kiss. You know?" [124]

- MITSKI

I know. And then there's, *"I've been big and small and big and small and big and small again. And still nobody wants me"*.

"I have gained weight and I've lost weight. I've been big and I've been small. I've tried these clothes. I've had this haircut. I've done everything I could to my body. And still, nobody wants me. Why?" [124]

- MITSKI

I don't think that's exactly the truth.

Finally, there is the chorus that goes, *"Nobody, nobody, nobody, nobody, nobody, ooh, nobody, nobody, nobody"*.

"When you sing along to it at my show, don't worry about the pitch. Just the words are fine. Because it goes all over the place." [124]

- MITSKI

And then... there was *that* video. Shot in Kansas city, it is the first but not last Mitski video directed by Christopher Good. It came out on the same day as the single release (June 26th, 2018).

"We shot this video over five days in both sides of Kansas City. I've never been able to take this much time to shoot a video, so it was wonderful to have the space to get the details right, as well as actually hang out and have fun with everyone involved. This video made me fall unexpectedly in love with Kansas City." [124]

- MITSKI

The clip did not hold back, delivering the song with a very elaborate, surreal, and colourful piece that is difficult to decipher and even more difficult to describe. There's Mitski singing into a hairbrush and arms coming out of walls and people with missing faces and diaries within diaries... it's best you just watch it yourself.

"That was Christopher Good's idea. He sent me a treatment and I was, like, 'This is great.' One of our inspirations was Michel Gondry's stuff with Björk, like the 'Bachelorette' video." [85]

- MITSKI

"Putting yellow stage makeup on the wall-arms. Later we discovered the makeup really does not want to wash off, and I wondered what kind of industrial-grade makeup remover is used by actors playing Elphaba in Wicked." [125]

- MITSKI

"It was actually hard to get this one little shot where the magnifying glass goes directly in front of my eye, because, in one swift motion, I had to raise the magnifying glass at exactly the right angle where the camera catches my blurry eye right behind it. We did a lot of the shots in this video over and over, it had to be precise. And I loved every minute of it." [125]

- MITSKI

The critical crowd lost their nuts over this song. Pitchfork? Dubbed it a Best New Track. Consequence of Sound? Said it was Mitski's best song ever. TikTok? Insanely viral, thanks to a 2021 trend where people ran away from the camera during the chorus.

"I'm 31 years old now and I guess I'm just a clueless millennial because sometimes... I mean, I really really appreciate your use of my music,

but I don't understand why there was a trend of people running away from the camera while my song 'Nobody' is playing? I don't understand what everyone's running away from? I don't think the song is that scary." [25]

- MITSKI

That little TikTok boost pushed the song back into the Billboard's Top 200 in 2021, three years after its release.

"My friends keep sending me ways that my song 'Nobody' has been used in TikTok. TikTok has been very good to me. I don't know what I did to deserve it, but people have continued to use my songs on TikTok. Thank you, TikTok. Thank you, teenagers." [25]

- MITSKI

In 2022, reports showed that "Nobody" had been streamed nearly 200 million times on Spotify with 2.5 million user-generated TikTok videos.

"Even though it's been a long time, I still haven't wrapped my head around it. My brain doesn't know how to process how somebody else has understood and heard something I made." [19]

- MITSKI

• Two Slow Dancers

"So much of pop music is about infatuation and attraction. That is most definitely one side of love but I would love to explore more sides of it in music. Like, with 'Two Slow Dancers,' I wrote about two people who once had some kind of history but they're much older now. They have lives, but for one dance, they're coming back together to experience that and realising they're both the same

people they were when they were teenagers. I would like to hear more love songs about all the complexities of it." [28]

- MITSKI

I'm so tired of the youthful song. The song about 'I'm on the dance floor, and I meet you, and I have sex with you, and we then don't talk about the rest.' There's so much more to sing about!" [33]

- MITSKI

"Two Slow Dancers", the album's final single, came out on August 9th 2018. Again the movie theme took over the cover with *"Mitski presents..."* at the top.

It's not about a romantic relationship, it's about two real lives lived. And there's something very visceral and real about that. These two people have lived their whole lives, and they're older and they have problems, and their lives are complicated and they're just experiencing this one dance together where they get to pretend that they're young again. But it's in this context of life mess." [85]

- MITSKI

They used have something together that is no longer there and they're trying to relive it in a dance, knowing that they'll have to go home and go back to their lives." [96]

- MITSKI

No official music video blessed us this time, but an official lyric video came out featuring a slow disco spinning ball as the words come up, karaoke style. I have to include a line stolen from the Mitski Fandom Wiki, which reads, *"Interestingly, instead of singing along to the karaoke, the viewer tends to cry quietly, alone."* Classic Mitski fans.

• Washing Machine Heart

"I remember trying to think of my heart pounding, and then thinking of when you put shoes in a washing machine. Which I don't know if you're supposed to do, but I've done it before. I think we all have, so we shouldn't have shame about it. And it goes DA DUM DA DUM DA DUMM. That's what I wanted to express lyrically." [18]

- MITSKI

Full disclosure: "Washing Machine Heart" is not a single! But it's so insanely popular that it charted and got a music video, so we might as well treat it as one.

"I just thought of the heart as a washing machine that this other careless person just tosses their dirty shoes into. I don't know if you've ever tried to clean your shoes by throwing them in the washing machine but they go DOOM DOOM DOOM. Something about that, just like someone else making your heart pound really loud but also someone else using your heart to clean themselves." [28]

- MITSKI

That is some strong stuff. But what about the nonsensical *"Do, mi, ti, why not me?"* line?

"Fun fact: at first, I was, like... I mean, it didn't end up being this, but I was being very silly [...] I wanted to do a solfège-based lyric, and I was really really trying to figure out a way to say 'miso', because I wanted to talk about miso soup. But it just didn't... I had to give it up [...] It wasn't a novelty for me. It was very serious for me." [118]

- MITSKI

What a treat, we got a lot of Patrick quotes about the composition on this one.

"I think I was trying to go for, like, a Prince type thing." [118]

- PATRICK HYLAND

"One of my favourite things about this song is that there isn't that much going on. There's one keyboard doing the chords, one doing the lead." [118]

- PATRICK HYLAND

"We found surfaces in the studio to bang, essentially." [118]

- MITSKI

"Yeah, it was like the floor. And some road cases and boxes and stuff." [118]

- PATRICK HYLAND

"We were just like the two of us with one mic." [118]

- MITSKI

"I was quite proud of the melody because it was so different." [118]

- MITSKI

Despite not being a single, the charts yanked it up, hitting 93 in Ireland and 26 on the UK Indie charts. The song was certified Gold in Norway, Sweden, and UK, while it reached Platinum status in the USA.

So what does an artist do when they have such a winning song on their hands? Film a video, obviously! Released on November 1st, 2018, it was a black and white affair where a sophisticated-looking Mitski sings the song while suggestive imagery brings a subtly erotic yet very classy atmosphere. As for the credits, let Mitski tell us about it:

"We got to make a video for my song 'Washing Machine Heart' thanks to TIDAL! Directed by Zia Anger who also did the videos for my songs 'Your Best American Girl' and 'Geyser.' Movement by Monica Mirabile who also choreographed my 'Be the Cowboy' tour. Cinematography by Mia Cioffi Henry who also filmed 'Geyser.' The list goes on, all in the family." [126]

- MITSKI

The song is so loved that the TV show *You* featured it in season 5, episode 4, "My Fair Maddie". But, hey, do you wanna hear something extra crazy? "Washing Machine Heart" nearly wasn't on the album at all!

"The thing that people might not know is that most of your most popular songs are songs that you wanted to cut from their respective albums. This was like towards the end of Be the Cowboy, and as we were finishing the album, you were, like, 'Yeah I don't really know about this one, I kind of want to cut it.' And I was, like, 'No I think we should keep it on.'" [118]

- PATRICK HYLAND

"Why I wanted to cut it was because I was, like, 'This is a silly song. This is not part of my serious album.'" [118]

- MITSKI

OTHER NOTEWORTHY SONGS

The best thing about having so much public interest in *Be the Cowboy* is that people have drawn quotes from just about every song.

• Why Didn't You Stop Me?

"I think it's actually one of the more cowboy songs, just because there's a certain amount of selfishness in saying 'I know I did this, but why didn't you stop me?' And there's a sort of very cowboy power thing going on, where you kind of ride into town, wreak havoc and be like 'this is your fault.' That's where I was coming from with that, like, 'I know I fucked up, I know I was the one who left, but why didn't you stop me?' It's a power move." [85]

- MITSKI

The Japanese release of the album features an alternate version of this song called "ほうじ茶バージョン" aka "Hoji Tea Version". Mitski's vocals are a totally different recording.

• Old Friend

"If you'll meet me at Blue Diner, I'll take coffee and talk about nothing." When imagining the "Blue Diner" in "Old Friend" Mitski paints a picture of it like this:

"It's not pretty. It's very run-down, but been there for a long time. It's just like the local spot that's not on Yelp, but everyone knows it. It may be a little more discreet so the people in the spot can meet there without running into any of their other friends. It's like their spot that no one else knows about. The perfect place to talk about secret desires, which is everything that's unsaid in this song." [85]

- MITSKI

"I don't really attach as much fetish to [the all-night diner] as a lot of Americans do, or as much as David Lynch does. But because I've always lived a transient life, there is something really charming

about one specific place where everyone you know goes, and where people know you." [45]

- MITSKI

Another visceral image comes with the line *"Every time I drive through the city where you're from, I squeeze a little."*

"In my mind visually it's like squeezing the steering wheel a little, just thinking about it. Just trying to hold it in; feeling emotional but just being like 'nope.' Gritting your teeth." [85]

- MITSKI

This song can also be found on the *Rough Trade Shops: End of the Road 2019* compilation.

• A Pearl

"I think what's more surprising to me is when you're okay, but you're not used to being okay. And when you've been unhappy for so long that being unhappy is your norm and what you're uncomfortable with, so when you're not unhappy, when you're finally fine, you don't know what to do with yourself. You repeat self-destructive behaviours because it's what you know, it's what you feel you deserve and what you're comfortable with. If it's just your life then you can be as self-destructive as you want. But what makes it complicated is if you have someone else in your life who cares about you. If you're in a relationship, and you're supposed to be fine and you have someone asking about you and caring about you, but you just can't stop being unhappy, because being unhappy is what you want. That feeling of someone else being involved in your wellbeing, and not being able to

be well for them. [It becomes a pearl] because it's this little thing that's very pretty to you, and you roll it around in your hand. It's almost like Smeagol from Lord Of The Rings, where it's just a pretty little thing in your hand that you hold on to. You don't have to hold on to it, but in your mind you feel you have to, and at night instead of going to sleep you wake up and look at it. And that's a metaphor for something unhealthy, something that's no longer serving you, but you can't stop rolling it around and looking at it." [85]

- MITSKI

"I want you to get caught up in it. But for me, it was actually about when you have some kind of toxic relationship to yourself, or to another person, for so long that it becomes your identity. Even when you don't need it anymore and you've stepped away from it, you still hold on to it because it's scary to let it go—because if you actually let it go, it feels like erasing yourself. That song is about likening that sort of toxicity to a pearl. Even though you're in this great relationship with somebody who loves you and wants to take care of you, you still don't talk to them about what's toxic in you. You just roll around this pearl in your hand every night and just look at it, like it's a pretty thing." [45]

- MITSKI

Lucky, lucky, there's a music video for "A Pearl" too! Premiered on January 31st, 2019, it was directed/animated by Saad Moosajee (who has worked with Woodkid and Apple) and co-directed/cel-animated by Danae Gosset (who has worked Hermes and Warner Music) while the collective Art Camp (who've worked with Coldplay and Nike Jordan) were involved. Spotify commissioned it, and it's a gorgeous piece of work.

"The guiding concept of this video was an image that Santiago and I both shared when we listened to the song: a small character—Mitski, but not Mitski—flying through an untethered universe on an abstract emotional journey. The lyrics are very visual, and it was tempting to try to illustrate the imagery, but we chose to focus on the feelings contained in the song instead of the words. Not that we didn't make dozens of animations of floating pearls [...] We all knew of her. We listened to all the albums, but we obviously listened to Be the Cowboy the most. One interesting thing I found is that none of us got tired of the music, somehow. No matter how much we listened to it, it was always good." [127]

- JOS DIAZ CONTRERAS

Animated using 1480 frames, printed, painted, then rescanned to create the dreamy animation, we see a Mitski-like figure running through houses and falling through sky in flawless time to the music.

"We wanted the fall to be very long and emotional, a physical drop to represent the rupture of one's heart of one's soul." [127]

- JOS DIAZ CONTRERAS

"I wrote so many songs about being in love and being hurt by love. You think your life is horrible when you're heartbroken, but when you no longer have love or heartbreak in your life, you think, wasn't it nice when things still hurt? There's a nostalgia for blind love, a wonderful heady kind of love." [95]

- MITSKI

Here's a different thing: keen-eared Mitski fans have noted that around the 1:40 mark of "A Pearl", Mitski hums a little melody which is undeniably similar (if not identical) to one found on *LUSH*'s song "Pearl Diver." Mitski has never acknowledged the rumour but considering the title connection and Mitski's smarts, I find it hard to believe this is coincidental even if the debate goes on.

"I'm always winking." [11]
- MITSKI

• Lonesome Love

This title was probably an allusion to *Lonesome Dove*, either the 1989 American epic Western television miniseries (directed by Simon Wincer), or the 1985 novel that the series was based on (written by Larry McMurtry). But, to be honest, nobody cares about that. They were more interested in the lyric *"because nobody butters me up like you, and nobody fucks me like me".*

"Thank God I was able to put it into words." [45]
- MITSKI

Because of this, "Lonesome Love" is the second of only two Mitski songs to be marked *Explicit* on streaming services.

• Remember My Name

"It's about wanting something that's just... you will never get that; you will die and you will be forgotten. In the chorus, it's 'I want something bigger than the sky,' and there's nothing bigger than the sky. But you still want it." [85]
- MITSKI

According to the credits, the "Ripping Sax Solo" was by, of course, Patrick Hyland. This song was also heard on the TV show *13 Reasons Why*, season 3, episode 6, "You Can Tell the Heart of a Man by How He Grieves".

• Me and My Husband

Wait, is Mitski married? She has a lot of explaining to do!

"I mean, I'm not married, so... I think a lot of marriages are like that because that's what it is; it's no longer about being in love. It's really hard to stay in love and keep the spark. When you get married and you're with someone for years and years, it no longer becomes about infatuation or having your heart aflutter. But the song is just about, 'You know what? This may not be love anymore, and I may be unhappy, and I'm going to die one day and this is just going to be my life.' But then turning around and saying, 'This is the decision I made, and you're the person I chose, so I'm just going to stick with you. We have our problems, but this is our life and we're going to live it.' And that's what it's about. I think a big part of me is retaliating against youth culture, because I'm getting older, but I'm in the entertainment business, where I'm expected to be young forever and sing about going to the club and being infatuated with someone and having your first love. But I'm 27, like... I can't keep doing that and still being truthful. Because the reality is I'm an adult now, and I'm getting older. And as you get older you see a lot of sides of love, and you experience relationships that aren't just your first love. I think so much of music is so youth-oriented, when there are so many more stories to tell. A pop song doesn't just have to be about that young love, because there's so many more experiences that are worth singing about." [85]

- MITSKI

"I try to keep a sense of humour about all this stuff. I'm not married, I don't have a husband, but I was just thinking about being

a woman with a man in a long term relationship. I used a stereotype of the suburban, old-fashioned housewife to kind of accentuate my point. But I think that dynamic still exists today even in like urban people or people who consider themselves no longer old-fashioned. There's something about being the person in the relationship who is dependent on the other person—whether it's financially or it's just in terms of identity—and maybe not being happy, but saying, 'This is the life I chose and this is the person I chose and this is my identity, so I'm going to hold onto it and I'm going to do this until I die. Maybe in the next lifetime I will be somebody else. But in this lifetime I'm sticking with my husband. I am maintaining my position in this relationship. And it doesn't matter if I'm happy.'"[85]

- MITSKI

"I don't think of any of my songs as fiction because they're all things I've felt and things I wanted to express. It's just that sometimes using a character or using a narrative that didn't actually happen in my own life better expresses what I really felt in that moment. Sometimes the things that trigger your emotions in your own life are actually incredibly mundane and wouldn't make for a great story. So, for example, the song 'Me and My Husband.' I don't have a husband, but I've experienced what the character has experienced in terms of emotion, so I thought, well, what is the most exaggerated way I can express this emotion? And I used a stereotype of a housewife in the suburbs. Someone who's just been married for a really long time and being dependent on your spouse and just kind of deciding that that was your life."[28]

- MITSKI

• Come into the Water

"The water is a metaphor. It's like, 'Are you gonna leave me alone in this? Or are you going to come in and join in and be in it with me?' Because a lot of the lyrics are about 'I'm not gonna move until you show me how to.' It's like literally taking the plunge; 'Are you going to take the plunge with me?'" [85]

- MITSKI

• Pink in the Night

"It's very Old Hollywood: 'Let's make this kiss mean so much because we can't show any more.' I always feel like a kiss is so much more intimate than any other act. Maybe because it's one of the first acts you do with somebody, so it's the most special." [1]

- MITSKI

• A Horse Named Cold Air

"This song encapsulates the album a lot. A horse that used to be young, used to be vibrant, but now is sort of still and cold and old." [86*]

- MITSKI

"I think, actually, the most cowboy song might be 'A Horse Named Cold Air', not just because it's about a horse, but also because it's about someone who has ran like a storm but sort of has grown old and kind of looks back on that." [85]

- MITSKI

"There's something about animals that are forced to compete by humans... something about that really fascinates me. I'm really fascinated by race horses and dog fights or dog races or just kind of like situations where animals are made to compete. There's something incredibly horrible about it, and human about it. So I always come back to those themes." [28]

- MITSKI

"Racehorses always have interesting names. I saw somewhere that there was a horse named Cold Air, which I thought was beautiful. But then I went back on Google and I couldn't find it, so maybe I actually dreamed it? But I just imagined a racehorse that was named Cold Air and people used to say, 'That horse ran like a storm but now it's old and tired and its heart is like a lake with no fish, an unmoving still lake.' Something about that image was very beautiful to me." [28]

- MITSKI

• Blue Light

Like "A Pearl" there is another (possibly coincidental) relation between *LUSH* and *Be the Cowboy* found through this song. On Mitski's debut, the song "Eric" mentions a blue light. Coincidence? Maybe, actually.

Also, listen closely at 1:30 for the mouse click.

COWBOY CONCLUSION

Before we round off, I have to mention the mini-EP called *Nobody* by Gumi and Miku who cover three Mitski songs from *Be the Cowboy* ("Washing Machine Heart", "Me and My Husband", and "Nobody") in super J-bitpop vocaloid style. It's cute and fun and weird.

Alright! So after the crazy whirlwind of writing on tour, feeling depleted yet pushing out this album anyway, did Mitski learn anything?

"I did. I learned that I need to put limitations on myself during the creative process or else my anxiety takes hold and I give my brain room to doubt. For Puberty 2 I only had a two-week span to do it, so when I was recording I was very much making decisions based on instinct and wasn't looking back every time I made a decision. It was just about trying to get it done. I think that actually helped my creative process. For this album, the process was really stretched out. It was whenever I had time between tours over the course of two years. That gave me a lot more time to doubt myself, to second guess, to go back and try to fix something and then forget what I was even trying to say in the beginning. So yeah, I've figured out that I need to be my own mom. I need to create a mom for myself or an authoritarian figure in my head or some kind of limitation to make sure that I actually follow the creativity and I don't get in my head too much about it. I actually need limitations, which is counterintuitive because you'd think that creativity is about being unlimited. I also realised I am smarter than I thought. I think because my previous records were so much about following instinct there was a part of me that doubted that I had the brains to create music rationally. For this album, I made a lot of very thoughtful, rational decisions because I had a lot more time. I realised, 'Oh, my music degree did do something.'" [84]

- MITSKI

Nevertheless, the post-*Cowboy* release part of this story will go down in Mitski's history as surely the most mentally testing of her career, as we shall dive into shortly.

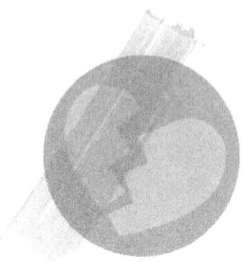

5.2.
INTRODUCING MARY BANAS

"The design [must] function as another gesture of the music." [87]
- MARY BANAS

Mary Banas designed the Grammy-nominated packaging for *Be the Cowboy*, which must've pleased Mitski. So much so, that the two have worked together on many projects since, earning Mary Banas this separate section.

"I am really lucky to collaborate with Mitski because she has great respect for the creative process. Collaboration across disciplines is special, because of that relationship of mutual admiration and understanding." [87]
- MARY BANAS

Mary is based in San Francisco. She runs her own studio called Yes Is More while she teaches at California College of the Arts.

"The work needs to amplify the photography and mood of the albums, but each one has a different path to getting there." [87]

- MARY BANAS

Their process starts with the photos coming in (often shot by Ebru Yildiz). Mitski and Mary then spend a "period of seclusion" where they brainstorm and "chip away" until they have a coherent theme Mary can bring to her marketing team. This always includes a heavy focus on typography.

"Typography is vital to any design project. It is a form that communicates, in addition to the language it makes." [87]

- MARY BANAS

Look out for her name as we go!

"Mitski's fanbase are the nicest and most thoughtful group of people, and they have expressed appreciation for most things in the Mitski universe. I am always thinking of them when I design and I aim to delight them with work that reflects the depth of the art Mitski creates." [87]

- MARY BANAS

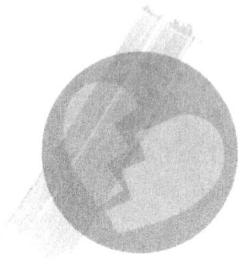

5.3.
MAC DEMARCO BEEF

Roughly nine months after Mitski released *Be The Cowboy*, Canadian singer Mac DeMarco released his fourth studio album called *Here Comes the Cowboy*. As if that wasn't enough, get this: the first single was called "Nobody".

"The word 'cowboy' is like a pet name for me. I often use it when I talk about people in my life [...] Where I grew up, there are many people who wear cowboy hats and do cowboy things with conviction. But these are not the people I'm referring to here." [87]

- MAC DEMARCO

Mitski fans being Mitski fans attacked with their fangs dripping, accusing DeMarco of stealing from their goddess. Thankfully, Mitski herself stepped in before anyone got hurt.

"My god, why is everyone mad? I'm laughing!" [29]

- MITSKI

"I'm 100% sure Mac and I just went fishing in the same part of the collective unconscious! What's wild is we have the same PR, so I LOVE my personal conspiracy theory that [my PR] heard the album and track titles, but kept quiet thinking maybe some Mac fans will mistakenly find me. lol." [129]

- MITSKI

Mac DeMarco did eventually release a statement.

"[I was] not trying to troll Mitski. [I] didn't know who Mitski was! [But Be The Cowboy is] really cool, and I think we might even cover one of the songs because it would be fun and we could try to make sense of the situation." [130]

- MAC DEMARCO

Mitski later referred to the incident as a "non-issue".

"Anyway thanks for the laugh, Mac! Happy release!" [129]

- MITSKI

5.4.
TOUR THE COWBOY

"The jumping around onstage, getting everyone pumped up, doesn't come naturally to me." [33]

- MITSKI

The *Be the Cowboy Tour* brought a dramatic shift in Mitski's stage show. With the help of choreographer Monica Mirabile, they developed a style in the vein of the 1950s Japanese dance theatre called "Butoh", characterised by slow, ever-flowing movements that can be playful or even grotesque, intended to illustrate the primal condition of being human.

"I was dealing with being an object that's looked at. Being a woman— an Asian woman—there are all these different projections that people put on me, and I guess the choreography was me trying to figure out how to deal with that. And playing with it. I would signify to people that I'm being sexual, but I would have a stone face. There's a sense of security, like you can go out and take risks." [93]

- MITSKI

"The concept is that she's initially this robotic, repressed woman who is very rigid in her behaviour and actions, and that slowly starts to dissolve over the course of the show, so she becomes more the person she actually wants to be, drawing on a confidence that's less rigid but still choreographed." [33]

- MONICA MIRABILE

Mitski officially took *Cowboy* on the road on August 12th, 2018 (even though she was already busy touring before then), and ended on September 8th, 2019.

"I don't want to do pyrotechnics. I don't want to do big LED screens. I want to make sure that everything onstage exists because it has to be there. I want the whole show to feel essential. I don't want anything superfluous. Performance can be as deep as you wanna make it." [2]

- MITSKI

Her intended stops were cities where she did not usually play. These landed across the USA, UK, Ireland, France, Belgium, Germany, Netherlands, Denmark, Canada, New Zealand, Australia, Japan, South Korea, Taiwan, Malaysia, Indonesia, Singapore, Norway, Sweden, Finland, Austria, and Portugal. Supporting acts included Katie Von Schleicher, Sidney Gish, Jay Som, and Jessica Lea Mayfield. Of course, there were festivals too, such as Lollapalooza in Chicago.

Look, ma, Mitski is on TV! During these promotional gigs, she stopped by on *The Daily Show With Trevor Noah* to play "Geyser", and she visited *Jimmy Kimmel Live!* to play "Two Slow Dancers" and "Nobody".

Around this time and maybe even before, Jeni Magaña joined Mitski's live line-up on bass, and has remained a core part of this stage crew right until today.

During her *Cowboy* shows, Mitski would also dare debut new songs, to which she'd request:

"Promise you won't put them on the internet. The temptation will be very strong when you go home. But you have to imagine my broken heart before you press upload." [6]

- MITSKI

Naturally, people didn't listen and uploaded them. How could they not? For at this stage, Mitski was transcending the realms of normal stardom. In the eyes of many bloodthirsty fans, she had become a deity.

"I was just trying to get through it every day. I was disassociated through most of that." [1]

- MITSKI

5.5.
TOXIC MITSKI FANDOM

"The sad girl thing was reductive and tired like five, ten years ago, and it still is today [...] let's retire the sad girl shtick. It's over. Sad girl is over." [131]

- MITSKI

ad but true, Mitski fans are notoriously negative to the point of venomous. Across the internet, you'll regularly find Mitski's most depressing slices of lyrics pasted together with comments like "too real" or "literally me."

"You're more than that. You're more than just my lyrics glued together, and you know it. Don't put yourself down." [13]

- MITSKI

These albums became the go-to music for sad girls, leading to (admittedly hilarious) observations such as:

"Bought my ticket to Mitski and they offered a 30-day trial for Headspace. They know their audience." [50]

- ASH (MITSKI FAN)

"I'm not sponsored by Headspace. I want a free Headspace." [131]

- MITSKI

Numerous articles have likened her following to a cult, with shows regularly punctuated with deliriously screamed confessions of love.

"You don't know me. But thank you. I get that you really love my music. Thank you very much." [123]

- MITSKI

Other common names you will hear thrown at Mitski include "God", "Queen", and "Mother".

"I am not your mother." [132]

- MITSKI

At first, like anyone would, Mitski appreciated the recognition.

"They're the reason I'm here. Because the music industry didn't want me, didn't know what to do with me. And even to this day, I feel like the industry at large doesn't quite know what to do with me, doesn't really understand me. But then I can show them all these other people who do understand me, and be like, 'This is what they're saying.'" [133]

- MITSKI

"The music business didn't wanna have anything to do with me. [But] I trust in the power of the listener." [17]

- MITSKI

"It's incredibly validating. It makes me feel useful. I think what I want most in the world is to feel useful and I don't have many other skills. I don't have another trade. So just knowing that something I made or something I contributed actually means something to other people is really validating." [28]

- MITSKI

"When people finally started to hear [my music], it was more a relief than anything. I wasn't surprised, because I had just pushed so hard for it. I think it really started to sink in when the tension became sustained, like, 'What I'm saying is being understood by other people that I haven't met.' That sensation, in and of itself, is why I keep doing what I do. Just that very raw phenomenon of it being clear that something you feel is something other people feel. Just that sheer sense of connection, because in that moment you're not alone. You're just a normal human being. That's what keeps me doing this. Just constantly having it be reaffirmed that I'm normal and other people have felt the way I feel." [42]

- MITSKI

"My best fan encounter... everyone's been really nice to me, but I still have this Princess Mononoke blanket that someone gave me." [31]

- MITSKI

"I don't want to put too much pressure on Gen Z, but we're really counting on them." [1]

- MITSKI

But soon the joke where everyone was crying to her music became excessive, tiresome, and less humourous.

"I was always bothered when people say, 'I cry to your music, it sounds like a diary, it sounds so personal.' Yes, it is personal. But that's so gendered. There's no feeling of, 'Oh, maybe she's a songwriter and she wrote this as a piece of art.' Every time someone on social media is like, 'I can't wait to cry to your new album,' I'm like, 'I don't know if you'll cry. I'm sorry.'" [6]

- MITSKI

"I got so much flak on social media. It was weird. 'What's wrong with crying to your music, I love your music.' It was so funny, because I was being scolded, but also being told that people love my music. I'm glad that people cry to my music. What I was trying to say was that my music is so often understood as a diary entry that has not had any sort of composition or thought put into it, and that's really frustrating. I've found that I've become a sort of emotional vessel, and I think that can be unhealthy. The point of my music isn't to make you cry. I'm not trying to make torture porn. I want to express, I don't know, the whole gamut of human experiences." [45]

- MITSKI

This onslaught of tears started to worry Mitski as she was treated more as therapy than an entertainer.

"It's embarrassing. Not to play the songs but to hear about other people listening to my music with a sober mind. Because when I'm writing it and when I'm performing it, I'm kind of in my own world. I'm not thinking about other people when I'm just rational normal everyday Mitski. And then someone's, like, 'Hey I love your lyric about blah blah blah,' I'm like, 'Ahhh! Stop stop!'" [23]

- MITSKI

"It's always really wonderful when people open up to me. I feel a connection with people, like, 'Oh, they understood my lyrics!' or, 'Oh, they related to what I was saying!' But it's a fine line between that and then feeling like they're entitled or I owe them a friendship or I owe them guidance. Because I'm not qualified to do that. I'm a musician. And I'm a young person, just like them. I don't know the answers and I can't be everybody's best friend. So that's a painful thing for me, actually, because I do want to relate to and help all these people who are reaching out. But I can't... I don't know how to." [15]

- MITSKI

"It's like, I'm sending out messages in bottles, but very picky and stubborn and selfish in that I only want the right person to receive it. I want to connect, but I also want to be left alone." [18]

- MITSKI

"The US is in political turmoil so people want change. They're unsatisfied with their life, understandably, and then they see my face all the time and they put it together and think, 'This person should fix it for me'. But I took, like, maybe one American history course. I don't

know anything about politics or law. I'm just a dumb musician. I'm just as mystified as the person looking at my face. I don't think it's wise to turn to me for revolution, because I'm not equipped for that." [88]

- MITSKI

"It's not healthy. We prop up artists as if they were politicians. Artists are often fucked-up people. I don't know anything about policy. I don't know how to run a country or a state or a city or even a community. There's a lot of push towards 'correct' art, art by outstanding citizens who are 'perfect' in every way. But we need artists that represent every emotion. Some of our emotions are destructive. It would be unhealthy if people didn't have an outlet for sadness or anger. I don't want artists to be shitty people but I don't want artists to be held up to the same standards as politicians. We shouldn't have to be superheroes." [17]

- MITSKI

"I get a lot of messages and emails from people I don't know who listen to my music. And I think because of the emotional content of my music people really relate to both my music and to me as a person. Which is a really beautiful thing. But sometimes it seems forgotten that they don't actually know me. Or they feel like they know me. But they don't actually, and they email me or message me as if we've been friends for a long time. And they share a lot of things with me. They kind of unload on me. On one hand, I think that's like a wonderful and an honourable position to be in, where people trust me with their personal issues and lives. But on the other hand, I can't always answer that. I can't always emotionally fulfill them or reply with good answers as to what they're talking to me about.

There's so much expectation for me to be a counselor, in a way. Or it seems, like, if they message me and I don't know how to respond or I don't feel comfortable responding so I don't respond or I just respond with a shorter email, and then like I get another email, like, 'I thought you would understand!' or 'I shared this with you, why are you ignoring me?' or, 'I thought you were in my scene' or I get these resentful messages afterwards when I'm not who they thought I was. And that's always painful because it seems to be forgotten that we've never met or I don't actually know them. I don't owe them anything." [15]

- MITSKI

"I really do want to connect with people in that way because I know what it feels like. I know it makes all the difference when there's just even one person out there who says, like, 'I'm sorry' or 'I know how that feels.' But I can't. I have a really complex life to live as well and I'm really fucked up too. So, it's, like, you can't hand me your life and expect me to do something with it." [15]

- MITSKI

"I think it does affect me in my day-to-day. It's quite sad—maybe I turn everything into a sad thing—but what I've noticed is that so many people think that they know me now. It's very weird, because they don't. And what's paralysing is getting messages or emails from people I've never met acting like they're my best friend or expecting me to do things for them. I've had people say, 'So, my mother is in the hospital and she has cancer. Can you please come visit her?' That's been paralysing." [10]

- MITSKI

345

"I started getting messages where teenagers would threaten to hurt themselves if I didn't respond, and I realised that I didn't want to be that accessible [...] Sometimes [fans] think, 'Me and this artist are meant to be together. We're the same person.' And you have to know when to disengage." [123]

- MITSKI

Mitski's inability to cope with the pressure of her fans only made her more relatable, and the delusions escalated to the point where she started to grow concerned, not only for the mental health of her fans, but for her own safety.

"It's usually great. People are usually nice. But I had one show recently where I had to go through the crowd in order to get from the stage to the outside, and the show didn't have security. So I just said, 'I'm gonna have to go through the crowd,' and I thought explaining would make everyone understand, but I got grabbed a lot. I kept saying, 'Please let go, I need to go, please stop.' But it was like everyone's eyes were sort of glazed over, and they didn't see me as a real person telling them to stop. And that's weird. That's when the whole 'being a projection' thing can be really uncomfortable and dangerous. But I don't know how to negotiate it, because I also think it's healthy. I think humans need symbols—or rituals, like going to a show—in order to organise our thoughts and understand the world. So when I'm on stage, I think it's really healthy that people are not seeing me as a person. But it's hard when that doesn't stop." [13]

- MITSKI

"I was saying, 'No, please stop, please let me go', and everyone's eyes were glazed over. I realised I wasn't actually a fellow person; I was an idea. That's what I'm uncomfortable with. People want to take

something of me to keep with them, and I don't want to be owned like that. I want to be a fellow person standing on the same ground, I don't want to be someone's little treasure in their pocket." [88]

- MITSKI

"People were unrelenting. Everyone needed a piece of me, whether it was a photo, or my autograph, and then I was so overwhelmed being surrounded by hands grabbing at me that I was crying, but they still didn't seem to see my crying face. People started to grab at my shirt and, by the time I got out, my shirt was basically off. It was an emblematic moment. That has been happening to me in different ways." [13]

- MITSKI

"I'm terrified of crowds. I've always been someone who's outside of crowds and either at the mercy of crowds or just observing them. So seeing mob mentality unfold in front of me, because of me, is just terrifying." [33]

- MITSKI

"It's funny. It's, like, there's no way around being an object, whether it's an object of hate or an object that people want to possess and consume. What really just eats at my soul is that I'm actively being consumed as a person. It's not just my music that's being consumed."" [33]

- MITSKI

"It's difficult to write from an authentic place in yourself when so many projected versions of you are invading your brain." [50]

- MITSKI

"I am a musician, but the reason they really pay me the big bucks is to be the place where anybody can put all of their feelings, their ugliness, that doesn't have a place in their own lives. I'm like the black hole where people can dump all their shit, whether it's a need for love, or it's hatred and anger. So I've seen a lot of the ugliness of people [...] I've put myself in this position where anyone can really do anything they want to me. I'm always fearful of somebody who might not have good intentions finding me and doing something to me." [93]

- MITSKI

Sadly, this strained relationship continues to this day. But, please note that Mitski truly does love her fans.

"I really do love you. I think it's possible even though we don't know each other." [83]

- MITSKI

"I want you to know, and I mean this sincerely—I love you. It's a selfish kind of love, because it's about what you do for me. But thank you for connecting. Thank you for making me feel less alone." [33]

- MITSKI

5.6.
CHILD TRAFFICKING ACCUSATION

TRIGGER WARNING: SEXUAL ABUSE

If you need additional evidence that Mitski's gravitational pull attracts a toxic atmosphere, here is one of the more harrowing stories.

On Tumblr in 2019, user Amberdollars accused Mitski of sexually abusing them from the age of 11 until 2015. They further claimed that Mitski was part of a sex trafficking ring. The posts have since been removed and, apparently, the username has been taken over by someone else. But the posts on that page still revolve around the topic.

Mitski took to Tumblr to address the rumours, with her full statement below:

"The allegations made on Tumblr of child sex trafficking and abuse against me are completely false in every respect. I don't know the accuser, and I don't know how or why they have come to associate me with their trauma. I have not ever been part of sex trafficking or child abuse in any form. I initially did not acknowledge the

allegations because I feared bringing harm to a person who may be struggling with mental health, either by drawing further attention to them, or by involving myself and thereby giving reality to their claims. I hope those of you on the internet treat them with kindness and compassion, and I truly hope they find the help they need. But it became clear that I need to address this after learning from a child sex trafficking survivor that, because of these false and conflicting accounts, incredibly harmful misinformation about the reality of child sex trafficking is being propagated, and existing survivors are being triggered and re-traumatised by the continued and confusing discourse, which I am hoping to bring an end to by responding here. I am also motivated to make this statement because my family has somehow been falsely accused of being involved alongside me, and for their sake I need to make absolutely clear these accusations are false; they do not deserve any of this. Again, the allegations are not true, there is clear and overwhelming evidence that they are unfounded, that is easily corroborated many times over. This pains me to say because we should continue to practice believing in victims, and I hope that survivors out there are not discouraged to come forward with their own experiences because of this instance. Thank you, Mitski." [135]

- MITSKI

5.7.
MITSKI QUITS SOCIAL MEDIA

"When you're writing a song, you need a lot more stamina. My mind has switched into trying to fit things into 140 characters, so when I'm writing a song I feel like I don't have the attention span to finish a thought. To actually let something sit. To let the creative process happen naturally. Because I'm not thinking about anything when I'm writing, except for being in the moment. I think that's why I love it, because everything goes quiet. Only after I write a song, I get myself into trouble because, 'Shit! This is really really personal.' But... it's my job now!" [18]

- MITSKI

Before Mitskimania, our protagonist was cherished for her social media presence, posting several times a day. Here are some of her long-since deleted Tweets to brighten your day.

"ppl quit naming ur cats mitski I'm trying to twitter search my name like any regular girl +all I get's anime porn +cat owners gushing to no one."[135]

- MITSKI

"Is there nowhere in this godforsaken town a girl can have a breakdown in peace?"[136]

- MITSKI

"whenever my bb acts like they don't deserve the world I'm like, excuse me darling do u forget that I am a *goddess* + I chose only u to love?"[137]

- MITSKI

"what kind of.......sex do you have...to my music, because...does it end happily? is everyone alright?"[138]

- MITSKI

"boys assign me a role then say i've deceived them for not fulfilling that role all while I've just been standing here looking up at the sky"[139]

- MITSKI

"once I was talking to a dude about this band Mitski +he went "oh yeah I know those guys, super nice, we go way back"[140]

- MITSKI

"Today in a pause between songs someone yelled really loud "you're so weird" and then there was silence and another quieter voice said "thank you" This short interaction fed me for the rest of the set and will probably fuel me for the rest of this tour. Thank you" [141]

- MITSKI

"I'm not doing this for the white boys saying I'm living wrong, I'm doing this for all my former selves out there who need to see me doing it" [142]

- MITSKI

"fuck i just woke up from a performance anxiety dream where the guitarist kept playing Wheatus songs i didn't know and my drummer was EEYORE" [143]

- MITSKI

No doubt about it, Mitski loved her growing social media outreach.

"I am on the internet a lot." [51]

- MITSKI

"That's why I love social media so much; it's a great way to let everyone know I'm a real person and that I'm out there just trying to do the best I can as a person." [74]

- MITSKI

"As much as [the internet] often is the bane of our existence it also has given us so much it's connected us to other worlds that we never had access to before." [25]

- MITSKI

"I try to tweet useful information, or things people would actually benefit from seeing, and try not to make it self-indulgent. Before I tweet anything, I think, 'Is this content that would actually benefit someone, or am I just looking to be validated?' If it's the latter, then I try to refrain. If it's the former, like a good book that I feel is not getting enough attention, or a useful link with phone numbers of local politicians and other representatives, or resources for conflict resolution when you're talking to a family member who you don't politically agree with, for example—then I'd usually post that. I don't tweet too much sad or angry personal stuff either, only because I am fully aware that my having a bad day isn't anyone else's problem or responsibility, and no one wants to see that; everyone is already going through their own shit." [95]

- MITSKI

"I just see it as something I have fun with. I hope it stays that way. Maybe one day I'll have to quit it, because I make myself too accessible on it, but right now I'm just having fun with it." [56]

- MITSKI

One guaranteed way to destroy everything is to get a large group of people involved. The more keyboards lined up beneath her posts, the less fun it became. And then it turned ugly.

"Honoured to serve as a minor clickbait profit generator and light distraction from the hellish real world for the day. But I feel very empty from looking at this phone screen for so long, so let's all please stop and get out of here. Thanks to everyone who cares for my music, truly!" [33]

- MITSKI

"For better for worse, now teenagers grow up in public. So all the mistakes you make and all the stupid tomfoolery you go through and the shit you regret that you don't want people to know about, is posted everywhere and will be on record. That's terrifying to me." [9]

- MITSKI

"It's hard [not to interact], because I just have a really strong understanding that the person talking behind the screen is a real person with a real life, and I don't want them ignored or neglected. I'm trying to figure out how to balance my own personal energy and also be a good person to other people. I think a lot of people on the Internet interact with me... not really understanding that I'm a person behind the screen. I'm more than just an image or a symbol. I've started to understand that. Before, I'd be so confused why people were throwing such strong emotions and words at me. I think it's because young people who grew up on the Internet sometimes forget that thing they are throwing all this stuff at is an actual person." [49]

- MITSKI

"I have a weird relationship with social media. To be real, I'm afraid of people. Especially people in groups. As someone who has been an outsider all my life, I understand the danger of being alone right outside a circle of people. Human beings instinctively group into groups or seek out other humans because it's just safer. I grew up on the outside of it, so I have seen firsthand the kind of shit people do when they feel safe within anonymity. People feel strong in a group. People feel justified in a group. And social media is that times 100. It's anonymous people in a big group against me. It's my biggest fear. So I think by going on social media, I'm also confronting my fear, or just

trying to keep that channel open and stay connected and communicate to remind myself that these people in groups are individuals. I can communicate with them and I am one of them. So I think that's why I stay on social media even though it scares me. The herd mentality is very very scary for me. But I go on there to try to keep negotiating my humanity and keep my faith in people. People in groups have started revolutions, you know. People in groups are powerful and that can be so positive. But it also starts wars. So when people rally around me I need to learn to trust it. But I still don't quite trust it. There's a part of me that's still sniffing the air for when the mood changes and everyone turns on me. That's not anyone's problem. That's my problem. But I have trust issues, basically, if we're really getting into it in this interview." [11]

- MITSKI

"Lately it's been stressful because it puts me in a vulnerable position, where people I don't know who I've never met can come at me with whatever their emotions or issues are and hold me responsible for them. I've had a bunch of angry boys threaten to rape me, for example. And I'm, like, 'Do you know that I'm a person? I'm not just an image on a screen?' I guess that's also why I hope I can keep interacting with people on a real personal level, to remind them that I'm not a symbol but a real person with a real life, and I, in turn, always have in mind that whoever is reaching out to me is a real person with a real complex life, and I don't want to treat them like they're just another tweet or email." [48]

- MITSKI

"I think maybe she didn't realise how much it would change her day to day life. The increased obligations and the mixed bag of experiences that you get from having a larger fanbase, of interacting online with the nicest people in the world and the worst people in the world, I think she didn't realise how much attention there would be on herself as a person when the music started to get more attention." [18]

- PATRICK HYLAND

On her quest for greater self-care, Mitski experimented with short bursts of social media detoxes.

"I'm thinking of scaling back. I'm slowly trying to wean myself from it, because it's taken up too much of my energy [and] my time. I don't want it to start affecting my artistry, because I don't want to make music that caters to people or is worried about what people will think or say." [18]

- MITSKI

"I took a break from Twitter because I realised I was spending five hours... and, like, everything is so dramatic. And I already have enough bullshit in my life. I don't need to watch other people's bullshit all day. But I've slowly eased my way back into it. Like alcohol, like anything else, just in moderation." [43]

- MITSKI

"I'm not on Instagram anymore because I can't remember my password. I lost my iPhone and I can't remember my password, so it's going to be a whole thing to try to get back on it. I can't bother." [11]

- MITSKI

These breaks were not enough, and then one day in 2019, after one fan attack too many, she logged out for good.

"I don't remember my tweet exactly. I was like, 'I'm tired.' I was tired of being on tour. The comments I got were: 'How dare you! You have so much privilege! You have the best job! Why don't you quit then?!' Twitter didn't feel compassionate any more." [17]

- MITSKI

"I understand the importance of connectivity, you know? A lot of great change has happened via the internet and social media. But I want us to figure out a way to have that without having our livelihoods depend on it." [60]

- MITSKI

"[I] could finally leave socials without it devastating my income." [33]

- MITSKI

"I always hated what social media did to my brain, and now that I'm not on it I feel a significant difference. It shortened my attention span, created a feeling of anxiety and distraction throughout the day, even when I wasn't physically on it, and it demanded that I accept hundreds of strangers' daily cruelty, simply for making them aware that I exist." [33]

- MITSKI

If you love Mitski content spilling across your newsfeed, there are some active accounts that I recommend. Get your XTwitter kicks from *@mitskidata*, *@dailymitski_*, and *@randomitskis*. Some fresh Insta-Mitski vibes can also be found on *@mit.skil0v3r*, *@iamnotmitski*, *@queenmitski*, and *@lloveme_afteryou*. Cool Tiktok crew includes *@mitskistuff*. And if Facebook is your safe place, try the *mitski fandom* or *Mitski Fandom 2* groups on for size. Meanwhile, Mitski's official social media accounts still exist, business as usual, find her *@MitskiLeaks* across the board. But these platforms are under the control of her management now, which apparently was an easy solution for all involved.

"It wasn't a point of contention. It was more just a problem we had to solve, like, okay, the problem is, I have to have socials, but being on socials is bad for my brain. How do we make it work?" [60]

- MITSKI

"My social media is run by my manager. Apparently he gets threats on his email, saying, 'Put Mitski back online!' But, you know, those threats just make me want to not be online. So, yeah, I live in blissful ignorance of whatever is being said about me on Twitter." [131]

- MITSKI

"I'm not on social media. I very thankfully have a manager who runs my social mediums. I think it got really unhealthy very quickly for me to have access to thousands, tens of thousands of strangers' opinions of me and whether it's positive or negative feedback. I mean, obviously, no one wants to hear mean things. But also all the sort of aggrandising, strangely worshipful commentary about me, it doesn't make any sense, and it's not good for my self-image. Like, I can't read that and then go through my life with the commentary in my mind that there are people who think I am perfect and great. It's not good." [19]

- MITSKI

Like anyone who has tried to quit social media, did Mitski face the temptation to sneak a peek every now and then?

"No, no, no. I used to in the very beginning, mostly because I was weaning myself off of socials. But every time I would be bad and lurk secretly, it would just ruin my day. Even you, any kind of self-employed person, has to have socials now to continue to be employed, which is a really messed up situation we've put ourselves in. A resume no longer suffices? Now thousands of strangers also have to like your online persona for you to be employed? It's wild." [60]

- MITSKI

For obsessive superfans, this loss of Mitski accessibility was an absolute horror show. But little did they know their nightmare was only beginning...

"So much of my income is directly based on external validation, which is quite unhealthy. I might, just to get away from it, get another job and take a break from music, not because I don't want to make music anymore but just to have a sense of stability." [42]

- MITSKI

5.8.
MITSKI QUITS MUSIC

"It's hard. I don't do it for fun. I do get some kind of deep satisfaction out of it, but it is anxiety-inducing, and hard, and you have to investigate parts of yourself that maybe you don't want to." [45]

- MITSKI

"Day after day, it got harder and harder, and I was just unhappy and in distress all of the time. Looking back, I actually think Be the Cowboy was a cry for help." [60]

- MITSKI

"I basically dissociated through many years. I don't remember most tours, except for the performance. My hair was greying. I had a lot of medical issues that went undiagnosed because I never went to the doctor. My body was breaking down. The only way of getting through it was dissociating." [60]

- MITSKI

Mitski got everything any artist could wish for, but it landed so fast and hard upon her that she could no longer hold the weight. So, on September 8th, 2019, Mitski announced that the final show of the *Cowboy Tour* in Central Park, NYC, may be her last show... forever.

"This will be my last show indefinitely. And I'm glad it's ending in NY where I came up. It's time to be a human again. And have a place to live." [144]

- MITSKI

"I was thinking this was the last show I would perform ever, and then I would quit and find another life." [1]

- MITSKI

The root of her problems came as she started questioning where to place her art in the world.

"I had quote-unquote 'made it,' I guess. And I started to hear this voice in my head: 'Now you have to keep this up. Now, you can't lose this.' And I was afraid that that voice would lead me to writing songs for the sake of staying in the game and I just felt like something in me was dying a bit and I felt like I needed to step away before it completely, irreparably died." [19]

- MITSKI

"This is what really made me quit. I could see a future self, who would put out music for the sake of keeping the machine running. And that really scared me." [1]

- MITSKI

"I was really thinking, okay, my music career is over. I need to find a new career. It really occurred to me that I'm just moving from one set of exploitation to another, you know?" [60]

- MITSKI

"I felt it was shaving away my soul little by little. The music industry is this supersaturated version of consumerism. You are the product being consumed, bought, and sold. Even the people on your team who are your friends, the very foundation of your dynamic is that they get a percentage of your income. Every time I turned something down, it would mean that they would make less money." [1]

- MITSKI

"I don't think I had any room to acknowledge how other people reacted. I was really on the edge for a very long time." [60]

- MITSKI

Lucy Dacus opened for Mitski's final show, so she witnessed the process turning in real-time.

"I asked her, 'How do you feel?' The first thing she said was, 'Oh, I've made a huge mistake.' She verbalised it, and I felt a shade of terror for her." [1]

- LUCY DACUS

"A lot of my decisions are made very instinctually without much thought. Like, my biggest decisions." [73]

- MITSKI

It's only natural she'd have her doubts following such a monumental swerve.

"I really thought, 'What have I done?' I had strived and built towards this point in my career, and I felt like, 'Oh my god, I'm just throwing it away.'" [60]

- MITSKI

"I was filled with regret and grief because I thought maybe I'd made a big mistake. You know, I'd worked so hard to get to that point in my career and, in my mind, I was throwing it all away [...] I would think, 'Oh my God, I wish I was still doing [it],' and I would just tear up, which is pathetic." [117]

- MITSKI

"In order for me to survive in the music industry as it exists, I had to stuff a pillow over my heart and tell it to stop screaming, and be like, 'Shut up, shut up, take it.' After a few years of doing that every single day, my heart really did start to go numb and go silent. And the problem with that is that I actually need my heart—my feelings—in order to write music. It was this paradox." [1]

- MITSKI

To deal with these life changes, Mitski made another life change by moving to Nashville, Tennessee, around 2020. Some say she still lives there today, but who knows? Before this, she was living just outside of Philly.

"I moved [to Nashville] knowing nothing about it." [34]

- MITSKI

"I'm becoming attached to Nashville. I didn't want to do LA or New York, because I felt I shouldn't live in incredibly competitive, expensive cities when I'm quitting my job." [1]

- MITSKI

It's debatable whether the move helped much.

"It got so bad, to the point where I was living in a white room with nothing in it." [1]

- MITSKI

5.9.
HIRED GUN, PART 3

Mitski may have "retired", but for those who knew where to look, there were additional songs popping up here and there around this time.

On 31st August, 2018 (a mere two weeks after *Be the Cowboy*), Wild Nothing's fourth studio album *Indigo* manifested with Mitski's backing vocals on the final song, "Bend".

"Mitski and I got set up to work on some stuff together, and we hit it off, and we ended up opening up a few songs that I had been working on, and that was one of them. So basically, when I was working with her the music was more or less done, but there were no vocals. No vocal melody or lyrics. And she just helped me spitball ideas for vocal melodies. It was great! It was really really fun working with her. It's kind of rare that I open myself up to working with other people, at least in terms of the writing side of it, but it was really actually so beneficial to that song. It really helped open up that song in a lot of ways." [45]

- JACK TATUM (WILD NOTHING)

Fast forward closer to where we are up to, and Mitski gave her unreleased song "Cop Car" to the 2020 horror movie *The Turning*. Fans were overjoyed for a recorded version of this tune because it had floated around live from as early as 2014 (you can find Mitski performing it on YouTube, just search for *"Mitski: The Red Barn @ Hampshire College - 11/24/2014 (COMPLETE PERFORMANCE)"*).

The movie bombed with a 12% Rotten Tomatoes score. The Thrillist stated that *"'The Turning' Soundtrack Is Even Better Than 'The Turning' Movie"*, which seemed accurate, considering other awesome artists featured, such as Courtney Love, Soccer Mommy, Kali Uchis, and Alice Glass.

On February 21st, 2020, Allie X's second album came out, called *Cape God*. Mitski sang on the ninth track, "Susie Save Your Love" which musicOHM called *"unaccountably sad yet impossible not to dance to"* and Paste enjoyed it as a *"solid track"* with their two voices *"almost too perfect of a match"*.

"I discovered Mitski's music a couple of years ago and was instantly smitten. She has such a singular voice—it was so authentic, so sad, so relatable [...] Mitski's taking a break from the music industry at the moment—she's not on social media, she's not touring. And so when I asked her to sing on the track, she was like, 'I love this song so much, but I'm saying no to every feature right now.' But then one day, I was flying somewhere, and when I landed, there was a text from Mitski saying, 'Hey, no pressure, but if you still want me to do the feature on the song, I think I would like to do it.' And I was like, 'Oh my god, yes!' She doesn't really do features, so I feel very lucky." [146]

- ALLIE X

The following month (13th March, 2020), out came the fourth studio album by the band Porches called *Ricky Music*. The song "Madonna" features Mitski's backing vocals. The album wasn't loved that much. However, it's no surprise that everyone said the Mitski song was the best piece on offer.

"The only time Maine manages to rouse himself from his funk is 'Madonna,' which dazzles like a night out on the town. Mitski sings hushed backing vocals, and synthesisers fan out like a royal flush. It's too bad the rest of the record can't match its energy." [147]

- PITCHFORK REVIEW

Finally, Lucy Dacus' third studio album *Home Video* arrived on June 25th, 2021. The song "Going Going Gone" featured Mitski's backing vocals, but don't get too excited as she is just one of 14 voices which includes Patrick Hyland and the rest of Boygenius.

"When I wrote this one, I didn't like it so much because it had that campfire vibe, and I thought it was too twee. For a long time, I've tried to establish myself in people's minds as Not Americana, because people go to such lengths to show girls with guitars as country adjacent. People have called me alt-country. Genre is dead, and yet, I make rock music. But I felt more comfortable doing whatever the song wanted this time around. So if it's a campfire song, then let's get people on the refrains, and let's do it with acoustic guitars and make it super cozy." [148]

- LUCY DACUS

5.10.
SECRET SESSION WRITER

"Y'all, I'm not quitting music! I've been on non-stop tour for over five years, I haven't had a place to live during this time, and I sense that if I don't step away soon, my self-worth/identity will start depending too much on staying in the game, in the constant churn." [1]

- MITSKI

Reading the previous section, one can't help but be confused as Mitski flooded us with mixed retirement messages. There is clear evidence presented earlier that she certainly did contemplate quitting music forever. Then again, with quotes like the one immediately above, what was anyone to believe? Some fans concluded Mitski was transitioning into the world of session writing. As it turns out, there was truth in that.

""It really is joyful getting to be almost like a craftsperson, just walking into a room and putting puzzle pieces together." [50]

- MITSKI

In typical Mitski fashion, any songs she may have written for other artists are shrouded in mystery, and we have no idea how many we may have already heard. Reportedly, she contributed to numerous genres, including pop, hip-hop, and country.

"I'm just trying to plant as many seeds of investment as possible." [6]

- MITSKI

"It's great. I'd like to do more of it. I currently don't have time, but over the years, I plan to do more [...] Sometimes I write a song and know that I can't do it justice with my voice or persona, and it'd go really well with somebody else's voice. An extra need is filled when I get to write for other people, because I get to be creative in ways that might be limited if I was just working on my own stuff. I don't think my creativity is a limited resource. I can write a great song, give it to somebody, be happy that I wrote a great song—and then write another one." [45]

- MITSKI

"It's liberating. I've been enjoying it because sometimes I write songs that I feel like I can't serve with my own voice or with my own persona. I just couldn't live up to it. And so writing for other people, I feel like I can channel all these different personalities in me that maybe I can't even express very well, but someone else can express for me. So I've been really enjoying writing for other people." [61]

- MITSKI

"I've always felt like I needed to put my eggs in as many baskets as possible, because what I do has never felt sustainable, never built to last." [50]

- MITSKI

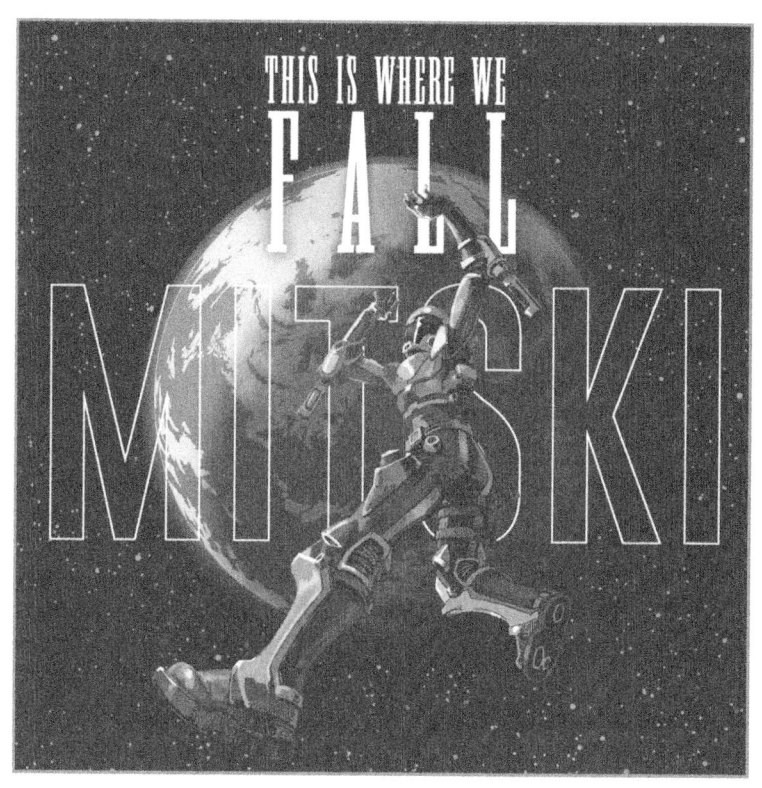

5.11.
EP: THIS IS WHERE WE FALL (2021)

1. The Baddy Man (02:15)
2. The Beginning (02:55)
3. The End (03:15)

TOTAL RUNTIME: 08:25

A little-known EP from Mitski appeared around May 5th, 2021. Interestingly, it was a soundtrack to the graphic novel *This Is Where We Fall* published by Z2 Comics. To fit in with the scifi Western themes, the music genre has been labeled anything from rockabilly to Spaghetti Western to post-rock.

"It was exciting to make a soundtrack for a comic book. It allowed me to work outside of my usual songwriting form and try to approach it like a score, but without any of the cues that come with working alongside a moving image, which ended up being both freeing and challenging. I hope the end result helps to immerse you in the story!" [149]

- MITSKI

If you haven't heard this (or even heard of it) don't feel too bad. The three-track vinyl release was limited to 2,000 copies, sold with the deluxe edition of the comic... for $100. Other than that, it is not on any streaming platforms, although you can download the digital files for free on Bandcamp.

"A project and partnership like this is the perfect marriage of a visual art form like comics, and music. Fans of Mitski's music will not only get something new from one of their favourite artists, but a companion piece that completes the experience. Comics readers will find an original work of science fiction from top creators that is enhanced by the music that accompanies it." [149]

- JOSH FRANKEL (Z2 PUBLISHER)

Reviews for the comic and the EP have been mediocre, to put it lightly. The rating for the graphic novel sits around 3/5 on Goodreads while one Mitski fan wondered, *"Why did she agree to do this? Did she owe someone a favour?"*

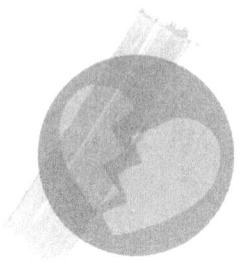

5.12.
AND THEN THERE WAS THE PANDEMIC

"Suddenly, I was in this city I don't know anything about, locked down, and existing in this weird bubble for, I'd say, two years." [117]
- MITSKI

Everyone has their story about the world collapsing in 2020. With Mitski, she turned 30 while in lockdown.

"No exaggeration, I woke up and shed one single tear because I was so fucking glad to be out of my twenties." [1]
- MITSKI

There were two types of people when it came to the pandemic: those who lost their minds without social interaction; and those who enjoyed the alone time to dabble in different projects. No prize for guessing in which category Mitski fell.

"I am introverted. I have a home, thank goodness. I have a roof over my head so I've been safe. But, well, it was funny, I remember in

the very beginning of the pandemic, the extroverts were kind of going wild online, being, like, 'I can't take it!' and it was, at that time, just a month into the pandemic. Meanwhile, I was, like, 'This is great!' Obviously it wasn't great the entire time, but I'm just remembering the very beginning of it, where I was fine." [30]

- MITSKI

"I'm just on a couch, watching T.V. My fans should not meet me because they would be disappointed." [1]

- MITSKI

Mitski busied herself making vegan pies, bingeing horror films, and gardening.

"[I learned] how to live like a regular person. I started baking. I learned how to garden. It turns out I don't have a green thumb, because I'm so used to getting things done on the fly. But, with plants, you can't force them to grow in a soil they don't like. You can't rush their growth. Each thing needs its own amount of water, its own environment." [93]

- MITSKI

"Baking was a hobby that stuck with me because it takes such a long time and I had a lot of time to fill. It's a lot of precise work. For some reason I don't really care about cooking, but I love baking. Especially during the pandemic. It was, like, this recipe told me exactly what to do so I knew for the first time in my day what I was supposed to be doing. And then it took a really long time, so it was a process that I could just get into and forget about everything else for a long time. And then at the end of it, you get a sweet treat! You're rewarded for doing exactly what the recipe said,

and taking a long time to do it. It was just like that's what I needed during the pandemic." [30]

- MITSKI

But her musical calling did not shush, even if she found the idea difficult.

"[I felt the] complete inability to feel motivated. Just getting up in the morning and doing something became so hard for no reason. So that got in our way." [11]

- MITSKI

"Some people do writing sessions on Zoom, but I realised I can't work like that. So I just had a lot of food deliveries." [117]

- MITSKI

Nevertheless, once the airborne disease cleared up, so did her brain fog.

"I felt like we needed some infusion of possibility, some sense of things happening again." [50]

- MITSKI

5.13.
MITSKI DOES NOT QUIT MUSIC AFTER ALL

I believe I speak for everyone when I say, "Thank God Mitski returned to music!" Then again, some of her reasons for doing so are less romantic than others. For example, contractual obligations, as she still owed her label another record.

"I contractually had to release it. I just didn't know whether I would ask the label to take it and keep me out of it, or I would actually go out and present it." [1]

- MITSKI

But deep down, I think we all know the truth...

"What it came down to was, 'I have to do this even though it hurts me, because I love it. This is who I am. I'm going to keep getting hurt, and I'm still going to do it, because this is the only thing I can do.'" [1]

- MITSKI

"It was simpler to just explain it away as physical exhaustion which, of course, was part of it. But looking back, it was more mentally [about] being a working person in the music industry, which is like this super-saturated version of consumerism. I got really scared because I could see myself caving in and being swept away by that current, and putting out music that I don't really care about. I needed to step away to get out of that mechanism and just learn how to be human again, I think."[117]

- MITSKI

"You could say that I was just exhausted because I had been touring and popping albums out one after the other for a while. I'd just been grinding so hard, for so long, that I think I just—I needed a break. Being in the music industry requires a lot of compromises, or doing things you don't want to do. When you make those kinds of compromises—even though your heart or soul is crying out against them—you do them every day, year after year."[60]

- MITSKI

"Sometimes pursuing [music] isn't even good for me. And there's something in me that needs to come out and it's not being fed by this career in music or this act of creating music. But then I go back to thinking... it doesn't even matter if it's good for me. I will be whatever it needs me to be. I'll do whatever it needs me to do in order for me to continue to be able to make music."[68]

- MITSKI

Like everyone will find in their lives, one needs to go through one thing to get to another, and now here she is.

"I think this break has been good for me. I had physically neglected my health because I was on tour so much. I didn't have health insurance. Basically during all of my twenties, I had no time or space to figure out who I am. I needed to actually figure out how to take care of my body."[1]

- MITSKI

"To clarify, I never intended to leave music. But I think it was about whether I should do this as a job. Mostly I was uncomfortable with being in the public eye. So I decided to leave the industry for however long it would take for me to get my heart and soul back. But eventually, I kind of looked around and realised just how lucky I was to get to create the music I want to make and have my music reach other people. And I just realised, you know what? I need to buckle up, in a sense, and just take all of the good that comes with the bad. Nothing was consciously empowering in the moment. I really made that decision to leave out of desperation because I felt like I was just at my limit. I couldn't see a way out of my situation. So I just left it all. But walking away, and sort of sitting with myself helped me realise what were my choices and what I could control. And that in, and of itself, I think in retrospect was very empowering. I mean, granted, you know, I have had one of the more luckier lives. So maybe if I were pushed a little harder, I would be down. I did go quite down mostly of my own doing. I was at a point where everything around me felt completely dark. And I realised that if there's no light around me, it's kind of up to me to be the light for myself. And I think that light is love for me as long as I just hold on to my love for people, for the world, for getting to live. Then my world will have love in it."[121]

- MITSKI

"I'm still mentally and emotionally negotiating the music industry. It's still what it was in 2019, if not worse, but I never intended to quit music. I'm always going to be a musician. I'm always going to be making songs and singing. It was just a matter of whether I would continue to try to make a living off of it and continue working in the industry. And I sort of came to peace with it. It's still exploitative. It's still not a great place to be. But I looked around at other people's jobs and I was, like, 'You know what? If it's not this job, it's going to have to be another job.' And other industries are also messed up in their own ways. Every job has good and bad. I figured I'm willing to take the bad of this job to get to have the good of this job, because if I worked in another field, I'd probably have the same problems. It's just a matter of deciding what you're willing to take for what you're willing to get."" [92]

- MITSKI

Because, in the end, Mitski doesn't make music without having a big reason.

"Everyone has a different reason for making music. Mine is I want to feel connected to other people. I've always grown up feeling lonely or other, but through my music, I can be like: 'Look, we're the same, we've felt the same thing, so we're not so different. I belong here.' It's almost like a hungry monster that's just a constant need to feel connection." [88]

- MITSKI

"I went to music school and I met some great musicians who really get off on the music theory. And they really make music because they

enjoy the mathematics of it, or the puzzle of it. And as much as I
enjoy that, that's not the reason I make music." [68]

- MITSKI

"The difference between making something really obscure versus
making something people like, there are a lot of different kinds
of musicians. Some musicians really love music for the sake of music.
I don't think I'm that kind of musician. I'm kind of a selfish musician
who uses music in order to express something I want to express. So
music is just my medium whereas a lot of musicians, especially
in Conservatory, who genuinely get off on chord progressions and
love the math of it. And that's fine. [But] I think of music more
as little baskets that carry the baby. The stork metaphor. Is
anyone following me? Whereas a lot of people's baby itself is
the chord progression." [11]

- MITSKI

Without a shred of exaggeration, music is Mitski's calling and her fate.

"Sometimes I listen to other artists' music and I can tell which of
those artists definitely don't have any other options in their life,
and which artists could do something else for a living. It has nothing
to do with how good you are as a musician. There are great
musicians who are also great visual artists. But there's a
desperation in my music." [68]

- MITSKI

"[Music is] the one thing that truly, fundamentally makes me happy,
and that's why I keep doing this. There is the ecstasy of being in

the zone, as they say, but there is also the contentment that comes from songwriting—for me, anyway. There's a feeling that I did a job or that I fulfilled a role, and I think that's why I keep going back to it. I think that songwriting and composition is actually very healthy for me because it's not just about the high, even though that exists as well. It's just about feeling okay." [26]

- MITSKI

"Maybe this is a made-up belief to preserve myself, but I do believe that everyone has a purpose, and my purpose is to put out music that means something. Every time I would almost just not make it, I would be like, 'But I have this thing that I can do, this thing that gives me a passport that allows me to be here.'" [80]

- MITSKI

"Not to be cheesy, but I do think music helped me not die." [80]

- MITSKI

But things were going to be different around here. A new sheriff was in town. Maybe not *Be the Cowboy*... but *Be the Mitski*.

"I don't want to make another Be the Cowboy. I knew that I didn't want to make music that was putting up walls against the listener. At the time I felt I needed to in order to protect myself, but that's not why I make music. At the end of the day, the music that touches me and has saved me is the stuff that goes right to my heart and feels personal, authentic and true." [60]

- MITSKI

Part Six
LAUREL HELL ERA

6.1.
ALBUM: LAUREL HELL (2022)

1. Valentine, Texas (2:35)
2. Working for the Knife (2:38)
(first single)
3. Stay Soft (3:16)
4. Everyone (3:47)
5. Heat Lightning (2:51)
(third single)
6. The Only Heartbreaker (3:04)
(second single, written by Mitski and Dan Wilson)
7. Love Me More (3:32)
(fourth single)
8. There's Nothing Left for You (2:52)
9. Should've Been Me (3:11)
10. I Guess (2:15)
11. That's Our Lamp (2:24)

TOTAL RUNTIME: 32:25

"How does it feel to be releasing a record again? Terrible. Absolutely terrible. It's like, 'Oh Jesus, here we go again.' I thought I was having fun and now it's no fun anymore." [117]

- MITSKI

Mitski came out of her hiatus like a machine gun. On October 4th, 2021, she announced a tour along with her next single, "Working for the Knife". The following day, it was out, just like that. A month later, the second single, "The Only Heartbreaker", arrived along with the announcement of her sixth studio album, *Laurel Hell*.

Laurel Hell was completed during the lockdowns, then finally released on February 4th, 2022, through Dead Oceans. Interestingly, Mitski had been sitting on these songs for several years, some of them reportedly written and even recorded as early as 2017.

Mitski sang and played keyboard on the record. Patrick Hyland was our reliable producer, but was also credited for guitar, percussion, and synthesiser. Beyond them, there were many other magic fingers dabbling the pie, including various *Be the Cowboy* people who made it across. Evan Marien played some bass just like he did on "Nobody" from *Cowboy*. The mastering genius behind

Cowboy, Ted Jensen, also returned for this record's levels. Ryan Smith did the lacquer cutting and vinyl mastering on both albums. Additionally, *Laurel Hell* featured the piano skills of Brooke Waggoner, who is known for his work with Jack White.

TITLE

"'Laurel Hell' is a term from the Southern Appalachians in the US, where laurel bushes basically grow in these dense thickets, and they grow really wide. And, I mean, I've never experienced it myself, but when you get stuck in these thickets, you can't get out. Or so the story goes. And so there are a lot of Laurel Hells in America, in the South, where they're named after the people who died within them because they were stuck. And, so the thing is, laurel flowers are so pretty. They just burst into these explosions of beauty. I liked the notion of being stuck inside this explosion of flowers and perhaps even dying within one of them." [150]

- MITSKI

"They're supposed to be hells that you can't get out of. I like the notion of being trapped inside this maze and possibly dying within it, but also being surrounded by these beautiful, explosive flowers." [34]

- MITSKI

"It was just too perfect. I'm stuck inside this maze... I can't get out, but it's beautiful." [1]

- MITSKI

SOUND

"This album went through so many iterations. This album has been a punk record at some point, and a country record. Then, after a while, it was like, 'I need to dance.' Even though the lyrics might be depressing, I need something peppy to get me through this." [1]

- MITSKI

Another shift in Mitski's sound was noted by everyone with ears, calling *Laurel Hell* synthpop, indie pop, electro-rock, art pop, new wave, ambient pop, and disco... all very much dictated by the 80s.

"[It's] more uptempo and dance-y." [151]

- MITSKI

"At first, most of the songs were kind of maudlin, slow rock songs. But, as the pandemic progressed, Patrick and I just stopped being able to handle these overtly morose songs. We needed something big, something extravagant, because we were just inside the same room every day. And what better era than the 80s to draw from for that?" [117]

- MITSKI

"We were in lockdown, and I was, like, 'I cannot handle sad music production! I am going crazy, and I need something that I can overtly dance to! That is overtly more upbeat than what I usually do, because I can't write my usual sad songs and put melancholic accompaniment to it because then it would just be too much. I just needed something lighter for the pandemic!'" [152]

- MITSKI

"[The 80s influence] less deliberate and more of a resignation. Patrick and I were like, 'Let's just allow it to happen, we can't fight this anymore. We love Hall and Oates.'" [117]

- MITSKI

Hall and Oates, yes, but the list of influences spread much further across the decade. Names frequently mentioned include Vangelis, Ultravox, Phil Collins, Giorgio Moroder, Arthur Russell, Beverly Glenn-Copeland, and, of course, ABBA.

"ABBA were a huge influence on the record." [117]

- PATRICK HYLAND

"At first, I wanted a lot of songs to be more disco. But then it just wasn't working, and so we took it up a decade." [152]

- MITSKI

"When was a time when everyone felt hopeful and everything is happening and everything is good? The 80s bubble! That feeling of possibility, having lots of money. I wanted to channel that feeling, just to get out of the fog of the pandemic. [Patrick and I] had time to consider every detail, for better and for worse. It's not good for mental health to have no limitations and just be focused for so long." [93]

- MITSKI

"I think it's fair to say that each record we make is written more and more for Mitski herself [with] less of an interest in trying to appeal to any type of imagined audience. It's more about making something that she enjoys." [60]

- PATRICK HYLAND

"You can do what you want. It doesn't have to be this pop formula, and you don't have to have this voice or look this way." [33]

- MITSKI

ARTWORK

Ebru Yildiz is one of Mitski's go-to photographers, and she is here again, behind the lens of *Laurel Hell*. What's interesting about Yildiz is that she was born and raised in Ankara, Turkey, but now lives in Brooklyn, NYC, USA, so I'm sure she and Mitski had a lot of geographical similarities to chat about.

Mary Banas took over the design as before. The typeface used was "Resolve" by Corinne Ang.

THEMES

"Laurel Hell is a soundtrack for transformation. A map to the place where vulnerability and resilience, sorrow and delight, error and transcendence can all sit within our humanity, can all be seen as worthy of acknowledgement, and ultimately, love. I accept it all. I forgive it all." [153]

- MITSKI

As anyone already assumed, this album provided an outlet for Mitski to heal from the pandemic as well as her misalignments with her career.

"This album, in general, has been a process of me trying to figure out how to forgive myself and other people. In my actual moments of tragedy or joy, I do tend to turn towards black-and-white thinking, and often that hasn't served me. [Writing Laurel Hell] has been a process of learning how to be kinder to myself and, through that,

be kinder to other people. I want to get out of being a hero of the story and being the villain." [93]

- MITSKI

"I needed love songs about real relationships that are not power struggles to be won or lost. I needed songs that could help me forgive both others and myself. I make mistakes all the time. I don't want to put on a front where I'm a role model, but I'm also not a bad person. I needed to create this space mostly for myself where I sat in that grey area." [150]

- MITSKI

"I've often found myself in a situation where, narratively speaking, I'm the bad guy. We can acknowledge more than just black and white. If you present something that feels true to you, there will be other people who are like, 'This is true to me too.'" [1]

- MITSKI

"This album is full of resignation. A feeling of ending, but wrapped up in 80s-inspired pop music." [60]

- MITSKI

CHARTS

The currency of Mitski's name delivered hard. *Laurel Hell* sold like the hottest cakes on the market, Mitski's best achievement yet. She hit the top 10 on the charts for Australian Albums (7), Irish Albums (7), UK Albums (6), US Billboard 200 (5), Scottish Albums (4), UK Independent Albums (3), US Independent Albums (2), US Top Alternative Albums (1), and US Top Rock

Albums (1). This was the highest she's reached on any of them, including her first ever to reach the top 40 on the Billboard 200. It's also Dead Oceans' first top 10 record. During its release, Laurel Hell was the best-selling album in the US. Woooo, go Mitski!

CRITICAL

The peculiar thing about *Laurel Hell* is that it was arguably her worst received record since her college days, and some may even argue before then. But don't get me wrong, it was still mighty in acclaim! With full marks, the Observer observed, *"This is an album that wrestles with the sisyphean slog of remaining engaged—with love, with work, with life. And you can dance to it."* Similarly, Consequence of Sound gave it 100%, stating, *"The resulting album is a sophisticated and magnetic collection of songs. But more than that, it's Mitski trusting herself, confidently blazing forward into the next decade of her storied career."* The majority of publications went for 80% or higher, including Variety, The Telegraph, The New York Times, Rolling Stone, The Independent, NME, Mojo, and Spin.

Nevertheless, there was a sense of people feeling let down. Pitchfork noted, *"To say that it is the least compelling of her Dead Oceans records is also to acknowledge the stratospheric standard she has set."* with 7.8/10, missing the Best New Music mark she was almost guaranteed in the past. The A.V. Club had a hard time, complaining, *"For someone who has historically bared it all in her work, it's frustrating to hear Mitski craft songs with such surface-level musicality,"* with a B- score. The worst review came from Slant Magazine, who said, *"Mitski's adoption of the decade's tropes comes across as muddled and at times mismatched to her songwriting,"* with three stars out of five.

I'm sorry, but grant me this rare moment to get personal: I call bullshit. I revisit *Laurel Hell* more than most of her albums, and while I note some tiny dips in consistency, I consider many of these songs the most enjoyable from her career. And, besides, an 83% aggregate Metacritic score, while her lowest, is no joke. It's a testament to her craft that even when she "misses the mark" she still does so with utter Universal Acclaim.

The End of Year lists did not ignore the album either, featured in the Top 25 for Slant Magazine (25), The Ringer (25), Northern Transmission (24), NME (21), Under the Radar (11), Gigwise (10), and The Forty-Five (4).

SINGLES

• Working for the Knife

"It's about going from being a kid with a dream, to a grownup with a job, and feeling that somewhere along the way you got left behind. It's being confronted with a world that doesn't seem to recognise your humanity, and seeing no way out of it." [154]

- MITSKI

What was the best way for Mitski to return to the industry she grappled with? To address the situation head-on. In every way, "Working for the Knife" cut through the crap and splayed her position out to dry like only Mitski would know how.

"'Working for the Knife' was the one song that I wrote almost immediately after my last show in 2019. I was like, 'I have time now, I'm going to sit at a guitar and just work through this.'" [60]

- MITSKI

Mitski told Rolling Stone that "Working for the Knife" became *"the beacon of the record"* and *"the compass"* she used if her writing veered off track.

"I would like for 'The Knife' and 'Working for the Knife' to be whatever the listener needs it to be. For me, I think a knife was a good metaphor because it's something that's sharp and that hurts you and it's also cold and it doesn't care about you. It's hard. It was important that it was an object without feeling or empathy. The idea of the song can apply to any working adult. The song is basically about when you're a kid, you have dreams, and then you grow up, and you enter the working world, and you have to make compromises,

and you might not like the way your life is, you might not like the things you have to do, but you're an adult and you have to work. I mean, sure, there are things specific to my work that are hard for me, but I think if it wasn't this job, it would be another job, you know? I don't know how to negotiate trying to stay an artist, but also being a working person. I always thought, like, 'I'm just going to have to struggle.' And then I got there and it's like, 'Oh, no, now what?'" [19]

- MITSKI

"There are different shades of that feeling that we're all unable to escape throughout the album. I had this feeling that we're being exploited and there's nothing that we can do about it. To be really real and cynical with you, now I've been discovered as a real source of money for people, I feel kind of trapped. Sometimes I feel—how do I put this?—like institutions have discovered that they can make money through me, and they're not going to let me get in the way of making money from it." [50]

- MITSKI

"I don't think I ever write autobiographically in the confessional sense. What I do is I feel a feeling, and then what I want to express is that feeling. So, the lines are 'I always thought the choice was mine, and I was right but I just chose wrong.' It means a lot of things to me, but to say it simply, it's that you've grown up. You've lived your life or you've lived your childhood. It's over. Time has passed and you can't take back the choices you made. And now you have to live with them. I also think when you're younger you make all these choices that you don't even realise shape the rest of your life forever and you can't do anything about it." [69]

- MITSKI

The song splattered everyone, from NPR (*"[only Mitski could] transform a song about feeling hollow and adrift... into something transfixing and staggeringly alive"*) to Clash (*"a work of supreme confidence"*) to MTV News (*"[Mitski's] power is on full display"*) to Stereogum (*"gives [Mitski's anxiety] cinematic grandeur"*). Pitchfork later called it the 7th Best Song of 2021.

"Three words to describe 'Working for the Knife' would be: 'late capitalist', 'blade runner', 'resignation'" [60]

- MITSKI

That's five words, Mitski.

So, was there a video? Hell yes, there was a video! Directed by our longtime pal, Zia Anger, it was released the same day as the single, on October 5th, 2021.

"An artist returns to the cruel stage that gave birth to her [...] It's all about how hard it is to be travelling somewhere in one's career, and then you get there–or maybe you don't get there–and it's never what you wanted it to be. Mitski speaks from this really specific point of view and it allows this access that is not too universal. You still feel like you're part of a secret club, but there is this universality to it." [60]

- ZIA ANGER

After a dramatic build-up, we watch Mitski walking around, bursting into small theatrical moves before ending on the stage, dancing energetically to musicless applause. From some perspectives, it resembles an extension of her live performances. From another perspective, it looks like a cry for help.

Again, the media cheered, calling it *"forceful"* (Pitchfork), *"emotional"* (the Fader), *"disconcerting"* (Slate), *"startling and magnetic"* (NPR), and *"gritty"* (Hot Press).

I have to note that in this video, Mitski takes her shoes off and, like, never puts them back on again. Indeed, in all her following videos, you are more likely to see Mitski barefoot than wearing in any footwear.

• The Only Heartbreaker

"When there's a sad message under a veneer of danciness and happiness, you almost trick people into going on that journey with you. Like: 'Oops, too late! You're sucked in!' Have you heard 'Gimme Gimme Gimme' [by ABBA]? There's a desperation to those lyrics, but you don't notice until you really listen." [50]

- MITSKI

The second *Laurel Hell* single, "The Only Heartbreaker", was released on November 9th, 2021.

"Three words that pop into mind when I think about 'The Only Heartbreaker,' are: 'the bad guy', 'relationships', 'dance beat.'" [69]

- MITSKI

"The person always messing up in the relationship, the designated Bad Guy who gets the blame. It could simply be about that, but I also wanted to depict something sadder beneath the surface, that maybe the reason you're always the one making mistakes is because you're the only one trying." [155]

- MITSKI

"I wanted to induce this realisation that maybe you are the one making mistakes all the time because you're the only person fully in the relationship. The other person isn't making mistakes because they're not in it with you. So you're just sort of shadowboxing in this relationship alone." [117]

- MITSKI

"The first layer I wanted to express in the dynamic of this relationship that's being sung about is that you, or the protagonist, always ends up making mistakes in the relationship somehow. You're just always the bad guy. Always the one hurting the other person and the other person is always forgiving you. And you just feel ashamed and bad about yourself. But also I wanted to express another layer where you stop and think about how maybe you're the only one continuing to mess up because you're the only one trying. You're the only one revealing yourself to the other person. And when you reveal yourself, you always reveal yourself to be ugly. So I wanted to get closer to expressing the fact that people are usually never good or bad. You're usually in between. For my own sake, I wanted to express that I am not a dichotomy. I am complex. I am bad and good and neither. And I just needed that for myself. So I wrote what I needed." [69]

- MITSKI

Here's something uniquely interesting about "Heartbreaker": it marks the first time ever that Mitski's writing credit is shared with someone else. It was against Mitski's nature, but after the song went through 20 revisions and was almost discarded, she swallowed her pride and reached out for assistance.

"I needed that Breakfast Club dance-sequence music. [Collaboration] was a real struggle. I'd held on so long to my music being mine." [1]

- MITSKI

Dan Wilson of Semisonic helped pen this piece. He had the CV for the job proven by his band's hit "Closing Time", as well as co-writing collaborations with Adele ("Someone Like You"), and producing credits with Taylor Swift ("Treacherous"). He's also worked with Pink, Celine Dion, Halsey, Weezer, Panic! at the Disco, My Morning Jacket, John Legend, and Laufey.

"The song was sitting in my head for too long and rotting. I was, like, 'This is a person who has much more experience than me. Maybe I could punt this to him.' And I'm glad I did, because he did come through and lead me to conclusions that I wouldn't have arrived at otherwise." [1]

- MITSKI

"This is the first song in my entire discography of... however many albums I've made... where I have a co-writer, and it's because this song was this puzzle that I couldn't solve. And I was just sitting on it forever. I have so many iterations of it. Nothing felt right. And right when I was stewing over it, I was actually in LA, doing co-write sessions for other artists. And we had this one day, or I had this one day with Dan Wilson. I had every intention to write for somebody else, but then I just sat down at his piano, and I was like, he's one of the best, smartest songwriters in the world. Maybe he can help me with this song. And so I brought the song to him, and it turned out he's really good. He helped me solve so many of the problems and kind of lead me out of the labyrinth of it. And yeah, I'm really glad that I took that chance with him." [156]

- MITSKI

Something certainly worked because the single became Mitski's first #1 on the US AAA charts, with another hit at #4 in Iceland. The track was also included on Barack Obama's revered list of top listens of 2021.

Good songs make good singles make good videos. Maegan Houang (remember her from "Happy"?) directed it with Jeff Desom. Here, Mitski sets fire to a forest via her touch alone, dancing through her passionate anxiety as the world burns around her and then literally blows up. Talk about escalating quickly. It was filmed entirely in front of a green screen.

• Heat Lightning

"Three words to describe the song 'Heat Lightning' are: 'heat lightning', 'insomnia', 'giving up'. But in a good way!" [6 9]

- MITSKI

Third single? "Heat Lightning"! Date? December 7th, 2021. Video? No! What?? Whaaa!

"Initially, 'Heat Lightning,' the whole song basically sounded like the first half of it. But something didn't feel right. It just felt a bit boring. And then Patrick came up with the idea of having it depart into this whole new sound. We drew inspiration from Prince and sort of a little bit more of an R&B feel to it." [69]

- MITSKI

• Love Me More

"Three words that I think describe 'Love Me More' are: 'The Exorcist', 'urgency', 'running'." [69]

- MITSKI

Here comes the fourth and final single from *Laurel Hell*: "Love Me More", released on January 12th, 2022.

"As 'Love Me More' was written pre-pandemic, lyrics like 'If I keep myself at home' had different meanings than what they would now, but I kept them on the album because I found that some of the sentiments not only remained the same, but were accentuated by the lockdown. [The song] went through the most iterations out of all the

songs on the album. It's been too fast, too slow, and at some point, it was even an old style country song. Finally, I think because we had watched The Exorcist, we thought of Mike Oldfield's 'Tubular Bells' and experimented with floating an ostinato over the chorus. As we steadily evolved the ostinato to fit over the chord progressions, we began to hear how the track was meant to sound." [157]

- MITSKI

There's a music video directed by Christopher Good. As the same mind behind that wild "Nobody" video, it's not surprising that this is another one of Mitski's surrealistic pieces that are better watched than described. But highlights include a creepy Mitski doll, an injured Mitski covered in casts, and Mitski trying to unlock a door with piano keys.

For those who can't get enough of the song, you're in luck! The Rough Trade version of *Laurel Hell* has a demo for this song as a bonus track, and there is also a remix of the tune by Clark out there.

"Artists generally, unless they're geniuses, we tend to kind of go back to the same three to five themes throughout our life. So, for 'Love Me More', I guess it's a repetition of that same theme. It's almost like somebody else loving you really hard is a really convenient distraction from yourself. And maybe that's one of my themes. Where I'm always trying to find fulfillment via other people's love. Can't be healthy, but it is what it is." [69]

- MITSKI

OTHER NOTEWORTHY SONGS

What a time to be alive, Mitski was asked by Pitchfork to explain every song on *Laurel Hell* using "three words" each, giving us more quotes than we can handle.

• Valentine, Texas

"Three words I would use to describe 'Valentine, Texas': 'dust devils', 'clouds', 'desert motel.'" [69]

- MITSKI

Valentine is a real town in Texas, named because it was founded on Valentine's Day in 1882.

"A long time ago somewhere in a vast expanse of America, I was in a motel room. I had closed up the curtains, made it really dark mood for myself, and just wrote the first and then the second verse. I wrote basically in the car ride over to a show in Marfa, Texas, because on the way to Marfa there's a town called Valentine and it's just desert. It's, like, the most deserted desert you've ever seen. I saw my first dust devils and the clouds and everything was just so beautiful. And that's where the second verse comes from." [69]

- MITSKI

Both the Japanese edition and the Rough Trade edition of *Laurel Hell* features a demo version of this song.

• Stay Soft

"Three words that describe the song 'Stay Soft' are: 'sex', 'trauma', 'disco'." [158]

- MITSKI

"'Stay Soft' was a more straightforward rock song when I wrote it on guitar, but the darkly sexual lyrics sung in that context felt too heavy and melodramatic. So we couched the depressing lyrics in an inviting dance beat, which is a trick people have used for hundreds of years. The remnants of the original grungy feeling can be heard starting at the instrumental interlude, when the distorted guitar comes in." [159]

- MITSKI

"I can't put myself into a sad song that's outwardly sad. I find it's easier to allow a song in when the message might be depressing or dark, but has a veneer of happiness. Otherwise, it's off-putting. It starts to feel like whining." [60]

- MITSKI

"This song, frankly, is about hurt people finding each other, and using sex to make sense of their pain. This is by no means the correct way to cope with trauma, but it's a thing people do regardless, and I always want to write songs about what we actually do, so that we don't feel alone in them." [159]

- MITSKI

"Stay Soft" may not be a single, but it sure was a video. Another Maegan Houang directed-masterpiece, it popped out on February 4th, 2022. Watch it and you'll see Mitski tending to her garden by feeding blood to her Venus flytrap before being attacked by weird masked people. After a dance sequence, she murders them all for more flytrap food. Simple stuff.

"This video is heavily inspired by Romanticism and paintings and artwork from the Victorian era. Like the lyrics of the song 'Stay Soft,' paintings from that era have a gentle quality, but they still evoke a certain feeling of unexplored darkness and danger. I want the audience to feel safe within this fabricated world and then realise that the character Mitski plays is being hunted. The violence lurking beneath the surface emerges, and yet is still transformed into something beautiful via dance. Through the dance sequence, Mitski's character is able to conquer the violence, but not without irreparable harm to her psyche." [60]

- MAEGAN HOUNG

The Rough Trade edition of *Laurel Hell* has an acoustic version of this song. And perhaps I don't need to state the obvious, but I will anyway: this song provided the lyrics after which this biography was titled.

• Everyone

"Three words to describe 'Everyone' are: 'minimal', 'solitary', 'Beak'. Beak is actually an electronic group from the UK and they were a big reference for this song. I drew inspiration from how a lot of their production is very minimal but it still feels significant and emotional." [69]

- MITSKI

"I wrote this song when I didn't have an instrument around, so it was just me singing to myself. So I wrote the words and the vocal melody, [and] I think I got too used to not having any accompaniment because

when I tried to add chords to it or I tried to add accompaniment to it, nothing was satisfying. So I finally decided I should allow it to be this minimal thing with just a simple beat and a few notes on a synthesiser and call it a day." [69]

- MITSKI

"It's basically my one shot at truly connecting with the listener and expressing myself to this person who hopefully will connect. I'm trying to give everything I have so that I can get my feeling to that person." [69]

- MITSKI

• There's Nothing Left for You

"The three words I would use to describe the song 'There's Nothing Left For You' are: 'big waves crashing'. I just used the narrative of somebody who had spent most of their life pursuing one singular goal. And I envisioned a person who could no longer pursue this one thing that they had spent their entire life pursuing, and realise they have nothing else. I wrote this song basically as I finished my last show. So that was the end of something that I had been working towards feverishly and I guess I was reflecting on that." [69]

- MITSKI

Quick lol: this song's title was initially released on digital platforms as "There's Nothing Left **Here** for You." No idea how this happened, but it was certainly an accident on someone's part as it's since been corrected.

• Should've Been Me

"Three words to describe the song 'Should've Been Me' are: '80s', 'compassion', 'nuance'." [6 9]

- MITSKI

"It's about your partner cheating. But because you love this person and you know yourself, you understand their perspective. You understand your part in it. And, through somebody straying and betraying you, weirdly understanding that they loved you so much. You just weren't there for them—they needed something and you couldn't give it to them, so they tried to find it elsewhere. I wanted to portray a narrative of compassion, even after being lied to." [93]

- MITSKI

"I wanted to write a song about cheating that came from understanding and compassion and empathy. The thing is, when you're in a relationship, you get to know a person. And you love a person fully for who they are and you understand all of their flaws and their good side and their bad side. In a real relationship, a person doesn't just become a villain because they did something wrong. The more I need forgiveness, the more open I become to forgiving. I just needed a lot of forgiveness and acceptance of myself and that made me open to writing about forgiving other people. I needed to lighten the load and not have so much anger and shame and sadness and I think forgiveness is the way to go for that." [69]

- MITSKI

"The imagery I was thinking of in terms of the lyrics for the second verse [...] I was thinking of, like, a minotaur in a maze [...] I would often go somewhere else in my mind. I would be doing dishes and then suddenly I would look up and realise 20 minutes have passed because I've just gone somewhere else in my mind. How could I be anywhere and then some invisible hand can just pick me out of where I am and put me in a mental maze and then I'm just trapped in that maze for however long until I can get myself out of it. And then I can go back to doing the dishes." [152]

- MITSKI

"I think this is the first song where [Patrick] gave me songwriting criticism which I hate [...] 'This verse melody is too busy!' I clutched my pearls first. But then, I was like, 'You know what? You're right.' And I took it back to my room and was, like, let me rework this." [152]

- MITSKI

Patrick also confessed that Phil Collins' "You Can't Hurry Love" was a huge inspo for the song.

"If you bring a sad song in a sad song tone, people usually don't want to hear it. Whereas, if you hide a sad feeling or a negative feeling in a really upbeat song, then you get to trick people into listening. And then by the time they realise it's a sad song, you've got them." [152]

- MITSKI

Side props to Elizabeth Chan, the drummer on this song, who laid her tracks down for "Should've Been Me" in one take.

"One and done!" [152]

- MITSKI

• **I Guess**

"Three words that describe the song 'I Guess': 'quiet', 'still', 'piano'." [69]

- MITSKI

"This song is the oldest song on the album. I don't even remember when I wrote [it]. I guess that's how old it was. It just sat in my notebook for a really long time. I wrote [one] part alone randomly on the keyboard. I heard that melody, and I quickly recorded it and then went about my day. That was years ago, but I found that that melody kept coming back to me. I realised I should give that melody a home somewhere." [69]

- MITSKI

"Sometimes you've been with an idea or a goal or a person so long that it's a deep part of you and without them it's like you have to figure out a whole new person to be. When someone or something has made you who you are, even if it's the end, there's a gratefulness for how you came to where you are together. You wouldn't be who you are without them. There's a real beauty and peace to that." [69]

- MITSKI

• That's Our Lamp

*"Three words that describe the song, 'That's Our Lamp': 'carnival',
'happy', 'goodbye'."* [69]

- MITSKI

*"What I wanted to express was walking down the street with
something ending inside of you in your life. But no one around knows
and life is going on as it always had around you. I wanted this feeling
of liveliness and a lot of people being around. At first we tried to just
make the sounds louder, [but] nothing felt right. And then I realised,
'Oh, if I want to feel like people are all around me, I should just put
crowd sounds in.' We also mixed in our own room sounds and talking
sounds and we also sang parts over and over together, so it sounded
like a chorus. That really did the trick."* [69]

- MITSKI

*"I've tended to end my albums on a quiet note. With everything that's
going on and with the tone of the album, Patrick and I both felt it
best if we ended with a carnival and a party."* [69]

- MITSKI

• Bonus Track: Glide (Lily Chou-Chou)

We've already mentioned the bonus tracks from both the Rough Trade and
Japanese edition of *Laurel Hell* except for one: "Glide". It's a cover! The song
was originally performed by Lily Chou-Chou, a fictional musician invented
for the Japanese experimental coming-of-age film *All About Lily Chou-Chou*
by Shunji Iwai. That same song was later found on their debut album *Kokyū*
(which means "Breath"). Mitski recorded her own version of the song which
was first heard in the 2021 film *After Yang* by Kogonada. And now it's here too!

The four bonus tracks were compiled separately under the curiously familiar name *Stay Soft, Get Eaten: Laurel Hell Demos*, and released through Rough Trade as limited edition coloured vinyls (white and opaque bone). There are only 750 copies in existence. For neatness, here are those songs again, in order:

1. Valentine, Texas (demo version)
2. Love Me More (demo version)
3. Stay Soft (acoustic version)
4. Glide (Lily Chou-Chou)

6.2.
HIRED GUN, PART 4

Mitski has been involved with some big-name songs, but one could argue there were none as monumental as "This Is a Life". Written and performed with Son Lux and David Byrne (from Talking Heads), it was the first single from the *Everything Everywhere All at Once* soundtrack. The 2022 film smashed the Oscars to pieces, winning seven of its eleven nominations, including Best Picture. Sadly, it did not win for Best Original Song, beaten by Naatu Naatu for the film *RRR*. Nevertheless, you can add "Oscar Nominated" to Mitski's list of achievements while you're keeping score.

"Yeah, it still doesn't feel real. Also, it kind of felt like cheating a little bit, because this was just this amazing film. Like, it's one of my favourite films, it would be even if I wasn't a small part of it. But I wasn't part of the film making. I wasn't part of anything that made the film great. And then, of course, Son Lux and David Byrne... Son Lux did the majority of the writing of the song. I contributed just a little tiny bit. So it felt, like, just sheer improbable luck that I got a quote-unquote 'Oscar Nomination'. It doesn't really feel like my Oscar

nomination. I feel like I'm piggybacking on everyone else's great work. And I'm really grateful to be a tiny part of it, but, again, I'm just kind of, like, 'Well, this is nice, but I don't know if I can claim this.'" [30]

- MITSKI

Coming out on February 25th, 2022, Mitski lent her background vocals to two songs on Sasami's second album, *Squeeze*. As the title suggests, you may have to squeeze your eardrums to hear any Mitski. I almost didn't believe she contributed if it weren't for her name on the credits. The two have toured together, too, so it checks out.

Finally, on June 24th, 2022, Mitski's co-writing skills were added to Muna's self-titled third studio album on the song "No Idea".

"I just want to say, first of all, I'm always inspired by Mitski, because Mitski's one of my favourite living songwriters, and I just learned so much about myself from listening to Mitski. But we did talk about disco when she came over. It was January of 2020 [...] we knew that she was listening to a lot of disco. Josette and her bonded over ABBA. It was kind of funny that we ended up working on that song together, but she was definitely encouraging of us going down that route with that song and making it really dancey and some combination of Daft Punk, Zapp & Roger, and the Backstreet Boys." [1 61]

- KATIE GAVIN (MUNA)

6.3.
LAUREL HELL TOUR

"My whole life has been about adapting to new environments. I don't know any different, so I don't know if touring would have been harder or easier if I had a home base. Because I don't know what that feels like. [But] touring is great for me. I feel like I'm in my element when I'm on tour, when I'm like heading towards something. On tour there's such a sense of purpose, where you go somewhere, and you do your job, and then you go another place, and you do your job. I feel like I'm so in my element when I'm on tour." [15]

- MITSKI

The *Laurel Hell Tour* ran from February 17th to November 18th, 2022, although Mitski did continue onward to Primavera Sound on November 20th. Other festival appearances took place at the 2022 Glastonbury Festival, the 2022 Lollapalooza in Stockholm, and the 2022 Pitchfork Music Festival in Chicago. She also performed "Stay Soft" on *Jimmy Kimmel Live!* as part of this promo run.

If you were lucky, you may have caught her in the USA, Canada, UK,

Ireland, Belgium, France, Netherlands, Switzerland, Germany, Denmark, Sweden, Norway, Austria, Czech Republic, Turkey, Brazil, Argentina, Chile, Peru, or Mexico. Supporting artists included Cassandra Jenkins, Chai, Hurray for the Riff Raff, Indigo De Souza, Michelle, Sasami, Sorcha Richardson, Stella Donnelly, and The Weather Station.

Like the rest of the world, the tour was plagued with positive COVID tests. Shows in Washington, D.C., Philadelphia, and Boston had to be postponed.

"The stakes are so high. If anyone on the crew tests positive, whether we feel sick or not, we're gonna have to cancel the show. And the reality is, if any show gets cancelled, I'll be paying. Which, you know, has helped me reassess my priorities because I would pay to play. I still love to play. But it is a bit of a bummer." [117]

- MITSKI

COVID aside, things were looking good again in Mitski's orbit, especially when, in some glorious full circle moment from her One Direction love, Mitski opened for Harry Styles during this period. This was on his *Love On Tour*, specifically the shows in Scotland and England from 11th to 19th of June 2022.

6.4.
THE PHONE INCIDENT

Hey, remember Mitski's fans? Remember how we said some of them were toxic? Well, they be toxic-ing!

In February 2022, Mitski made a small announcement expressing her feelings about the use of phones at her shows. It read something like this:

"Hello! I wanted to speak with you about phones at shows. They're part of our reality, I have mine on me all the time, and I'm not against taking photos at shows (Though please no flash lol). But sometimes when I see people filming entire songs or whole sets, it makes me feel as though we are not here together. This goes for both when I'm on stage, and when I'm an audience member at shows. I love shows for the feeling of connection, of sharing a dream, and remembering that we have a brief miraculous moment of being alive at the same time, before we part ways. I feel I'm part of something bigger. When I'm on stage and look to you but you are gazing into a screen, it makes me feel as though those of us on stage are being

taken from and consumed as content, instead of getting to share a moment with you. Thank you for reading my woo-woo thoughts about shows lol—I just love and believe in them so much, and I want to share them fully with you! Thanks." [162]

- MITSKI

Mitski's cult responded how you'd imagine: with backlash that went from zero to a million within minutes. Certain fans claimed their ADHD, depression, and dissociation meant that phone-recording the shows were the only way they could enjoy it later. The other side then fired up in defence, stating it was Mitski's right as a performer to request privacy. These two opposing forces ripped at one another's throats until the original Tweet was quickly deleted.

"It was naive of me to post that, frankly. I've been away from social media so long, I forgot that on Twitter, our words are regularly misconstrued and used by whoever has an argument to make. People picked and chose parts of sentences that helped further their own arguments. Some ignored every word, and simply used me to start different arguments altogether. Somehow, my statement led to online fights about race, gender, sexuality, generational rifts—you name it!" [50]

- MITSKI

"This underlying fact will always be true, as I am indeed providing a service in exchange for income. But it does feel sad to be told directly by people I'm hoping to share my heart with, that to them I'm a product they have bought for the night, and they will do what they want with me while they have me. It is sad to go on stage and now be conscious of the fact that, to some of the people in front of me, I am a dancing monkey, and I better start dancing quick so they can get the content they're paying for." [50]

- MITSKI

6.5.
MITSKI FASHION

Rather than end this chapter on that slightly tangy note, let's lighten the mood by discussing outfits! If you've watched Mitski grow, you will note how her presentation has evolved from not caring to nailing a plethora of classy looks.

"It's very complicated for me, because I spent all my teenage years being obsessed with beauty. I'm very resentful about it. I'm very angry, where I had so much intelligence and energy and drive and instead of using that to study more, instead of pursuing something, instead of going out and learning about the world, changing the world, I directed all that fire inward and burnt myself up. I tried to make myself beautiful and perfect, and so I'm not exaggerating when I say: when I was a teenager, every second of my waking hour and even my dreams were focused on, or were somehow about being as perfect and beautiful as possible. So when I came to New York, it wore me out. I was tired and I did a 180 and decided, 'You know what? I'm gonna ditch all of this. I'm not gonna do anything that is

femme.' And if you see early footage of me, you can see where I'm very butch, because I didn't want to have anything to do with beauty. Because it ruined my life. And it ruined my sense of self. And it ruined me. And I wasted my youth on it. But slowly, little by little, I'm realising that now that I've found a balance. I enjoy all the rituals. I enjoy the classical ideas of femininity. And maybe it's something that's been ingrained in me. I'm still researching it in my mind. But I'm realising I don't have to be one or the other. I can investigate what I like and I can think about whether it's problematic. I can think about how it's healthy or how it's not. I'm still searching. I don't know the answer but, in the meantime, I'm letting go of that other extreme of not doing anything to kind of make myself look nice. Because I'm realising I enjoy these silver slippers." [11]

- MITSKI

Sounds good! But does Mitski have any fashion tips she'd like to share with us?

"I have a few, actually. Number one: I don't wear shoes that I can't run away in. And number two: I always want to be clean and neat, even if what I'm wearing is very simple and not expensive. [...] I always wear gold. I love gold. It just goes really well with my skin tone. I'm not interested in the whole ragged-clothes thing or just wearing whatever and looking dirty and not showering. Most people who dress like that come from privilege. They can dress like that and still have their privilege. They can move through the world comfortably like that. People who don't come from that privilege, if we dress that way, we just won't be considered real people. I have crust-punk friends, when I meet them and think, you know, the fact that you can *dress that way, means that if at any point shit gets real, you can go home to mom and dad."* [74]

- MITSKI

"It's so important to have a comfortable shoe. Because going through your day in an uncomfortable shoe just ruins your day. It's so important to have a durable, well-made shoe that's comfortable to walk around in. It truly makes or breaks your day. When I say shoes, I'm not talking about Sex in the City stilettos." [25]

- MITSKI

She's also had her say on the "man bun" hairstyle.

"The hairstyle itself is fine, but the term 'man bun' is overrated. It's a bun. Like, I could put on a man bun right now. There are so many things going on in the world. Does it really matter whether a man is wearing a bun or not?" [40]

- MITSKI

And with that, the *Laurel Hell* era closes. It may seem like there was less information in this chapter, but that's not because Mitski wasn't busy. Quite the opposite. For, with the end of 2022, came 2023. And with 2023, came a whole new album, ready to serve. And, while no Mitski album could be called ordinary, this wasn't any ordinary Mitski album...

Part Seven

THE LAND IS INHOSPITABLE AND SO ARE WE ERA

7.1.
ALBUM: THE LAND IS INHOSPITABLE AND SO ARE WE (2023)

1. Bug Like an Angel (3:32)
(first single)
2. Buffalo Replaced (2:40)
3. Heaven (3:44)
(joint second single with "Star")
4. I Don't Like My Mind (2:25)
5. The Deal (3:52)
6. When Memories Snow (1:44)
7. My Love Mine All Mine (2:17)
(third single)
8. The Frost (2:48)
9. Star (2:59)
(joint second single with "Heaven")
10. I'm Your Man (3:29)
11. I Love Me After You (2:48)

TOTAL RUNTIME: 32:21

"In terms of whether the [pandemic] isolation helped with the creative process, I'm not sure. I think I was more actively isolated during the creation process of Laurel Hell, my previous album. I feel like I went through the isolation and the hard stuff in Laurel Hell and after that I was, like, 'Okay, now I can move on and do maybe what I want or do.' Something different. So I did make some of this album during the pandemic, but that was more Laurel Hell, and now this is my sprouting out of Laurel Hell album." [30]

- MITSKI

Mitski's 7th studio album, *The Land Is Inhospitable and So Are We*, came down from the heavens on September 15th, 2023. It was recorded in the studios Bomb Shelter (Nashville) and Sunset Sound (Los Angeles). Sunset Sound is particularly notable, as those studios have recorded over 200 Gold records within their walls. Some of these include Prince's *Purple Rain*, the Rolling Stones' *Exile on Main St.*, Neil Young's *After the Gold Rush*, the Beach Boys' *Pet Sounds*, Janis Joplin's *Pearl*, and the first two Doors albums.

A list of facts that won't surprise you about *The Land* include that all songs were written by Mitski, the album was produced by Patrick Hyland, and it was released on Dead Oceans. However, the list of credits rolled on to quite a length, so we'll detail those in a subsection later on.

"The best thing I ever did in my life was to love people. I wish I could leave behind all the love I have, after I die, so that I can shine all this goodness, all this good love that I've created onto other people." [163]

- MITSKI

The promotion for this record was a little different than usual. The announcement came on July 18th, 2023, via a voice memo recorded at Bomb Shelter Studio, sent to her newsletter subscribers as a link to an unlisted YouTube video. The full quote is here:

"Hi, this is Mitski, and I'm at Bomb Shelter Studios in Nashville where we recorded my new album that's coming out. It's called The Land is Inhospitable and So Are We, and its first single is coming out on Wednesday." [164]

- MITSKI

Six days later, on July 24th, Mitski's website changed into an orange teacup that was broken in eleven pieces, which fans later agreed was (most likely) to represent the eleven songs on the album. The next day, on the 25th, the same audio from before was released with video footage of Mitski saying those words while sitting at her piano. Then, the day after that, Wednesday 26th, as promised, the first single landed. It was "Bug Like An Angel". Another day later, and we had the video, which we'll elaborate on soon. Whew!

Mitski went even further for the album release. Pre-release listening parties took place in locations across the world (Chicago, Dallas, London, Los Angeles, Melbourne, Nashville, Sydney, New York, and Tokyo), and were each followed by a film of Mitski's choice (either Terrence Malick's *Days of Heaven*, Donna Deitch's *Desert Hearts*, Gus Van Sant's *Drugstore Cowboy*, or Federico Fellini's *La Strada*). The US events were presented in association with Spotify.

Some lucky fans got limited-edition posters. The Japanese event was different, as it took place in Tokyo's planetarium, so fans watched a projection of the night sky as they listened to the album. Sounds so lovely!

TITLE

"Very long album title. I pulled a Fiona Apple." [165]

- MITSKI

According to NPR, this was yet another title that came as a joke. Mitski imagined crossing state lines, but instead of reading slogans like *"The Land of 10,000 Lakes"* or *"The Constitution State"*, she envisioned the sign saying, *"The Land Is Inhospitable And So Are We"*.

"Love is always radical, which means that it always disrupts, which means that it always takes work to receive it. This land, which already feels inhospitable to so many of its inhabitants, is about to feel hopelessly torn and tossed again—at times, devoid of love. This album offers the anodyne." [166]

- MITSKI

"It's feeling really inhospitable in the United States right now." [121]

- MITSKI

"The greatest challenge right now is to keep fighting. It can become very hopeless when you try to make changes, and every day there's a new dystopian thing that's happening. There's so many mass shootings, just everything. Every aspect of America is falling apart right now. So the greatest challenge right now is honestly just holding on." [71]

- MITSKI

SOUND

"The Land, I think, like, half of it is just a collection of songs we had but didn't fit on Laurel Hell. A general influence for [Laurel], but maybe particularly for this one, is Patsy Cline. That era of country music where it's just like crooning and beautiful." [118]

- MITSKI

Almost sounding reactionary to the upbeat dance vibes of *Laurel Hell*, this record was far more stripped-down and darker. It has been called Americana, country, alt-Country, folk, indie folk, orchestral pop, and chamber pop. According to Hyland and Mitski, they found influence in spaghetti Western soundtracks, Arthur Russell, Igor Stravinsky, Scott Walker, Caetano Veloso, Faron Young, and Terry Riley.

"When someone says, 'I love this about you,' I make a mental note: I'm never gonna do that again. Maybe that's a psychological problem I have to deal with." [17]

- MITSKI

CREDITS

"Patrick and I knew that we really wanted to draw from Americana, from classic country, from folk and old-time music. And we knew that we needed a band that was versed in those genres, much more than, at least, I was. And since I live in Nashville, we were able to do that successfully. We got Brooke Waggoner on piano, who also did piano on Laurel Hell. We got Ross McReynolds on drums. We got Dominic Davis on bass. And then we got Fats Kaplin on fiddle, viola, mandolin,

pedal steel... I mean, Fats is a real Renaissance Man. Patrick did guitar because he usually does guitars on our albums together. So we got them. Patrick and I also knew we wanted it to be live. We wanted that live acoustic feeling to it so we rehearsed the band and I rehearsed for I think half a day and then the next day we recorded all the songs we would do together and it was just... perfect." [167]

- MITSKI

There are a lot of people smothered across this album, with some big names and some familiar ones.

Brooke Waggoner played piano and organ. He was also featured on *Laurel Hell*.

Fats Kaplin played pedal steel guitar, violin, mandolin, and viola. He is known for his work with Jack White and Beck.

Wayne Bergeron played trumpet because he has some deep skills in that regard. How deep? Disney/Pixar deep. You may have heard his work on *The Incredibles*, *Despicable Me*, *Frozen*, and *Toy Story*. He has also contributed to music for Christina Aguilera, Quincy Jones, Mars Volta, Seth MacFarlane, Meat Loaf, The Pussycat Dolls, Weird Al, and Neil Young. Oh, and the *Final Jeopardy* theme song? That was his cornet solo.

When considering the above and listening to the record, the orchestral layerings are an undeniable part of what makes this experience so special. These elements were largely constructed and arranged by Drew Erickson who has worked with Father John Misty, Angel Olsen, Weyes Blood, and Lana Del Rey. Speaking of Lana, his contributions to her 2023 album, *Did You Know That There's a Tunnel Under Ocean Blvd*, earned him two Grammy nominations, including Album of the Year.

"He's just a really great orchestrator. Anybody would be lucky to have him, but in our case, we were specifically looking for an almost Classic Hollywood Sound. Or a sweeping Disney soundtrack sound. Like, old school Disney. We also had some Ennio Morricone influence. We just felt like he is exactly the person who can do that, because he's provided sounds like that for other artists like Lana Del and Father

John Misty. I found out about him through Father John Misty. [His] most recent album features a lot of Drew's orchestration. And I was, like... 'Who did this?' And so I looked it up, and it was Drew." [30]

- MITSKI

Mitski got her Disney sound thanks to Drew's hired orchestral musicians who were literally on those Disney soundtracks.

"We managed to get them on our little record." [165]

- MITSKI

"It's amazing. We got some of the best players, and they were so... oh, God! I was just smiling ear to ear the entire day we were recording." [30]

- MITSKI

The album's 17-person choir was arranged by Mitski. There are some famous names there too, such as Erin Rae (folk pop singer), Caitlin Rose (country singer), Tristen Gaspadarek (pop singer), and Courtney Taylor-Taylor (lead singer for The Dandy Warhols).

Finally, Bob Weston mastered the record. He was the bassist in Shellac as well as Steve Albini's assistant engineer on Nirvana's *In Utero*.

ARTWORK

As we should be used to by now, Ebru Yildiz shot the cover photos and Mary Banas designed the art. The barely legible font choice is Ready Active by Plain Form (Lucas Descroix and Benjamin Dumond).

"I wanted to express the idea of 'unruly and free,' like the idea of the American Old West. Ready Active fit my vision, and I chose to further that notion by allowing it to break the border of the image *in the design. [I wanted to rebel against] clean sans serif fonts found on digital platforms."* [87]

- MARY BANAS

For official merchandise, they used the Tofino font by Alanna Munro so that you could actually read it.

THEMES

"My head was at very different places at various stages, because my last two albums, Be the Cowboy and Laurel Hell, were a lot about desolation and resignation and sort of giving up ideas I had held onto. The songs were very detached, a bit cynical, and really heartbroken. For The Land, I've kind of moved through that, and realised there is still love. There is still value. There's a lot of growth in this new album for me. I mean, maybe I'll find out more about the album in a few years. But for now, I think that's what it's about." [92]

- MITSKI

Like so much of Mitski's creative output, this record was used as a tool to better understand America and her place within the country, getting closer per every release.

"It's my most American album. Number one: aesthetically, because I drew so much from... not just American artists, but traditional American or what's considered to be traditional American Music, like country music. Americana. And folk. So there's that. But, also, I've lived in America long enough and I've identified as an American for long enough that I feel like all of my experiences that contributed to the writing of this [album] come from a uniquely American perspective

[...] There's no way to really pinpoint what is American and what isn't, but, for example, the freight trains through the American planes. I feel like that's so unique to America. Or just the landscape of America. So much of America you will never find anywhere else. It's such a big, diverse country." [30]

- MITSKI

"I'm always trying to figure out what it means to be American. But especially with this album, I'm trying to reconcile all my various identities with being American today. I feel like I've always been seeing my own identities through the eyes of other people who haven't lived my identities. And I kind of think maybe that's also very uniquely American. I'm Asian American. I'm half white, half Asian. And so I don't really fit into either community very well. I am an 'other' in America, even though I am American. And I almost feel like a majority of Americans are actually 'other', and that's kind of what makes America what it is." [121]

- MITSKI

"I've always wanted to be an American and I could never figure out exactly what made me American, how I could be more American. I really wanted to figure out this place that I was supposedly from, but I didn't really know how to connect to it. And a lot of the world outside of America connects to America through the movies that it's produced and the media and all these... almost American caricatures. And I think that's kind of my way into understanding this place that, again, I'm technically from but I will never fully understand." [30]

- MITSKI

"I don't think Americans realise how much the rest of the world is looking at America and wondering what it's going to do. The rest of the world kind of understands America through movies and music and media. So I kind of drew a lot from traditionally American Music, like country music, American folk music. And I also drew from Western films, like cowboy films and just ideas about America. I mean, while I'm trying to figure out what it means to be American, I'm almost approaching it as a foreigner and trying to understand it through its media and through outside perception of it. So that's what it means. Although probably in a few years I'll actually fully understand what this album means. But right now, that's as close as I can get." [22]

- MITSKI

CHARTS

Of course, *The Land Is Inhospitable and So Are We* sold well. Very well. How could it not? It hit the top 20 on just about every chart, including the Irish (20), Lithuanian (18), Dutch (18), Australian (13), US Billboard 200 (12), Portuguese (7), New Zealand (5), UK (4), Scottish Albums (2), UK Independent (2), US Independent (2), US Top Alternative (2), US Top Rock (2), and UK Americana (1).

CRITICAL

"This is the first record where I absolutely stopped caring what people think. Ironically, that's what people are the most attracted to." [168]

- MITSKI

Despite the long journey paved with gold we've taken, many have argued this as Mitski's finest half-hour. The album received full marks from The Telegraph (*"she stands alone in her lyricism and heart"*), The Independent (*"give it time and space at night, when you're alone, to allow its wild darkness to shine"*), The Guardian (*"in the best possible sense, Mitski feels out on her own"*), and The Skinny (*"a once-in-a-career masterpiece that synthesises difference through abstracted self-observation"*). Publications that gave it a 90+ score include Consequence of Sound, American Songwriter, musicOMH, Glide, Under the Radar, DIY Magazine, The Line Best Fit, Exclaim, and Slant. In fact, the only reputable review that fell below 80% was Sputnikmusic's 72, and who even are they? Nobody! Proven by Metacritic's final aggregate score at 90/100, not only Mitski's highest, but also the 8th highest out of every album from the entire year.

Speaking of the entire year, this record was naturally included on every list as one of 2023's best, including Entertainment Weekly (10), Consequence of Sound (9), NME (9), Dazed (9), Paste (8), Slant (7), Rolling Stone (7), Clash (6), The Guardian (5), Stereogum (4), Exclaim (2), and BrooklynVegan (1).

SINGLES

• Bug Like an Angel

As previously noted, the first single from *The Land Is Inhospitable and So Are We* was "Bug Like an Angel", fluttering out on July 26th, 2023.

"Most of the things you as a songwriter put in your songs, your listeners are not going to pick up on. That's just the name of the game. But also what's fun about writing songs is putting all these descriptors in there, these little Easter eggs, just for yourself and to kind of expand the world you're building if only just for yourself, even if no one else in the world gets what you're talking about. And I think that's the real fun about songwriting." [169]

- MITSKI

What's so cool about this song is that it's way smarter than anyone realises.

"'Bug Like An Angel' starts with these four chords in this order: D-flat major, A-flat major, E-flat major, B-flat major. And it's gonna stay in that sequence for basically the rest of the song, except for one time which we'll go over later. I wanted all the chords to just keep going in that progression because this song is about addiction and I wanted to show musically that addiction is basically a cycle. You're just stuck in this repetitive... it doesn't end, so that's the intention behind having the same chords over and over." [169]

- MITSKI

"So we have that chord progression twice, as an intro. Hopefully that leads the listener to think, 'Okay, I get it, the D-flat is the first chord, that's how it goes.' And then I wanted to do a little twist, a little change, a little surprise, by actually having the vocals come in the middle of what we think is the chord progression, at A-flat major instead [...] I wanted to do that because I wanted to give a feeling of being off balance because, again, this is a song about addiction and that's not exactly a balanced state. I wanted to figure out ways to express that state musically." [169]

- MITSKI

"It's useful to start songs with descriptions so that you can hopefully immediately paint a picture in your listener's head. For this, I wanted to paint a picture of someone drinking something out of a glass and there's a little bit left in the glass and [...] they realise there's a bug stuck at the bottom of their glass. And because it's stuck at the bottom and they're raising it, it looks like there's an angel in the sky." [169]

- MITSKI

In what may be the most dramatic moment in any Mitski's song is when the choir slides in to join her on the word *"family"*.

"My fans know that I love a jump scare. And I especially love a jump scare in the first track of an album, so I guess I'm doing that again. The choice of the choir, I mean. With music, the beautiful thing is sometimes you don't need to have a concise verbal explanation. Sometimes it's just a feeling [...] but if I were to try to explain it, the song without the choir is super simple. It's my vocal and then it starts with just acoustic guitar. Eventually there's some light keyboard and bass, but otherwise, there's not much else. And the song structure is also very simple. There's not really a chorus. So it's kind of a way to make the song a little bit more exciting than maybe it wouldn't be otherwise. And I just love choirs. I grew up in choirs. I'm looking for any excuse to put a choir in a song. And I wanted the choir to come in at really crucial words or lines that I wanted the listener to really hear. I think 'family' is a big multi-layered complex emotional word and I felt like it would make a big impact if an entire choir was singing it." [30]

- MITSKI

Another lyric you'd never find anyone else singing would be, *"Hey, what's the matter? Looking like your sticker is stuck on a floor somewhere".*

"I thought of that description because, you know, when you're a kid [...] I remember stickers were so important to me. And I had a notebook where I put stickers in it. I just looked at the stickers and they were just so precious to me. And I just thought of how sad a kid would be if their precious sticker was stuck on a floor somewhere and they couldn't get it off." [1 69]

- MITSKI

And, finally, there's the powerful conclusion of words: *"When I'm bent over, wishing it was over, making all variety of vows I'll never keep, I try to remember the wrath of the devil was also given him by God"*.

"I wanted the listener to have the option to take two main meanings away depending on what they want out of the song. I mean, of course you can take even more meanings from it. You might think of meanings I've never thought about, and that's beautiful. But for my intentions, it was one of two options: a positive or a negative. A pessimistic or optimistic option. The optimistic ending is that the protagonist is saying, 'Well, when I'm bent over and I'm at rock bottom, I try to remember that the wrath of the Devil I'm feeling right now, the suffering I'm feeling right now, was also given to the Devil by God. Because God created the Devil as well, so maybe all this suffering I'm feeling has some sort of meaning or some sort of thing I can learn from, something positive.' So that's option one. And then the pessimistic option is that, again, the protagonist is bent over and at rock bottom, and kind of making vows to God, like, 'I won't do this again, yada yada,' but then it occurs to the protagonist, 'Maybe the suffering was also given to me by God via the Devil, so maybe God intended this suffering for me and maybe there's no point in asking God for help because God wants me to suffer." [30]*

- MITSKI

If this endless depth blows your mind, you simply must watch Mitski breaking this entire song down on her video *"Mitski - Bug Like an Angel (Behind the Song)"* on YouTube. It's essential viewing for Mitski geeks!

"If you can't tell whether it's general information or it's deep, just think it's deep all the time." [11]

- MITSKI

The day after the song's release, the video appeared. It was directed by Noel Paul, who also has his name under clips for Slowdive, Danny Brown, Father John Misty, and Black Midi. The video features dance artist K.J. Holmes playing a drunk lady who stumbles around as a church choir in uniform sing their piece. Mitski plays guitar as one of them.

• Star

"I wrote 'Star' a long long time ago when we were out at [South by Southwest]. My friend Tyler was letting us stay at their house and I had an acoustic guitar and I was outside in the yard. I started writing this song. It was so long ago, I can't remember how I first started thinking about the song, but I started thinking about the fact that starlight that we see now is not necessarily light from stars that currently exist. 'Currently' is kind of like a weird word when we're talking about spacetime, but we're often seeing the light of dead stars." [118]

- MITSKI

"Star" is the first song from the "Star/Heaven" double-sided single, released together on August 23rd, 2023.

"This track is honestly all [Patrick's]. This is perhaps [Patrick's] masterpiece, I would say." [118]

- MITSKI

Well, let's hear from Patrick then.

"[We were] trying to basically cop the sound of Scott Walker and Angela Morley [...] and just all the amazing arrangements that they did together." [163]

- PATRICK HYLAND

"We took inspiration from Scott Walker, at the end of the day, and I'm so glad we did because I'm so proud of what it ended up being." [170]

- MITSKI

"I was trying to copy 'A Rainbow in Curved Air' by Terry Riley. Terry Riley was arguably the father of minimalism. Although, he probably doesn't like that term because nobody likes these things [but] 'A Rainbow in Curved Air' is probably one of the most ripped off pieces of music." [118]

- PATRICK HYLAND

"And then icing on the cake, my favourite part of this track, is the organ on top, which is inspired by composer Terry Riley, who is most famous in pop culture for inspiring the track 'Baba O'Riley' by The Who." [170]

- MITSKI

"[At the end], I'm just trying to have this sort of persisting chaotic ostinato that offsets how kind of restrained the track is up until that point." [118]

- MITSKI

"Very Moog. It's very Pink Floyd, isn't it? Sounds like all the drones on Wish You Were Here. The idea was that the bass synths are just one pitch until the last chorus... at that point, we're about 2 minutes into the song and it's just been one note... the idea was that you're thinking that bass won't change. Like, okay, this is it. If it was going to change, it would have happened by now..." [118]

- PATRICK HYLAND

"I love the point where it gets even louder. You think it can't possibly get louder." [118]

- MITSKI

Many months later, on April 23rd, 2024, a video appeared out of nowhere, with Mitski singing as she rowed a boat across the water. It's all very monochrome and reflective. Our good pal Maegan Houang was back in the director's chair.

• Heaven

"This song is about love. It's about how we should treasure this thing that we have. Maybe it's just within our own room. Outside of our room, maybe the world is terrible or hard to be in. But, for now, let's put the world aside and just treasure this precious love we have." [30]

- MITSKI

And here is the second of the "Star/Heaven" double-sided single, out on August 23rd, 2023.

"This is another old song." [165]

- MITSKI

"I remember when I first wrote it, it didn't have this country swing. But it does now. Just, like, a standard standard Mitski affair. And that just didn't feel right. It kind of sat for a while and then we demoed the swinged... the swung?... version." [118]

- MITSKI

This is one of the songs that got the big orchestral treatment from Drew Erikson.

"I remember we were trying to figure out the sound of the orchestra at the end. We were trying to decide whether to make it sound bigger like a big Hollywood film score or go the other route and just make it more chambery. And I remember thinking, 'Okay, instead of doing Los Angeles 60s wrecking crew type big smooth,' I wanted to do, like, Miss Bennett and Mr Darcy at the country ball."[118]

- MITSKI

"My notes for Drew [Erikson] on the end was... I kept talking about the last shot in [David Lynch's] Blue Velvet. I just can't say enough good things about all this beautiful work that Drew and the folks in the string section did. And the wind section. It's pretty close to what the original sounded like, just more competent."[118]

- PATRICK HYLAND

"I remember being at Sunset Sound and just being so happy that these real professionals were playing our music."[118]

- MITSKI

"I felt like it was one of your strongest songs. It was a bit weird that we just sort of put it away for a couple years."[118]

- PATRICK HYLAND

Sadly, there's no video for this one. However, another video worth checking out is *"Mitski breaks down her music"* from the BBC Music YouTube channel. The quotes for these songs are far more potent when you hear them in proper context.

• My Love Mine All Mine

"I was walking home with groceries and it was really heavy. I don't know if you've done this, but I had two bags in my elbows, and then I was holding my hands like this. And I tend to make up songs in my head when I really want to dissociate from the moment. I was, like, 'My love...' singing to myself. And I was, like, 'Wait a minute, this is actually good!' and then once I got home, I put the groceries down and I recorded everything and I got it." [168]

- MITSKI

The third single was "My Love Mine All Mine," released with a music video on September 15th, 2023, the same day as the album. Okay, deep breath, because while some of Mitski's songs were big, this one was a tsunami.

Peaking at 26, "My Love Mine All Mine" was Mitski's first US Billboard Hot 100 single. It charted hard, hitting the top 10 on the UK Singles (8), Ireland (8), Lithuania (8), Netherlands (6), UAE (6), New Zealand (5), Singapore (5), Philippines (4), US Hot Rock & Alternative Songs (4), Indonesia (2), Malaysia (2), and UK Indie (1).

Meanwhile, many publications placed it up high on their Best Song of 2023 lists, including Crack Magazine (14), NME (14), Slant (7), and The New York Times (6). Good old Barack Obama put this one on his 2023 favourites list.

Even crazier was how her TikTok fanbase had a million videos set to the song in less than two months. Or how it crossed the one billion Spotify streams after nine months. As Paste Magazine pointed out, it took Taylor Swift's "Look What You Made Me Do" six years to achieve the same feat.

"This love I have in me that I feel, not just for one person, but for people, for the world, for myself, for living... that's something that the world can't take away from me. No one can break me as long as I hold on to it. It just felt so powerful and important that I realised that for myself. Because it felt like, 'Oh, nothing can really hurt me.' I

mean, people can hurt my body. The world can take stuff away from me. But as long as I keep loving, that's all mine." [22]

- MITSKI

Yet, craziest of all... is that this song was the closest on the album to being excluded.

"It's always the song that almost doesn't make it on the album that ends up being everyone's favourite. For The Land it was 'My Love Mine All Mine', not because we didn't like it, but because we just couldn't figure out how to make it sound good for a while, and I was like, almost like, 'Just forget about it.'" [171]

- MITSKI

Imagine! Thankfully, they recorded it, we have it, and absolutely everyone adored it, talking about it so much that we have a stack of info to go over. Firstly, people wanted to know why Mitski was singing about the moon, so she told them.

"I was sitting outside and the moon was bright. I felt like it looked like a tent was actually covering the sky and the moon was a hole in the tent letting light in. I couldn't wrap my mind around the fact that that moon was there before I ever existed, it's going to keep being there long after I die. It's like a dog at two years old is an adult. And then it maybe gets 10 to 15 years, God bless. In moon years, I'm like a speck of dust floating maybe for a few seconds, completely insignificant and then I disappear." [168]

- MITSKI

"I was just thinking about how sad it was. Not that I had to die, but that I had to stop living. Because I love living life. I love people. I love the world. And so I was thinking, 'I wish this love in me that is temporary could go up to the Eternal Moon and keep shining down with it.'" [168]

- MITSKI

"It came exactly from the feeling I just described of being like, 'Wow, when I die, everything goes away.' I can't take any of my possessions with me. But I wish that I could somehow keep this beautiful love I have in me alive. And maybe, if the moon held it for me then it can shine it down onto the world after I die, as I can't shine it onto the world anymore. So that's kind of where it came from. I remember when I was writing it, I was literally sitting outside on a lawn chair and looking up at the moon." [130]

- MITSKI

"I grew up moving around. Nothing felt permanent. I wasn't from any anywhere. Everything was temporary. Nothing felt like it was mine. And then, suddenly, I realised, 'Oh!' But I have this thing in me that is actually fully mine. And there's something so wonderful and gleeful about that realisation." [168]

- MITSKI

For the second verse, Mitski brings it back down to Earth, so let's talk about that.

"Since I wrote something really abstract and vague in the first verse, let me ground it in the second verse by bringing another person in. I learned what my heart was worth and how beautiful my heart is through loving and caring for other people." [163]

- MITSKI

"I've found that everything in the world has a cost. There's, like, 'Do it for the exposure, you won't get paid but do it for the experience,' but that's still energy you're expending that still has a cost. I've done a lot of DIY tours that helped me get to where I am today but there was a cost to that. There was a cost to my health, my well-being, not to mention a lot of the time I was losing money, so there's a cost to everything... except for love [...] There was something about realising that my love is mine. Nothing else is mine. Everything else goes away, everything else including myself, is going to deteriorate. But as long as I hold on to my love, no one can take it from me. I can give so much love and it won't take away from me. It's this unlimited resource." [168]

- MITSKI

"This love I feel in me, that I've created in me, that I've built in me, that I've held onto. And it's mine for as long as I want it, for as long as I don't give it up or let the world take it away from me." [168]

- MITSKI

The album and the single and the music video all came out on the same day. Speaking of the video, go watch Mitski enter a room full of chairs then slowly stack them on top of one another, with the lowest chair balanced with one leg on an egg.

"For me, in Spanish, the video is about how 'a veces lo más frágil es lo más fuerte.' Which translates to: 'sometimes the most fragile is the strongest.'" [172]

- MITSKI

After which, Mitski climbs/floats to the top with lots of close-up feet shots.

"I was partially stitched into the wardrobe you see in the video, and under that I was wearing a full body harness, then under the harness I was wearing protective clothing to prevent the harness from digging into my skin [...] Going to the bathroom was a full team effort that stopped production for at least half an hour. Eventually, I just stopped drinking liquids so I wouldn't have to keep stopping just to pee, since we only had a day to get it done. After we wrapped and I got out of all the clothing for the last time, I downed a big bottle of water in one go. I was so thirsty!" [172]

- MITSKI

"It was so fun to be that high up! I told friends that I'm in danger of making every music video an excuse to do stunts for no reason other than my enjoyment. I also told the head stunt coordinator that I'm available to do stunts whenever he needs an extra person. A girl can dream!" [172]

- MITSKI

"The whole video concept was the director AG's idea. I'm so grateful to him for bringing so much beauty and depth to the video, as well as to the entire crew." [172]

- MITSKI

This fun spectacle was directed by A.G. Rojas whose talent can be found across videos from Skrillex, Jack White, Jamie XX, and Florence + the Machine.

"I spent a couple of months with my eyes closed waiting for images to appear while listening to the song. Instead of images, words kept

coming to mind: like touch, delicate, and effort. I put all the word shapes together and they formed a tower of chairs." [172]

- A.G. ROJAS

OTHER NOTEWORTHY SONGS

Like before, Mitski was kind enough to post a video with her explaining every song from *The Land Is Inhospitable and So Are We*, giving us a lot to talk about.

• Buffalo Replaced

"Unfortunately, it's quite a hopeless song, or it comes from a hopeless place. Especially the second verse makes it clear that the protagonist is wondering whether having hope is even beneficial. To the protagonist, having hope actually makes life more painful and harder to live, but still holding on to it because the protagonist loves hope. In this case, hope is a personified creature. I don't want to get too political but America feels kind of stranded and hopeless right now. In this song's case, the American perspective is hopelessness." [30]

- MITSKI

"For a lot of the albums I've made with my producer Patrick Hyland, we found the sound or the tone of the album by first finding the sound of a song, and then using that track as a guide or a reference for the rest of the album. For my last album, *Laurel Hell*, that track was 'Working for the Knife.' And for *The Land is Inhospitable and So Are We*, that track is 'Buffalo Replaced'. I remember Patrick said something about how often with novelists, the first thing they do is write a short story and then expand on that until it becomes a novel. Or with feature filmmakers, they first make a short film and then build on that and then turn it into a feature. It feels similar with this process, where you work on one song and try to pursue a sound until you come up with something that feels intriguing or interesting or generative. And then use that as a North Star for the rest of the album. It doesn't mean that the rest of the album is going to sound like that track. It just gives you a sort of hand to hold or a pathway so that you're not just fumbling in the dark trying to find this vague sound of the album." [173]

- MITSKI

"I remember we were very much inspired by The Velvet Underground. At first it was basically how it sounds in the beginning of the track, and then I absolutely love how Patrick thought of bringing in those keyboard sounds at the end. It really adds something beautiful." [173]

- MITSKI

• I Don't Like My Mind

"The lyrics are quite literal and self-explanatory, so I'm not even going to go over them." [174]

- MITSKI

"The demo was made in Philadelphia right after we recorded Be the Cowboy, which we also recorded in Philly. This is one of those tracks that ended up being really easy to make because the end result is so similar to the demo we made way back when. I think we even just kept the guitar track from the demo." [174]

- MITSKI

"After a while I found that I've started to write songs that are very comfortable for me to sing. But that also means I tend to not write songs that are very challenging for me to sing, so I'm sure you've noticed a lot of my songs just have me singing quietly and within a certain range. I think other singer-songwriters do that too. But so my point being, for this track it was actually really nice to belt at the end. I wrote for myself to belt and I remembered I could still do it."[174]

- MITSKI

• The Deal

"This song started a little differently than other songs. This song started when I misinterpreted a poem. I was reading this poem by Maria Mitchell, who was an astronomer in the mid-1800s. And this poem is called 'How Charming is Divine Philosophy'—which is a line from John Milton, but that's a whole other tangent I'm just not going to get into. Basically, it's a poem about when you go on a walk alone at night is when you can discover beautiful things about the world and about yourself that you probably wouldn't be able to discover if you were walking with somebody else, or you were talking and your ears were full of talk instead of listening to the sounds of the night. So that's basically what the song is about. There was this one line I read that went, 'There's a deal to be learned on a midnight walk when you take it all alone,' but when I read it, for some reason misread it as, 'There's a deal to be made on a midnight walk when you take it all along.' Before I realised that I was misreading it, I thought, 'Oh, that's an interesting thought! What kind of deal can you make on a midnight walk?' And then long after, I reread it and I was like, 'Oh, I just made a mistake.' I thought, well, what if it was about making a deal on a midnight walk? What does that entail? What kind of deal? What are you getting? What are you giving? And that just jogged my thought process and that's basically how this song started for me." [175]

- MITSKI

"There are some of us, including myself, who just can't help but give ourselves away. And for some people, it manifests in addiction. For some people, it means we can't help but give our power up to another person who wants to control people. And for some people, I think for a lot of people, it just means giving ourselves over to the market. You know, having it tell us who we are and what we need to buy in order to be ourselves. I feel like it manifests in a lot of different ways and I think we can't help but do it because, sometimes, it's just so hard to carry the full weight of our existence and actually be fully accountable for it. And so we give ourselves away or we hope to unburden ourselves by handing over the burden to another person or entity. And in the moment, it maybe numbs the pain. It makes things easier. But I wanted to write a song about how, in doing so, maybe you also give up your capacity to feel full, real, unbound joy [...] You give up the good with the bad, basically." [175]

- MITSKI

• When Memories Snow

"This track was an undertaking and I'm really glad it worked out. When I was first writing it, I was writing it on piano. I was learning about and experimenting with chords used by the shō, which is a traditional Japanese reed instrument. Its chords don't follow what we would consider standard Western harmonic structure. So I was playing around with the chords and in the beginning of the track you can hear the piano playing those chords [...] we do have a bit of the shō instrument sound in the resulting track, you can hear it especially towards the end. It's that really high reed-y sound. But, anyway, I wrote it on piano. I had the vocal melody. I didn't really know how to arrange it. The only thing I could hear in my head was, randomly, sopranos. That would be a weird track if it was just my voice and then random sopranos. So Patrick and I were trying to figure out how to produce the song and he came up with [dividing] it into two parts: the first part being inspired by Ennio Morricone's Western movie soundtracks, as well as the style of the Boléro. And the second half being inspired by British Invasion rock sound. We kept building and building on that. I don't know if you'd be able to hear the British Invasion part but that was the original experiment." [176]

- MITSKI

• I'm Your Man

"When I first wrote the song, it was just the first half of what the track is now [...] and after listening through, I was, like, you know, even for my standards, this is pretty short. I need to figure out a way to lengthen it. The problem was I didn't want to add other parts. I didn't want to add a chorus or a bridge or whatever. I wanted it to be exactly what it is. How do I lengthen it without adding any more?

[...] Then I thought, okay, well, what's my favourite thing? Choral voices! So I had the great privilege of writing the four-part harmony for the choir and then getting a choir at the end. I had the choir saying the words 'yoho' because 'yoho' is like a pirate thing, right? It's a pirate trope. Pirates say 'yoho'. Fictional pirates, obviously." [177]

- MITSKI

"I know it might sound like it's from the perspective of maybe a bad man character or a mean male partner, but actually what I wanted to do was write from the perspective of the man in my head. This sounds weird, I know, but stay with me! I think no matter what gender you are, there's the voice of a patriarch in your head because we all live in and we're raised in a patriarchy [...] I have found that the man in my head makes me believe some pretty unhelpful things, often toxic things about both myself and the world and other people. I always try to keep it in check but I thought, you know, maybe I should write a song where I give a voice to that man in my head, and maybe it'll help me come to peace with it? Kind of like that story of the Buddha when meditating to reach enlightenment... I hope I don't get this wrong... Mara [a demon] comes in and tries to distract him [...] and the Buddha responds by saying, 'I see you' and then inviting Mara for tea and treating Mara like a special guest. I think there really is something to that. I wanted to try something similar by being, like, Okay, patriarch in my mind. You have the floor. What do you want to say?" [177]

- MITSKI

"I'm so happy with it. And at the very end [...] is my final favourite part. You hear what sounds like a human scream. But then you realise it's not a human scream. It's some sort of bug [...] it was a public domain sound so we didn't know what it was. I did my little Googling, I listened to a lot of nature sounds, let me tell you, and I finally tracked it down to a type of toad, I believe. I think it's called the Fowler's toad that makes that kind of cry. So thank you to Fowler toads." [177]

- MITSKI

Click around to find the black and white video of Mitski performing "I'm Your Man" for La Blogotheque. She walks around a hundred-year-old French concert hall which is as live and as reverby as you can imagine, complete with stairs creaking, guard dogs barking, and Mitski messing up the chords. In the end, you hear someone coming, causing Mitski and the cameraperson to run and hide, giving off authentic breaking-and-entering vibes. It's a wonderful watch.

• I Love Me After You

"I made a grave mistake when trying to figure out the production for this song. I wrote [and] recorded myself playing it on just acoustic guitar and singing along. And I listened to that demo over and over and over. In my defence, I was just trying to figure out how the end result track should sound, and I couldn't hear what it should sound like at the end of the day, so I kept listening over and over. And the problem with that is, inevitably, you get used to things [...] and you start liking what you get used to [...] Patrick kept suggesting great ideas about how it should be produced, and every time I'd be like... 'But I just want it to be acoustic guitar and voice! I just want it to be the thing that I'm used to!' [...] Eventually Patrick convinced me to do the version that it is today [...] I'm glad he did. And what he said was his inspiration was that he wanted to try to figure out a way to make it sound like you're crawling through something in slow motion [...] In terms of how to make that sound, what we did was play it much faster and higher and then slow it down [...] and it kind of became this, almost... I hate to use this word because it's thrown around a lot, but... maybe shoegaze? No. I'm sorry I ever said that. Patrick didn't use that word. Forget I used that word." [178]

- MITSKI

And that's it! Damn, I always hate it when this album ends, leaving an empty space to wonder... what's next? And what will it sound like?

"I have this quote on my phone, a David Bowie quote. I'm going to paraphrase and butcher it, but it's just about how, if you're in a slightly uncomfortable spot artistically, that's where you should be. You shouldn't really be in a spot where you know what you're doing. You should go a little further into the deep end than you are able to swim. That's when things get interesting. I try to follow that. I don't know what I'm going to make next, but I know that I don't want to repeat myself. Even though it's very tempting to do so, especially because now this is my living. So people have to like my music and order for me to make a living, which is a scary thought. And so it's now very tempting for me to repeat what people have said they like about my music or just do what I know I'm good at. But on the other hand, in my mind, if I did that, I would no longer be able to call myself an artist because I think I should always be a little bit uncomfortable." [11]

7.2.
AMATEUR MISTAKE TOUR

The *Amateur Mistake Tour* ran from September 11th, 2023 until September 28th, 2024. The name comes from a lyric in "Bug Like an Angel". Many of her earlier venue decisions were aimed toward smaller rooms.

"I feel bad now because I realise that it's created this feeling of scarcity, which I didn't intend. Originally, my strong feeling was, for this album, I really want to present it in a room where everyone is seated, everyone can see what's happening on stage with their eyes and not have to rely on a screen. Just for this music, I wanted that intimate beautiful theatre experience instead of one giant venue. Of course, I also love arena shows because it brings all these people together. But just for this album, this was the best way for me to present it [...] I wanted a feeling of, like, 'Okay, I can see the person performing and feel them with my own eyeballs." [22]

- MITSKI

Shows took Mitski to Mexico, USA, Japan, Canada, UK, Germany, The Netherlands, and France. A festival stop happened at Primavera Sound, 2024, in Barcelona. Opening artists included Trust Fund, Tamino, Sunny War, Julia Jacklin, Richard Dawson, and Iceage. There was a special lottery in place that gave people the opportunity to win tickets.

Mitski's live band included many usual suspects, such as Patrick Hyland on guitar, Fats Kaplin (who played on the album) on guitar, Jeni Magaña on bass, Brijean Murphy on percussion, and Bruno Esrubilsky on drums.

"The vibes were incredible right from the start. There was this freedom to be myself as a drummer, no boxes, or restrictions, just trust." [179]

- BRUNO ESRUBILSKY (LIVE DRUMMER)

At the end of the tour, Mitski went back home to Nashville. But don't be sad if you missed it, because an official 104-page black and white photo scrapbook was put together by LA/Ohio photographer artist Lexie Alley. She has also worked with Sony Music, Red Bull, Universal Music Group, and Warner Music Group.

"It's just too difficult to go from one place to another and continue to lose things, or lose people; it's been nice to teach myself it's okay to become attached. Every day, the audience is different. You love them that day, but then you can't form attachments to anyone there, because you go to the next show. I'd found that I needed to guard my heart, so that I didn't just feel loss every day. So it is nice to be in this position where I have a home to miss. It feels really dear to me, actually, that I am expected back." [93]

- MITSKI

7.3.
HIRED GUN, PART 5

Before we even knew that the land was inhospitable, Miya Folick's album *Roach* came out on May 26th, 2023. It held the single "Bad Thing", co-written by someone named Mitski (and Andrew Wells).

"The day I wrote this song, I woke up with a first-class, absolutely soul-crushing hangover, after having slept for a couple fretful hours. I wasn't the kind of person who could hide a hangover, so I told Mitski and Andrew what was going on. We wrote this song. It's about being stuck in a cycle of behaviour that you can't get out of, but it's not bleak. There's hope in the song. I always knew that I would get out of that cycle eventually." [180]

- MIYA FOLICK

On 13th March, 2024, Mitski took part in the Spotify Singles sessions with two songs. The first was a new version of "Buffalo Replaced". The second was a cover of "Coyote, My Little Brother", written by Peter La Farge but made famous by Pete Seeger, originally on his sixth studio album, *God Bless the Grass* (1966).

Plucked straight from the tour band, these recordings featured Jeni Magaña on double bass and Patrick Hyland on acoustic guitar.Music Group.

On October 25th, 2024, previously mentioned Manu's Katie Gavin released her debut studio album, *What a Relief*. She managed to convince Mitski to join another collaboration, and our girl sings a whole verse for herself on "As Good As It Gets". Such a homely romantic song called for a homely romantic video, and Mitski makes an appearance there too.

Finally, Tamino's third album, *Every Dawn's a Mountain*, came out on March 21st, 2025. Mitski is here, dueting with him on the song "Sanctuary".

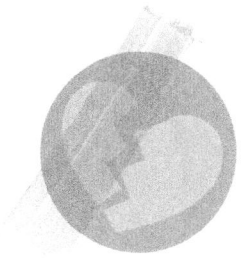

7.4.
THE QUEEN'S GAMBIT MUSICAL

"Before Level Forward even brought the idea of making a musical of The Queen's Gambit, I was a fan of the Netflix show, and an even greater fan of the original novel. So I was already determined to be a member of this team. And then I met Eboni and Whitney, and my determination grew tenfold! I absolutely had to be a part of this! I am ecstatic to get to work with all of these amazing creatives, who've each built beautiful and unique repertoires of their own." [181]

- MITSKI

As early as 2023, Mitski's name was tied into *The Queen's Gambit Stage Musical*, a stage show based on the hugely successful Netflix series and the best-selling novel by Walter Tevis. As you'd expect, Mitski is taking care of the music and lyrics. However, at the time of this book's publication, no further news has been announced. Just in case, it's worth checking if anything has changed via: thequeensgambitmusical.com

7.5.
MITSKI LIKE AN ANGEL

"I already know I'm not doing anything new. I just feel the need to make music. It's the thing that makes me happy. It's the thing that makes me feel like I'm part of something bigger than myself. In my day to day, I just feel insignificant. And when I make music, I am still insignificant, but I feel like a tiny insignificant part of something bigger. Or when I play shows, I suddenly start to believe in, maybe, some sort of higher power. I'm not religious but something more than just day-to-day. It transports you. Or, at least, it transports me. It makes me feel like there's meaning and there's purpose. There's something greater." [39]

- MITSKI

With her lyrical allusions to religion and the constant connecting of her songs to spirituality, you may wonder where exactly Mitski sits religiously? According to the above quote, she's not religious. Then again...

"There's no thought. It's like touching God. Once you taste that, you keep chasing it. I've recognised my tendency to want to know something for sure. I'm a very religious person, but I grew up in a non-religious environment that was...not cynical, but objective. I found music, and I devote myself to it." [14]

- MITSKI

So which is it?

"I don't have a religion, but I think I'm a very religious person. If I was raised with a religion, I think I'd be very religious. But I was raised very non-religiously so I think... it's just that I'm obsessive or I need something bigger to admire and to believe in." [56]

- MITSKI

Be that as it may be, the cult of Mitski persists, with many rabid fans likening her to a prophetic role model.

"I don't walk around thinking of myself as a role model because that would drive me crazy. You start thinking instead of following your own compass. You start following what you think is other people's compass for you, which is so confusing. So I haven't quite figured out what it means to be a quote-unquote 'role model'. I don't have a religion but it's kind of like having a religion in that you have this feeling of being watched and you have to be good. Isn't that what religion is? I don't really know." [11]

- MITSKI

Nevertheless, her lyrics frequently dabble in Biblical references, such as *"Would you kill me, Jerusalem?"* ("My Body's Made Of Crushed Little Stars"), *"Glory, glory, glory to the night"* (Thursday Girl), and *"Isaiah, Isaiah, Isaiah, Isaiah, Isaiah, Isaiah"* ("Strawberry Blond"). As you do!

"A good show allows me to feel connected with other human beings, and sometimes even with a higher power." [50]

- MITSKI

"I may not have a religion to keep me in check, but I do have people with tattoos of my lyrics who will forever have an embarrassing band tattoo if I do anything dumb. God bless." [182]

- MITSKI

Part Eight

LAST WORDS OF
A SHOOTING STAR

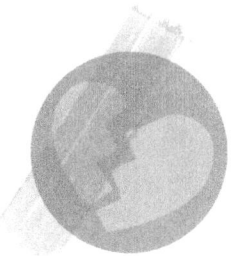

8.1.
AWARDS FOR MITSKI

While I know Mitski is the best, and you know Mitski is the best, and NPR knows Mitski is the best (calling her *"The 21st Century's Poet Laureate Of Young Adulthood"*), and The Guardian knows Mitski is the best (claiming her as the *"US's best young songwriter"*)... the general Mitski disregard from the music industry borderlines on criminal. Yes, she was co-nominated for an Oscar with the "This Is a Life" track from *Everything Everywhere All at Once*. Yes, *Be the Cowboy* was nominated for a Grammy... for the packaging of all things! But besides those crumbs, recognition from the award scene has largely eluded her.

"I wouldn't even get past the first round of American Idol. I don't have that sort of technique. It's just about, 'Am I communicating a feeling? Am I connecting with another person?' That's all that matters." [34]

- MITSKI

That said, she was nominated for three AIM Independent Music Awards, winning in 2022 as the Best Live Performer. Furthermore, "My Love Mine All Mine" was nominated at the 2024 UK Music Video Awards for Best Alternative Video. But it is only the Libera Awards who have clicked into Mitski's genius. With 12 nominations to her name, Mitski has won two Liberas, one for "Nobody" as 2019's Music Video of the Year, and one for *The Land Is Inhospitable and So Are We* as 2024's Record of the Year.

"The thing is, I want the art I make to be real, and in order for it to be real it has to be real to myself. I don't think there's any point in making art when it isn't saying something. I think I just accepted the scrutiny as a consequence of what I have to face in order to make art. I'm not going to make meaningless music. I just decided I'm going to face whatever consequences come. Because I want my music to mean something." [18]

- MITSKI

Then again, in some roundabout hipster way, there is something cool that Mitski, who is streamed by and screamed at by millions of fanatics around the world, remains in the hands of a select club. We should each feel special to be here, in the know. However, considering her endless productivity and her history of crawling up the fame ladder at a modest pace, we should not be surprised if she is drowning in awards within just a few short years. So enjoy these moments while they last.

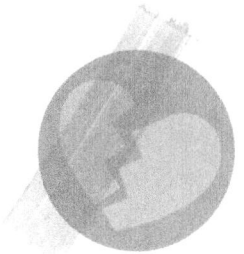

8.2.
PRAISE FOR MITSKI

But who cares about stupid awards anyway? What matters are those people who know about music. So, who better to ask than the music professionals themselves?

Let us not forget that, unlike so many songwriters in the pop world, Mitski is actually a trained composer who studied the artform before she delved into the industry. Silas Brown, a professor at SUNY Purchase College, said she was *"an articulate musician"* from the start.

"She can find those unusual notes. I think she makes a point of it and goes for that. 'Nobody' could be horrible pop drivel, but in her case, it's perfect. The further you go up into the extended notes above a chord—they still belong to the chord, but they cross over into the jazz threshold, and the more you do that, the more precision and technique is required to pull those notes off without it sounding out of tune. She has the vocal chops to do that and still sound like a pop musician. That's Mitski—that was true in the very first stuff of hers I was listening to." [34]

- SILAS BROWN

So proud is her former college that, for a brief time, the Wikipedia page titled "List of State University of New York at Purchase people" listed her as *"literally the most talented artist to exist and the greatest intellectual of the 21st century."*

And then, of course, there are her musical peers, some of whom have reached higher heights than Mitski but recognise that she is the more deserving talent.

"[Mitski has a] way of finding words for emotions you didn't even know you had." [83]

- LAUFEY

Michelle Zauner, the brain inside Japanese Breakfast, toured with Mitski, which was an experience that changed her for the better.

"I was from a DIY punk environment with a lot of rowdy guys and a lot of drinking. On tour with Mitski, I felt like I entered this much more professional, healthy, regimented realm." [33]

- JAPANESE BREAKFAST

"There are still a lot of things that happen on the road that are not the most supportive to women in music. [But Mitski would] go to the sound person, for example, and introduce herself and assert that she was going to be the one to talk to if they had any issues about tech. There are some dinosaur types who are rude to you, and a lot of times I would deflect to my male drummer—I didn't want to be condescended to. I was impressed that Mitski took that on every night." [33]

- JAPANESE BREAKFAST

Japanese Breakfast also told The Quietus that *Puberty 2* was her 11th favourite album of all time.

"I don't know what you would call her 'breakthrough record', but I love that album. She's obviously such a beautiful singer and amazing songwriter and a friend of mine. And watching her perform that album for five to six weeks was so inspiring. It felt like a real changing of the tides. It was her moment, and I was just happy to be along for the ride and watch her become the artist that she is. So that record always has a special place in my heart. I love the song 'I Bet On Losing Dogs.' I think that's one of her greatest. She's written so many great songs, but I especially love that song. I find that song to be really heartbreaking." [183]

- JAPANESE BREAKFAST

The supergroup, Boygenius, have spoken about Mitski every chance they get. Their 2023 record, *The Record*, was nominated for the Grammy Album of the Year and won the Grammy for Best Alternative Music Album. But they called into question the entire institution due to Mitski being snubbed.

"We're, like, what does it even represent if you're not representing one of the most listened-to artists of our lives in our genre? It's super weird." [184]

- BOYGENIUS

Speaking of Boygenius, member Lucy Dacus toured solo with Mitski and had nothing but glowing thoughts to report.

"Her music is really visceral. She's connected to a part in herself that wants to scream. Maybe you don't live in a space where you can scream, or maybe you don't have the words for what has happened to you. Mitski provides a space for that." [1]

- LUCY DACUS

Another solo artist/Boygenius member is Phoebe Bridgers. She has a funny story about when she attended a Mitski show with John Doe from the punk band X.

"He was, like, 'All these kids look like they're at a fucking church!' It looked like a punk-show crowd, but the kids were rapt with attention. He was blown away, and so was I. Mitski was playing solo, and the music was like this ethereal music from another dimension." [33]

- PHOEBE BRIDGERS

"[I admire the] weirdness of the creative choices that Mitski seems to make so confidently." [33]

- PHOEBE BRIDGERS

When Bridgers signed her first record deal, Mitski offered to be there to help.

"[She said] 'Let me know if you ever want to talk about anything.' I know she's done that for a ton of my friends, at varying levels of their careers." [33]

- PHOEBE BRIDGERS

These stories are not uncommon. Ask musician Sasami, for example, who was given $500 by Mitski so she could have shirts printed.

"[Mitski is] very conscious of who she brings on tour—having opening acts she wants to uplift personally, financially, and professionally. Mitski doesn't necessarily talk about feminism all the time on Twitter, but she has so many women of colour and queer people working with her." [33]

- SASAMI

One of Mitski's biggest fan names is the 44th US President, Barack Obama, who has included Mitski on two of his famed end-of-year favourite song lists (2021's "The Only Heartbreaker" and 2023's "My Love Mine All Mine").

The names keep growing, like when Nirvana/Foo Fighters legend, Dave Grohl, sang her praise.

"When I listen to a Mitski record, I'm like, 'This blows my mind.' There are things that I like, and then there's things that I become obsessed with, Mitski being one of them." [185]

- DAVE GROHL

But the most talked about of them all is, without a doubt, Iggy Pop.

"[Mitski's] a great talent. For me, she's probably the most advanced American songwriter I know." [186]

- IGGY POP

Mitski has frequently responded to this praise with immense levels of excitement.

"In that moment I was, like, 'Maybe I should just quit right now. Maybe this is it, this is the end. This is as good as it gets.' It's sort of strange because as much as I try to caution against it, I still very much idealise the artists I love and they don't seem like real people to me, they're more like ideas. So just the idea that Iggy Pop said he found my music on YouTube, [I thought] 'Oh Iggy Pop goes on YouTube!' like, oh, he's in the world right now listening to indie rock. The whole idea of it was just incredibly weird." [71]

- MITSKI

"I don't know where that came from but I'm grateful for it. I don't know how he found my music but, again, it's a miracle to me. He said

he found it on YouTube which is wild. Just imagining Iggy Pop silently in his room surfing the web. But it's great because Iggy Pop is one of my heroes. You have a specific amount of people you'd turn to whenever you're confused or you need guidance in your life and he's one of those people. I'd watch his live videos or listen to his music whenever I needed reminding of what I think music should be or what I think people should get out of a live experience. So, yeah, I don't know how to feel about it. It doesn't quite feel real. My mind doesn't know how to register it." [112]

- MITSKI

"You make your music, you put it out, but your life stays intact, sort of. But then, suddenly, these people you idolise are in your life in a weird way. Like, Iggy Pop said I was a great songwriter, and I will hold onto that for the rest of my life." [41]

- MITSKI

8.3.
HEALTH FOR MITSKI

"I've never gambled before.
I feel like my career is already a gamble." [7]
- MITSKI

A wards and praise are nice, but what's most important of all is that Mitski finds her happiness. And, thankfully, in recent years, our heroine has striven to locate a balance in her own special ways.

"I used to rebel by destroying myself, but realised that's awfully convenient to the world. For some of us our best revolt is self-preservation." [187]
- MITSKI

"I love cigarettes. Oh, so good. So tasty. Love them [...] I quit when I was like 18 ,19. Sometimes, when I drink, I like to smoke, but I try not to. And then, it's bad, because every time I smoke at a party, just

socially, I feel the effects. I have to control myself for the next two weeks after. It really sucks [...] I love cigarettes, especially when I'm touring through, like, Wyoming or that kind of country where it looks like a Marlboro ad anyway [...] You always have to be addicted to something. But it's, like, make it something else. Make it something better." [7]

- MITSKI

"I can't even do weed edibles because it's still going on when you feel done. You're, like, okay, I get it. I feel good, it's fine. And then you're still high? I can't do it." [7]

- MITSKI

"I don't drink on tour, so I don't drink at all because I'm always on tour, and I try to get as much sleep as I possibly can. I don't smoke at all, either. I think it's less about finding holistic balance and more about finding a unique balance within a fundamentally unbalanced situation." [84]

- MITSKI

"When I'm writing a song, I'm always thinking about the placement of things, how a composition will be balanced and how it will move. It's the same with emotions. Feeling really, really happy is actually scary for me because I understand that, in the balance of life, you have to bounce that much lower to balance things out. I guess it's very zen, but it's like caffeine or drugs. When you've had it, you know what it's like to have had it, and by taking it, you'll also experience the not-having it, and not having it will be more intense than having had it at all. And maybe that comes with maturity and

experience and stepping back and seeing how life goes. How getting up too fast is a little dangerous because nothing can stay up that way forever. It has to go down. But also, if you go really down, it means you'll go up soon." [5]

- MITSKI

Yes, it's about making those small changes from which we can all learn. For example, a healthy, conscious diet...

"I try to eat healthy in general. But I also can't eat right before I sing. So on tour, I would make sure I eat way before the show, just because I want to be satiated and not hungry, but I also don't want to be burping into the mic." [52]

- MITSKI

"I don't remember the first time I officially went vegan. It was just, like, my body doesn't like dairy. And so it was just easier to go with the vegan option instead of asking what's in something. Just go to a vegan restaurant or whatever. And then when I got out of the habit of eating meat, I started to think about what it actually meant to eat an animal and I just didn't wanna do it. And since I have the resources and access to vegan protein, I feel like I don't need animal protein. But on tour, it's hard. On tour I have eggs or whatever when I need my protein. It's all about whether you have access to it." [29]

- MITSKI

"I love dessert. I love sugar. You can tell me all you want how much sugar is bad for you, I don't care. It makes me happy. Especially crème brûlée, where it's, like... the top is this thin crackling that you *just put a spoon on it, and it goes... 'Ah'. I think you should be allowed to have beautiful wonderful tasty desserts."* [25]

- MITSKI

"Vanilla is the most perverted flavour of all the ice creams. I feel like it gets a bad rap because we say 'vanilla sex'. But I've realised that, after you go through all the flavours, you come back to vanilla and understand its depth and just how fucking nasty it is. A good vanilla is like touching God." [40]

- MITSKI

...swapping coffee for tea...

"I really love coffee, so I end up drinking too much of it and then it ruins my life. I really love tea. I'm a snob about tea. When I go to Starbucks, I insist that they give me the tea bag separately from the water because the water is way too hot all the time and it ruins the tea." [52]

- MITSKI

"I don't drink coffee. But I love tea. I need green tea specifically. I start my morning with sancha. I think it's, like, sancha all the way through until lunch, and then after lunch, I like to have a black tea. [There are] great black teas in the U.K. It's very exciting." [25]

- MITSKI

...logging off...

"You know, the cheapest way to get a break is just to not go on the internet. And that's it. When I really need a break I just don't look

at the internet. I'm just a working person. I can't be like, 'I'm so tired, I'm gonna go on vacation.' I have a life, I have my job, I have my responsibilities. Not going on the internet is free." [41]

- MITSKI

...staying organised...

"I'm a big fan of making lists, it helps me sort out my brain. The key to making a good to-do list is, among the things that will take a while to achieve, you put in really achievable stuff. Like, 'take your pill today', or, 'wake up', or 'remember to take a shower'. Put those things in there so that you can cross them out and feel like you're doing something. And then you can stay emotionally connected to the list." [43]

- MITSKI

...becoming aware of one's flaws...

"My worst habit is that I'm really impatient. Especially in subways. I don't know what comes over me, but if someone is slow in front of me in the subway? I just get so angry. And then I go above ground and I'm, like, 'Who was that person? Like, why did I become that?'" [187]

- MITSKI

...and, of course, recognising boundaries and learning to say "no", like Mitski did so easily when she was a child.

"I try to maintain balance in very practical ways. Maybe turning down some opportunities or turning down some tour dates to make sure that I go to the doctor or making sure I put breaks between tour dates. Just learning to say no to opportunities when everyone's telling you this is your only chance, because I realised everyone says everything is your only chance." [84]

- MITSKI

"It always ends up being smart when I pay attention to my limits and say, 'No, actually I can't do it.' Especially because there's so much pressure to say yes all the time. As an artist, it's made to seem like every opportunity that comes your way will be your last, and it's the best one, and if you don't take it, you're dumb. But often, that's not the case, and you have to keep reminding yourself you're still gonna have your job if you say no to this one gig or this one press opportunity. And it's better to preserve your health or your energy sometimes." [41]

- MITSKI

"I think I've gotten to know my limit of how many things I can do in a day before my brain stops working. So I set aside time for myself to just sit and do nothing in a place alone. That really helps me continue to be a pleasant person." [25]

- MITSKI

"Self-care isn't about specific material things. It's about listening to your own needs and being honest with yourself. Sometimes self care is about doing stuff you don't want to do, like admitting you were wrong, or cleaning your living space." [95]

- MITSKI

"Part of it is learning to say 'no'. Learning that I am not in a place of scarcity. That if I say 'no' to one opportunity, I have to believe that another one will come. And others have come. A lot of what was really making me unhappy was the feeling that I have to say 'yes' to every gig, no matter how unhappy it made me, because there will be no other gigs. I've come around to realising that, you know, of course, my job has its hard parts. But also every job has its hard parts. I am also very lucky to get to do what I really truly love in the deepest part of my soul as my work. I get paid to do it. So kind of putting things into perspective and realising I'm willing to take the hard stuff, like everyone takes the hard stuff in order to get to the really good stuff. And I've also realised how much performing feeds me. I've zoomed in on that, or locked in on that in my mind. Yes, there's such difficult parts about touring. But, also, I get to perform on stage and feed off the positive energy of the audience and really feel like I'm part of something bigger than myself. That really keeps me going even if some parts are hard." [30]

- MITSKI

But perhaps above all else, is Mitski working out how to maintain relationships in whatever context works for her.

"I've learned that just because you won't be able to see someone next year, doesn't mean that your friendship with them doesn't count. Every single year of your life counts. Every single relationship can be deep and meaningful, no matter how short or long they are. I used to close myself off because I didn't want to develop relationships that were going to end anyway, but I learned that right now is what matters most. If you have a great friend right now, then there's no

need for you to close yourself off. You can always think about the goodbyes later. Right now you can just enjoy your friendship." [44]

- MITSKI

These relationships include those with her cuddly friends...

"I love my cat so much. She's my soulmate, I've had my cat since I was, like, 13, 14. I look into her eyes and I just shake within my soul." [40]

- MITSKI

"I love animals. I think they're too good for us. We humans, even though we're animals, we're the one animal who seemed to only know how to destroy. I really think the Earth would be better off without us and we should all just disappear. That sounds very violent but I don't mean it in any concrete way. I'm not trying to destroy the world. I just think all the animals on the Earth would be better off without us and I think we deserve to go extinct." [25]

- MITSKI

...but also the relationship that matters the most: the one with herself.

"I found that as long as I love the world, and love other people, and love myself... sometimes that can be the only light in the dark. I found that if the world is dark, but if I'm also making myself dark, then everything is dark. But if I just create a light within myself with love, then at least I'll have that light to look to [...] I've said this before in my bio, but I realised as I got older, to love people and to love the world is really the best thing I ever did. It's better

than any song I've written, any achievement, everything is blown out of the water compared to getting to love while I'm living. And I feel like that has really helped me maintain a sense of happiness and warmth and lightness. Just holding on to the love inside me. Because that's something people can't take away from you as long as you hold on to it." [30]

- MITSKI

"Don't worry about me. First of all, I thrive in conflict, so that's one thing. But also, I get to make music for my job. I get to eat, I have a roof over my head, I get to travel, I mean... I don't have anything to complain about, really." [68]

- MITSKI

8.4.
AUTHOR THOUGHTS

"Everything I say is with the caveat that I'm a one-in-a-million luckiest person in the literal world." [1]

- MITSKI

As you've reached this far in the book, I can only assume we're on the same page. The Mitski-loving page! For that reason, I will treat this as a safe space to break down the wall between us: Jared, the author, and you, the reader, allowing me to gush my thoughts on Mitski, art, and myself.

Those who know me know I have a firm grasp of music. I am a musician. I listen to roughly 400 new albums annually. I have written a Top 50 Greatest Albums list at the end of each year since 2010. I have penned several books on music. I believe I can hold conversations with whomever about whatever genre. So when I say this, I say it with clarity and education: Mitski composes songs unlike any other in the history of the medium. Her subtle strangeness functions in a class where nobody else exists. It's as much about what she doesn't do as what she does do, a craft that vibrates between the lines, exploding silently within hidden reservations. That's why we can throw every accolade at her, but it will never be enough. She is the greatest we have. She's superior to everyone in every minuscule aspect of songwriting. We should be studying her musical contribution.

Anyone who has seen her live will tell you the same thing. Her devoted following is the epitome of cult madness, at times bordering on dangerous, as we've discussed. And yet, despite this intense heat of global admiration, there is still a sense that we're part of an exclusive club, where Mitski remains ridiculously undiscovered, hiding in the shadows of bigger popstars, even though we know she should be standing on top of their heads. Writing this biography has only heightened my dedication to her brilliance, and what's more, it has inspired my own creative pursuits. This hit me hardest during her earlier days when she knew her life was destined to revolve around her craft at whatever cost. She had to make it work because she had nothing else.

Like Mitski, I recognise my existence as one blessed with much fortune, but I am also constantly at war with my chosen path. When I inform you that I wrote a large portion of this text whilst travelling across Mitski's country of origin, Japan, you may say that I am lucky to have done so, and that is true. But when I also tell you that I slept in dirty hostel rooms with, at times, up to 20 other people snoring around me, or when I tell you that my every meal consisted of cheap rice balls from 7-Eleven, you start to understand the bigger picture.

Another similarity between Mitski and myself is that I do not have a home. I've lived out of a suitcase for over six years now, and my book sales fully fund my survival. Some months, I make money. Most months, I lose money. A masochistic part of me romanticises this starving writer lifestyle. I am willing to die for my work, which is why I persistently publish books across genres every year despite how little return I get for the many months they take to write. I do it for the love, against all odds, even as those odds continue to grow worse under the weight of AI crushing the entire writing industry.

What I am getting at, is you. By purchasing this biography, you have helped feed me. It's no exaggeration that one copy of this book sold pays for half a meal. So, from my heart, soul, and stomach, this is a message of thanks! Thank you, thank you, thank you!

Sales are, of course, the primary way independent artists make money. However, we also rely on recommendations from word-of-mouth and platform algorithms alike. Regarding DIY authors, Amazon has conquered the landscape as an extremely intelligent beast that judges products based on many factors. But inarguably, our most significant power comes from honest, verified reviews. So when you take a few minutes to tell the world what you thought of this book, the website wakes up and lifts the title to higher eyes, feeding itself in the process. I have no control over this side of the deal! It entirely relies on you! My everything is in your hands!

Hence, please consider reviewing this Mitski biography and help me work another day. You can do so at *https://mybook.to/mitski*. You wouldn't believe the difference a single rating makes.

Thankfully, dedicating so many months of research to Mitski's journey has validated my life choices and has made moving forward into the unknown much easier. We all have conflict within ourselves, our brushstrokes colliding with our spray paint, aggravating doubt, exhausting our confusion as we navigate this often troubling world. But if Mitski has taught us one thing, it's that this collision of inner contradictions is precisely where the magic lies. During the hardest times, we can fight onward using the unique combinations of our personalities as our strongest weapons. And once we reach the other side victorious, we can reflect on the mess and realise that our most extraordinary work was ourselves all along.

"This is my favourite thing to do. Thank you so much for making my dreams come true. You all saved my life." [6]

- MITSKI

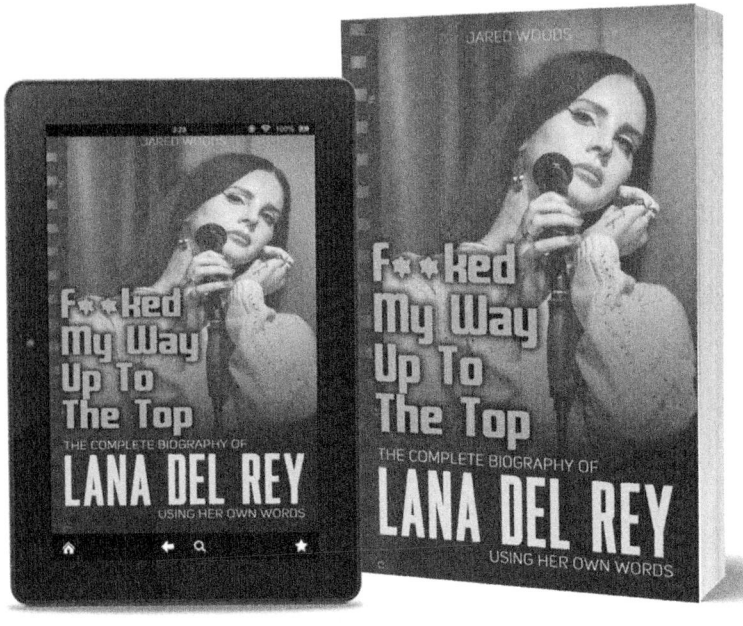

PLEASE REVIEW THIS BOOK!

Another casual reminder that only you have the power to spread the Word of Mitski!

Please consider reviewing this biography to help elevate the book into higher awareness!

Thank you so much!

mybook.to/mitski

ABOUT THE AUTHOR

Born in South Africa and now a homeless nomad, Jared does whatever he wants. His former scriptwriting for the YouTube channel *Pencilmation* has been viewed by billions of people, with scripts surpassing the 100 million mark. An additional million-plus viewers have enjoyed his blog, *Juice Nothing*.

Stay Soft, Get Eaten is the third of three biographies in Jared's *"In Her Own Words"* series. The other two are *When a Song Ends in a Minor Key* for Fiona Apple, and the phenomenally popular *F**ked My Way Up To The Top* for Lana Del Rey. Both of these are available right now.

As a traveller, Jared has explored and gathered inspiration from over 65 countries and counting. Additionally, he reads the central scripture from a different religion every year, deepening his understanding of numerous faiths and cultures. This curiosity and dedication to broad theology have greatly influenced his latest fiction book, *The Lamb Prophecy*, where Jared blends fantasy with deep spiritual themes, constructing a world rich with combined mythology.

His other publications include the spiritual philosophy of the *Janthopoyism Bible*, the self-help publication *Heartbreak Sucks! How to Get Over Your Breakup in 30 Days*, and the collection of short stories *Licking the Bottom of the Love Jar*.

Further creative projects include his one-panel Instagram comic *#legobiscuits*, his solo music under the name *Coming Down Happy*, his "singing" for the band *Sectlinefor*, and his film production called *Definitely Not a Cry For Help* which is already partially on YouTube.

Support Jared on *Patreon.com/legotrip*
Visit Jared at *JaredWoodsSavedMyLife.com*
Follow Jared on Instagram *@legotrip*

Other Books by Jared Woods
- F**ked My Way Up to the Top: The Complete Biography of Lana Del Rey (2023)
- When a Song Ends in a Minor Key: The Complete Biography of Fiona Apple (2024)
- The Lamb Prophecy (2024)
- Janthopoyism Bible (2022)
- Licking the Bottom of the Love Jar (2023)
- Heartbreak Sucks! How to Get Over Your Breakup in 30 Days (2021)

Stay Soft, Get Eaten

THE COMPLETE BIOGRAPHY OF

MITSKI

IN HER OWN WORDS

jared woods

REFERENCES

1 - https://www.rollingstone.com/music/music-features/mitski-new-album-laurel-hell-cover-story-1272973

2 - https://www.vulture.com/article/mitski-profile-laurel-hell.html

3 - https://www.youtube.com/watch?v=3RngQOHax5c

4 - https://gr8songpod.podbean.com/e/bonus-10-year-anniversary-of-lush-by-mitski

5 - https://www.stereogum.com/1874145/qa-mitski-goes-back-to-her-roots-on-puberty-2/interviews

6 - https://pitchfork.com/features/profile/dont-cry-for-mitski

7 - https://www.youtube.com/watch?v=ZKRePbNZQTA

8 - https://www.imposemagazine.com/features/mitski-interview

9 - https://www.youtube.com/watch?v=By9bb8V4YRQ

10 - https://www.loudandquiet.com/interview/mitski-revels-hurt-to-make-neo-grunge-but-would-trade-it-all-to-be-happy-and-dull

11 - https://pitchfork.com/features/podcast/in-sight-out-mitski

12 - https://fashionpost.jp/portraits/124246

13 - https://www.youtube.com/watch?v=QRXTmj9QvJ8

14 - https://www.thefader.com/2016/06/08/mitski-puberty-2-interview-gen-f

15 - https://www.youtube.com/watch?v=AmRC5B1J5v4

16 - https://chicagoreader.com/film-tv/mitski-i-dont-belong-anywhere-that-really-affects-how-i-write-songs

17 - https://www.gq.com/story/mitski-writes-bangers-for-the-loners

18 - https://jayw1023.medium.com/old-mitski-interview-5fc73db0d4c7

19 - https://www.pbs.org/newshour/show/indie-darling-mitski-asks-herself-now-what

20 - https://www.youtube.com/watch?v=25F4tJmoqSg

21* - https://www.reddit.com/r/mitski/comments/1cubjyc/mitski_interview_when_lush_was_released_2012 [UNRELIABLE SOURCE]

22 - https://www.youtube.com/watch?v=BMDOQW_YnMo

23 - https://www.youtube.com/watch?v=YFV50zCV9y8

24 - https://www.nytimes.com/2016/06/05/arts/music/mitski-puberty-2-interview.html

25 - https://www.youtube.com/watch?v=oPL0W0-6seY

26 - https://www.npr.org/2016/06/19/482375750/mitski-on-puberty-2-and-the-nature-of-happiness

27 - https://www.youtube.com/watch?v=bvIKoWCmgGI

28 - https://www.youtube.com/watch?v=tQ1m4ThDFeo
29 - https://www.youtube.com/watch?v=eWTWNCv9DCA
30 - https://www.youtube.com/watch?v=MmvdPmbK0v8
31 - https://www.youtube.com/watch?v=X4olgiySBqM
32 - https://www.theguardian.com/music/2016/jun/20/lo-fi-solo-rocker-mitski-new-album-puberty-2
33 - https://www.newyorker.com/magazine/2019/07/08/on-the-road-with-mitski
34 - https://ew.com/music/mitski-new-album-laurel-hell-interview
35 - https://faroutmagazine.co.uk/mitski-journey-j-pop-indie-songwriter
36 - https://misschryss.medium.com/interview-with-mitski-8cdd91c0ec87
37 - https://www.youtube.com/watch?v=jQKC3BaTZ6w
38 - https://www.thestranger.com/music/2015/06/24/22438250/mitski-talks-about-her-breakout-album-bury-me-at-makeout-creek-her-first-seattle-show-sat-june-27-and-more
39 - https://gr8songpod.podbean.com/e/ep-2-mitski-learned-how-to-sing-from-always-be-my-baby
40 - https://www.youtube.com/watch?v=zEaFRAK30tk
41 - https://www.spin.com/2018/12/mitski-interview-be-the-cowboy
42 - https://www.undertheradarmag.com/interviews/mitski_-_the_under_the_radar_cover_story
43 - https://www.youtube.com/watch?v=KqqsrNMN5Y4
44 - https://www.rookiemag.com/2017/05/an-interview-with-mitski
45 - https://www.thefader.com/2018/08/10/mitski-interview-be-the-cowboy
46 - https://www.youtube.com/watch?v=_E1NxKH47-M
47 - https://howlandechoes.com/2016/06/interview-mitski-puberty-2
48 - https://medium.com/@drewalllen/an-interview-with-mitski-aa3c238ce840
49 - https://flagpole.com/music/music-features/2015/11/11/mitski-manages-indie-stardom-in-the-social-media-age
50 - https://www.huckmag.com/article/mitski-interview-laurel-hell-huck-issue-77
51 - https://www.youtube.com/watch?v=tEIaBUuXDkc
52 - https://www.youtube.com/watch?v=qVerNxP9yaw
53 - https://rollingstoneindia.com/10-new-artists-need-know-february-2015/7
54 - https://www.thecurrent.org/feature/2016/07/26/mitski-on-lyrical-undertones-metaphors-and-puberty-2
55 - https://www.stereogum.com/1809020/mitski-ryan-hemsworth-predict-the-song-of-the-summer-2015/interviews
56 - https://chorus.fm/features/interviews/mitski
57 - https://www.youtube.com/watch?v=0Q4MDl_Iws0
58 - https://www.thelineofbestfit.com/features/longread/mitski-being-her-own-cowboy-interview-2018
59 - https://www.youtube.com/watch?v=hZOzIAaw6AI
60 - https://crackmagazine.net/article/profiles/mitski-new-album-laurel-hell-interview
61 - https://www.youtube.com/watch?v=hgmPpZZTtiI
62 - https://www.interviewmagazine.com/music/exclusive-song-premiere-and-interview-townie-mitski
63 - https://reverb.com/fr/news/interview-mitski-and-patrick-hyland-on-recording-puberty-2
64 - https://yeahiknowitsucks.wordpress.com/2013/08/20/mitski-retired-from-sad-new-career-in-business
65 - https://mitski.bandcamp.com/album/retired-from-sad-new-career-in-business
66 - https://www.reddit.com/r/mitski/comments/l1g9ve/whos_the_person_in_the_retired_from_sad_new
67 - https://radioutd.com/blog/2015/05/interview-mitski
68 - https://www.npr.org/sections/allsongs/2018/05/14/610868651/mitski-shares-and-talks-about-new-song-and-album
69 - https://pitchfork.com/video/watch/mitski-breaks-down-every-song-from-laurel-hell
70 - https://deadoceans.com/records/puberty-2
71 - https://www.undertheradar.co.nz/news/14738/Interview-Mitski-Talks-About-Her-New-Album-Be-The-Cowboy.utr

72* - https://mitski.fandom.com/wiki/Voice_Coils_(Band) [UNRELIABLE SOURCE]

73 - https://www.youtube.com/watch?v=dJnmPe6qyKU

74 - https://www.thecut.com/2015/05/mitski-on-writing-love-songs-and-giving-a-shit.html

75 - https://www.reddit.com/r/mitski/comments/17tg0oo/i_just_found_this_short_film_called_hoof_with/?share_id=OQs9AA_I0WO2x7pTRcOHC

76 - https://www.thefader.com/2015/03/09/mitski-get-animated-in-the-video-for-townie

77 - https://www.youtube.com/watch?v=wDrV9nnxkOw

78 - https://www.stereogum.com/1884504/watch-marceline-sing-a-mitski-song-on-adventure-time/news

79* - https://www.reddit.com/r/mitski/comments/1ckgg8u/mitski_has_a_sister [UNRELIABLE SOURCE]

80 - https://www.nytimes.com/2016/06/05/arts/music/mitski-puberty-2-interview.html

81 - https://www.eatsleepbreathemusic.com/2012/06/12/song-of-the-day-liquid-smooth-by-mitski

82 - https://www.davidmeermanscott.com/blog/people-pay-to-see-others-believe-in-themselves

83 - https://www.theguardian.com/music/2023/oct/13/mitski-how-the-us-songwriter-scored-the-years-quietest-global-chart-smash

84 - https://theoutline.com/post/5810/mitski-be-the-cowboy-interview

85 - https://savedbyoldtimes.com/features/2018/8/15/a-conversation-with-mitski

86* - https://www.musicianwages.com/w2/the-meaning-behind-the-song-a-horse-named-cold-air-by-mitski [UNRELIABLE SOURCE]

87 - https://www.itsnicethat.com/articles/mary-banas-mitski-album-covers-graphic-design-project-150824

88 - https://www.theguardian.com/music/2018/aug/23/indie-rock-star-mitski-new-album-rave-reviews-japanese-american-songwriter

89 - https://www.nbcnews.com/news/asian-america/mitski-says-doesnt-feel-either-fully-asian-american-fans-say-identify-rcna105606

90 - https://web.archive.org/web/20170818072720/http://deadoceans.com/blog/2016/03/album-announce-mitski-announces-puberty-2-out-june-17th-on-dead-oceans

91 - https://www.nytimes.com/2014/12/20/arts/music/mitski-leaves-her-mark-at-the-knitting-factory.html?_r=1

92 - https://www.youtube.com/watch?v=HSGIsZxgjAY

93 - https://www.theguardian.com/music/2022/feb/04/mitski-us-best-young-songwriter-im-a-black-hole-where-people-dump-feelings

94 - https://www.instagram.com/p/Cb229YSMqkX

95 - https://www.slugmag.com/music/interviews/music-interviews/real-whole-human-interview-mitski

96 - https://mitski.bandcamp.com/album/be-the-cowboy

97 - https://www.spin.com/2018/09/mitski-geyser-criticism-the-daily-show-video

98 - https://www.youtube.com/watch?v=HCShZiUGTWA

99 - https://www.npr.org/sections/allsongs/2016/03/02/468742138/mitski-talks-your-best-american-girl-identity-and-her-new-album

100 - https://www.billboard.com/music/music-news/mitski-your-best-american-girl-songs-that-defined-the-decade-8544166

101 - https://web.archive.org/web/20170612184329/http://deadoceans.com/blog/2016/05/listen-mitski-shares-new-single-happy-2

102 - https://www.thelineofbestfit.com/news/latest-news/mitski-uncovers-a-nasty-secret-in-her-happy-video

103 - https://web.archive.org/web/20180619063346/http://americansongwriter.com/2016/03/mitski-announces-new-album-puberty-2

104 - https://consequence.net/2016/03/mitski-announces-new-album-puberty-2-shares-lead-single-your-best-american-girl-listen

105 - https://www.rollingstone.com/music/music-lists/the-100-best-songs-of-the-2010s-917532/mitski-your-best-american-girl-single-917557

106 - https://www.newyorker.com/magazine/2016/06/20/mitski-miyawaki-and-chicago-rappers

107 - https://www.vice.com/en/article/mitski-happy-video-puberty-2

108 - https://www.factmag.com/2016/05/23/mitski-happy-video

109 - https://www.youtube.com/watch?v=qL-7SVtgQa8

110 - https://uproxx.com/music/mitski-donald-trump-voters-leave-show

111 - https://www.vulture.com/2018/08/review-mitskis-be-the-cowboy-album.html

112 - https://www.youtube.com/watch?v=J9TFkKmEToo

113 - https://www.npr.org/2018/09/06/642252679/mitski-is-the-21st-centurys-poet-laureate-of-young-adulthood

114 - https://www.talkhouse.com/mitski-talks-weezer

115 - https://www.talkhouse.com/one-projection-harry-styles-art-idealism

116 - https://www.thefader.com/2016/07/06/ryan-hemsworth-mitski-keaton-henson-wait

117 - https://www.bbc.com/news/entertainment-arts-59943542

118 - https://www.youtube.com/watch?v=QPBq_fMt0w8

119 - https://yesismore.us/Mitski-s-Be-The-Cowboy

120 - https://www.newyorker.com/culture/culture-desk/the-misreading-of-mitski

121 - https://www.npr.org/2023/09/19/1200167645/mitskis-most-american-album-is-united-by-love

122 - https://deadoceans.com/news/mitski-nobody-single-video

123 - https://www.theringer.com/2023/09/14/music/mitski-privacy-interviews-concerts-new-album-land-is-inhospitable

124 - https://www.youtube.com/watch?v=G30AtDEc5Do

125 - https://www.thecut.com/2018/06/new-mitski-song-nobody.html

126 - https://tidal.com/magazine/article/mitski-washing/1-53248

127 - https://www.thefader.com/2019/02/01/mitski-the-pearl-animated-video

128 - https://www.amazon.de/-/en/Here-Comes-Cowboy-Vinyl-LP/dp/B07P73PLVQ

129 - https://www.nme.com/news/music/mitski-responds-fans-accuse-mac-demarco-copying-2457404

130 - https://pitchfork.com/news/mac-demarco-discusses-mitski-metoo-and-alcoholism-in-new-interview

131 - https://www.youtube.com/watch?v=WhmS-KUP6d0

132 - https://www.youtube.com/watch?v=4We_UkHTIlo

133 - https://www.vinylmeplease.com/blogs/magazine/mitski-primer

134 - https://www.thefader.com/2019/08/13/mitski-issues-statement-denying-completely-false-child-sex-abuse-allegations

135 - https://www.reddit.com/media?url=https%3A%2F%2Fpreview.redd.it%2Fold-mitski-tweets-v0-ps7vdpn3apjd1.jpg%3Fwidth%3D736%26format%3Dpjpg%26auto%3Dwebp%26s%3D823a0c1a748f1a6f424c32b0d11a2212f9bcd3cd

136 - https://www.reddit.com/media?url=https%3A%2F%2Fpreview.redd.it%2Fold-mitski-tweets-v0-czh15e34apjd1.jpg%3Fwidth%3D735%26format%3Dpjpg%26auto%3Dwebp%26s%3D5fcd7e1b01448aee4250e34e9a4955eea3bbf820

137 - https://www.reddit.com/media?url=https%3A%2F%2Fpreview.redd.it%2Fold-mitski-tweets-v0-w4ayduq3apjd1.jpg%3Fwidth%3D415%26format%3Dpjpg%26auto%3Dwebp%26s%3De17b4f90e13ebd63a65868efc36614be4746ea6f

138 - https://www.reddit.com/media?url=https%3A%2F%2Fpreview.redd.it%2Fold-mitski-tweets-v0-ymuz5gw3apjd1.jpg%3Fwidth%3D620%26format%3Dpjpg%26auto%3Dwebp%26s%3D580e417b0b521b60d0931957b7e1524e4dac7b22

139 - https://www.instagram.com/p/CaJxkKcsQQk

140 - https://www.instagram.com/p/Ca7R-gxsdop

141 - https://www.instagram.com/p/CbX1kczsSO7

142 - https://www.reddit.com/media?url=https%3A%2F%2Fpreview.redd.it%2Fold-mitski-tweets-v0-2zeogsx3apjd1.jpg%3Fwidth%3D627%26format%3Dpjpg%26auto%3Dwebp%26s%3De17affc7d053e6664e4a52f9a4a721cf97991e5

143 - https://www.instagram.com/p/CciQFiIsUnb

144 - https://pitchfork.com/news/mitski-announces-last-show-indefinitely

145 - https://savedbyoldtimes.com/features/2018/9/4/a-conversation-with-wild-nothing

146 - https://www.nme.com/news/music/hear-allie-x-and-mitski-team-up-on-shiny-new-song-susie-save-your-love-2613294

147 - https://pitchfork.com/reviews/albums/porches-ricky-music

148 - https://pitchfork.com/features/song-by-song/lucy-dacus-interview-new-album-home-video

149 - https://uproxx.com/indie/mitski-graphic-novel-soundtrack-this-is-where-we-fall

150 - https://pitchfork.com/news/mitski-announces-new-album-laurel-hell-shares-new-song-the-only-heartbreaker-listen

151 - https://www.vulture.com/2021/11/mitski-album-laurel-hell-song-only-heartbreaker.html

152 - https://www.youtube.com/watch?v=VfnofOUXwi8

153 - https://variety.com/2021/music/news/mitski-new-album-laurel-hell-single-1235107444

154 - https://variety.com/2021/music/news/mitski-new-single-tour-1235080377

155 - https://www.nme.com/news/music/mitski-announces-new-album-laurel-hell-shares-single-the-only-heartbreaker-3091278

156 - https://www.stereogum.com/2166672/mitski-the-only-heartbreaker/music

157 - https://www.brooklynvegan.com/mitski-shares-new-single-love-me-more-from-laurel-hell

158 - https://www.youtube.com/watch?v=xLFnlCkhaIA

159 - https://diymag.com/news/mitski-new-stay-soft-video

160 - https://www.gaga.com.au/news/mitski-laurel-hell

161 - https://variety.com/2022/music/news/muna-album-saves-the-world-queer-interview-1235304208

162 - https://www.nme.com/news/music/mitski-asks-fans-to-stop-filming-entire-songs-or-whole-sets-at-her-shows-3169422

163 - https://www.clashmusic.com/news/mitski-details-new-album-the-land-is-inhospitable-and-so-are-we

164 - https://www.youtube.com/watch?v=vIAIcfxWs4U

165 - https://www.youtube.com/watch?v=TIGE2CSezcM

166 - https://deadoceans.com/records/the-land-is-inhospitable-and-so-are-we

167 - https://www.youtube.com/watch?v=5CXw4hSG9W4

168 - https://www.youtube.com/watch?v=DGoVFbbBYRU

169 - https://www.youtube.com/watch?v=U9Yy_3dk750

170 - https://www.youtube.com/watch?v=1Kiknae8H_c

171 - https://www.instagram.com/mitskicentral/reel/DDKH0xESE6L

172 - https://www.youtube.com/watch?v=RzlXZuKZGf0

173 - https://www.youtube.com/watch?v=KuzuqZBC1kI

174 - https://www.youtube.com/watch?v=ZgS9faasTSg

175 - https://www.youtube.com/watch?v=pwOVP8sZZ3o

176 - https://www.youtube.com/watch?v=eWLwIeY3mDc

177 - https://www.youtube.com/watch?v=6wWLDYgv9ZQ

178 - https://www.youtube.com/watch?v=pm5j-xIWSag

179 - https://www.brunodrums.com

180 - https://shemakesmusic.co.uk/new-music/miya-folick-shares-new-single-bad-thing-co-written-with-mitski

181 - https://deadline.com/2023/11/the-queens-gambit-broadway-mitski-1235613112

182 - https://www.reddit.com/media?url=https%3A%2F%2Fpreview.redd.it%2Fold-mitski-tweets-v0-7avbs224apjd1.jpg%3Fwidth%3D632%26format%3Dpjpg%26auto%3Dwebp%26s%3Deb-5b9a9184238b3a0aac355a4cb720c4047a9935

183 - https://thequietus.com/interviews/bakers-dozen/japanese-breakfast-bakers-dozen-favourite-albums/12

184 - https://exclaim.ca/music/article/boygenius-call-out-grammys-for-mitski-snub-it-s-super-weird

185 - https://www.vulture.com/article/dave-grohl-in-conversation.html

186 - https://soundcloud.com/deadoceans/iggy-pop-talking-about-mitski-on-bbc-6

187 - https://www.reddit.com/media?url=https%3A%2F%2Fpreview.redd.it%2Fold-mitski-tweets-v0-x8ry1ki3apjd1.jpg%3Fwidth%3D500%26format%3Dpjpg%26auto%3Dwebp%26s%3D3b667c2c349c14581b84ba2dc29790a652eba9d4

188 - https://thegrizzlygazette.org/2208/student-submissions/growing-up

189 - https://www.allmusic.com/artist/mitski-mn0003327534#biography

190 - https://atwoodmagazine.com/mitski-2018-review-lush-be-the-cowboy

191 - https://theabsolutemag.com/1226/music/mitski-retired-from-sad-new-career-in-business

192 - https://www.vogue.com/article/strawberry-dress-lirika-matoshi-popular

193 - https://slate.com/culture/2022/03/mitski-tour-fandom-tiktok-twitter-memes.html

194 - https://www.rollingstone.com/music/music-features/how-mitski-became-the-cowboy-710983

195 - https://www.stereogum.com/1788820/mitski-silences-the-rain-at-sxsw/photo

196 - https://www.allmusic.com/album/bury-me-at-makeout-creek-mw0002768049

197 - https://consequence.net/2022/02/mitski-best-songs-list/amp

198 - https://www.thefader.com/2014/11/04/mitski-bury-me-at-makeout-creek

199 - https://www.rookiemag.com/2014/11/sunday-video-mitski-townie

200 - https://www.imposemagazine.com/bytes/new-music/mitski-i-dont-smoke

201 - https://www.imposemagazine.com/bytes/new-music/i-will-by-mitski

202 - https://www.stereogum.com/1785985/mitski-townie-video-bury-me-at-makeout-creek-re-release-details/news

203 - https://web.archive.org/web/20170312193747/http://sheshredsmag.com/adventure-time-marceline-mitski

204 - https://www.nme.com/blogs/nme-radar/premiere-brooklyn-newcomer-mitskis-spellbinding-i-will-18904

205 - https://www.bbc.co.uk/news/entertainment-arts-59943542

206 - https://exclaim.ca/film/article/mitski-your_best_american_girl_video

207 - https://www.stereogum.com/1874719/mitski-happy/music

208 - https://www.pastemagazine.com/music/mitski/mitski-releases-music-video-for-happy

209 - https://americansongwriter.com/mitski-drops-happy-second-single-forthcoming-puberty-2

210 - https://xpn.org/2016/05/03/mitski-happy-single

211 - https://www.spin.com/2016/05/mitski-happy-stream-new-single

212 - https://web.archive.org/web/20160507192503/https://diymag.com/2016/05/03/mitski-happy-track-review

213 - https://www.npr.org/sections/allsongs/2016/03/01/468690106/new-mix-music-from-m-ward-nothing-marissa-nadler-a-chat-with-mitski-more

214 - https://atwoodmagazine.com/burning-hill-mitski-review

215 - https://www.stereogum.com/1968040/mitski-im-a-fool-to-want-you-frank-sinatra-cover/music

216 - https://www.stereogum.com/1965674/run-the-jewels-mitski-tove-stryke-to-open-for-lorde-on-tour/news

217 - https://www.billboard.com/music/rock/mitski-covers-one-direction-fireproof-exclusive-6531846

218 - https://pitchfork.com/news/mitski-reviews-weezers-new-album

219 - https://pitchfork.com/news/mitski-covers-billie-holidays-im-a-fool-to-want-you-listen

220 - https://archive.thetab.com/uk/2021/06/22/nobody-song-tiktok-211481

221 - https://www.pastemagazine.com/music/mitski/untangling-the-unique-private-and-meteoric-rise-of-mitski-in-the-age-of-tiktok

222 - https://www.out.com/music/2018/5/14/mitski-releases-new-geyser-video-announces-new-album

223 - https://uproxx.com/music/mitski-be-the-cowboy-new-album-geyser-song

224 - https://www.spin.com/2018/08/mitski-two-slow-dancers-listen

225 - https://deadoceans.com/records/be-the-cowboy

226 - https://www.undertheradarmag.com/news/mitski_announces_new_album_and_shares_video_for_new_song_geyser

227 - https://www.nme.com/news/music/mitski-responds-completely-false-child-sex-abuse-allegations-2537763

228 - https://exclaim.ca/music/article/mitski_responds_to_allegations_of_child_sex_trafficking_i_have_not_ever_been_part_of_sex_trafficking_or_child_abuse_in_any_form

229 - https://xpn.org/2018/05/15/mitski-geyser

230 - https://www.thefader.com/2018/05/14/mitski-geyser-music-video-new-album-be-the-cowboy-tour-dates

231 - https://exclaim.ca/music/article/mitski_soundtracks_sci-fi_graphic_novel_this_is_where_we_fall

232 - https://pitchfork.com/news/mitski-releasing-new-song-tomorrow

233 - https://www.ft.com/content/324eb48e-a06b-11e8-85da-eeb7a9ce36e4

234 - https://www.rollingstone.com/music/music-news/mitski-previews-new-lp-be-the-cowboy-with-geyser-video-628657

235 - https://www.rollingstone.com/music/music-news/hear-mitskis-bittersweet-new-song-two-slow-dancers-709245

236 - https://www.nytimes.com/2020/08/20/arts/things-to-do-weekend-coronavirus.html

237 - https://slate.com/culture/2021/10/mitski-working-for-the-knife-music-video-tour.html

238 - https://www.nme.com/news/music/mitski-new-single-heat-lightning-listen-3113007?amp

239 - https://pitchfork.com/news/listen-to-mitski-new-cover-of-pete-seeger-coyote-my-little-brother

240 - https://www.vulture.com/2023/07/mitski-new-album-bug-like-an-angel.html

241 - https://www.rollingstone.com/music/music-news/mitski-laurel-hell-annoucement-only-heartbreaker-1254681

242 - https://pitchfork.com/news/mitski-to-open-for-harry-styles-at-uk-shows

243 - https://www.rollingstone.com/music/music-news/mitski-bug-like-an-angel-new-album-1234794850

244 - https://consequence.net/2023/07/mitski-the-land-is-inhospitable-and-so-are-we-bug-like-an-angel

245 - https://www.rollingstone.com/music/music-features/mitski-working-for-the-knife-new-music-1236649

246 - https://variety.com/2023/music/news/mitski-new-album-1235679865

247 - https://xpn.org/2023/08/23/mitski-star-heaven

248 - https://uproxx.com/indie/mitski-my-love-mine-all-mine-video

249 - https://pitchfork.com/news/watch-mitskis-new-my-love-mine-all-mine-video

250 - https://www.rollingstone.com/music/music-news/mitski-the-land-is-inhospitable-and-so-are-we-2024-tour-1234838346

251 - https://www.billboard.com/music/chart-beat/mitski-hot-100-debut-my-love-mine-all-mine-1235432117

252 - https://www.officialcharts.com/songs/mitski-my-love-mine-all-mine

253 - https://consequence.net/2023/09/mitski-north-american-acoustic-shows

254 - https://diymag.com/news/mitski-the-land-is-inhospitable-and-so-are-we-film-double-features

255 - https://www.rollingstone.com/music/music-news/mitski-buffalo-replaced-coyote-my-little-brother-spotify-1234986680

256 - https://deadoceans.com/news/mitski-announces-new-album-tliiasaw

257 - https://www.youtube.com/watch?v=pLEilbUJP7o

258 - https://www.youtube.com/watch?v=FtQDj-3ps04

259 - https://www.youtube.com/watch?v=rM1WlDnClII

260 - https://www.wsj.com/articles/laurel-hell-mitski-review-dan-wilson-11643667169

261 - https://www.rollingstone.com/music/music-news/mitski-phones-statement-tour-1312596

262 - https://www.youtube.com/watch?v=EZj4cyozwwU

263 - https://www.youtube.com/watch?v=MS3Ul2sEXZc

264 - https://www.youtube.com/watch?v=cx4PTTozPHo

265 - https://pitchfork.com/news/mitski-announces-acoustic-tour-shares-new-songs-star-and-heaven-listen

266 - https://pitchfork.com/news/mitski-expands-2024-north-american-tour

267 - https://www.youtube.com/watch?v=fabSU_RliT4

268 - https://www.youtube.com/watch?v=xeO2yQB78zc

269 - https://www.youtube.com/watch?v=ahglDakG5CY

270 - https://www.youtube.com/watch?v=0lNFHD0lUAQ

271 - https://www.concertarchives.org/bands/mitski

272 - https://hannibaluress.com/podcasts/the-mitski-episode

273 - https://www.reddit.com/media?url=https%3A%2F%2Fpreview.redd.it%2Fold-mit-

ski-tweets-v0-dkvysdm3apjd1.jpg%3Fwidth%3D735%26format%3Dpjpg%26auto%3Dweb-p%26s%3D23ac135d5dbbe97353ecd7eb8ac1e524d6941f78

274 - https://www.elle.com/culture/music/a37003/mitski-interview

Stay Soft, Get Eaten
The Complete Biography of Mitski Using Her Own Words
by Jared Woods
proofreading by Milz Dechnik
cover photo by David Lee (CC Attribution 2.0 Generic license)
Published by The Goat's Nest Publishing
ISBN 9798282538090
ASIN B0F7G2CJ96
JaredWoodsSavedMyLife.com

Printed in Dunstable, United Kingdom

69065083R00288